BETWEEN
HUSBANDS
& WIVES

Sage's *Series in Interpersonal Communication* is designed to capture the breadth and depth of knowledge emanating from scientific examinations of face-to-face interaction. As such, the volumes in this series address the cognitive and overt behavior manifested by communicators as they pursue various conversational outcomes. The application of research findings to specific types of interpersonal relationships (e.g., marital, managerial) is also an important dimension of this series.

SAGE SERIES IN
INTERPERSONAL COMMUNICATION
Mark L. Knapp, Series Editor

BETWEEN HUSBANDS & WIVES

Communication in Marriage

Mary Anne Fitzpatrick

Sage Series

Interpersonal Communication 7

SAGE PUBLICATIONS
The International Professional Publishers
Newbury Park   London   New Delhi

For information address:

SAGE Publications, Inc.
2455 Teller Road
Newbury Park, California 91320

SAGE Publications Ltd.
6 Bonhill Street
London EC2A 4PU
United Kingdom

SAGE Publications India Pvt. Ltd.
M-32 Market
Greater Kailash I
New Delhi 110 048 India

Printed in the United States of America

Library of Congress Cataloging-in-Publication Data

Fitzpatrick, Mary Anne, 1949-
    Between husbands and wives.

    (Sage series in interpersonal communication ; v. 7)
    Bibliography: p.
    1. Communication in marriage.   2. Nonverbal
communication (Psychology)   3. Self-disclosure.
I. Title.   II. Series.
HQ728.F46   1988   306.8'72   87-28551
ISBN 0-8039-2618-9
ISBN 0-8039-2619-7 (pbk.)

92 93 94 10 9 8 7 6 5 4 3

CONTENTS

PART IV: THINKING ABOUT MARRIAGE

To Roman Kyweluk,
sine qua non.

SERIES EDITOR'S INTRODUCTION

This book is a godsend for two of my pet peeves about the study of marriage. *Between Husbands and Wives* should firmly and forever put to rest the following fallacious assumptions that permeate the marriage literature: (1) the assumption that any sample of married couples simultaneously qualifies as a sample of couples who are intimate or close, and (2) the assumption that any behavior uncovered in a sample of married couples can be used as the basis for generalizing about the behavior of married couples in general. Fitzpatrick's decade of research reported in this book makes it quite clear that "being married" does not necessarily mean "being close." Further, married couples who nurture distance in their relationship may be just as happy as married couples who nurture closeness. In short, "being married" means there is an opportunity for people to negotiate a variety of different types of relationships . . . and they do.

Fitzpatrick's research has uncovered and focused on three marital types and combinations thereof. The reader of this book will come to know these types well—the Traditionals, the Independents, and the Separates. They have different perspectives on life in general, marriage, and the roles husbands and wives should play. These marriage types are primarily distinguished from one another by the extent to which the partners subscribe to a conventional ideology, the extent to which the partners desire autonomy or dependence, and the extent to which they value confrontation or avoidance.

But the identification of marital types is not the only significant feature of this book. In a field dominated by psychological constructs, this is a book about communication. It is a book that demonstrates how different ideologies produce different patterns of communication. Traditionals, Independents, and Separates talk about different things, show affection in different ways, approach disagreement differently, undertake persuasion with different strategies, and engage in varying degrees of openness.

Readers will also find out why:

- Separates may be the most prone to violence due to frustrations associated with their beliefs about power and the way they deal with conflict.
- Criteria for what constitutes a "happy marriage" differs among the marital types.
- "Inexpressive" males may be quite expressive with their spouses.
- Couples who engage in a lot of conflict may not reflect an imbalance of power or necessarily be dissatisfied with their marriage.

The fact that married couples differ in what they desire and how they desire to express it has important implications for marital counseling as well. Appropriate communication behavior for one marital type may not be appropriate for another. Yet, as Fitzpatrick notes, there is a widespread uniformity in professional prescriptions for "good" communication. In this model, increased openness, confronting disagreements, and speaking in descriptive, consistent, and direct ways are valued. This fits the Independent marital type well, but may be problematic for other types.

The growing number of scholars interested in communication and relationship development will profit from this book in at least three important ways: (1) as an insightful treatise on the nature of marriage and marital communication; (2) as a resource for literature and instrumentation related to subjects, such as self-disclosure, conflict, and marital satisfaction; and (3) as a well-spring for generating research hypotheses to further understand the complex nature of communication between husbands and wives.

Mark L. Knapp

FOREWORD

What follows is an extraordinarily scientific story told by one of the most original and productive family scientists of our generation. For the reader who carefully follows the many plots and subthemes, this story emerges with great force and coherence. Thus the telling of the story needs no comment or exegesis; an explanatory or anticipatory preface is unnecessary. Nonetheless, stories accrue meaning not only in the telling but in the hearing. Like all readers who will follow me, I have generated my own sense of the import of what has been told. In effect I have begun a process by which this story becomes integrated into the collective awareness of our field; each subsequent reader will participate in this critical process. The story as told here, of course, will not change, but its meaning for our field will continue to be elaborated by the full engagement of readers with what they perceive as its central plot. Thus this preface is offered not as an exegesis but as an effort to facilitate the process of bringing these remarkable investigations into the center of our work.

My reactions to this manuscript seem to have fallen into two categories. First, I have been fascinated by the intellectual strategies Professor Fitzpatrick has used to develop her program of research on marital typologies. Second, many of the findings themselves strike me as providing novel insights into intimate human relationships. I would like to describe both sets of reactions because both may be relevant to the full integration of this work into our field. The fascinating intellectual strategies, from theory construction and integration of several disciplines to specific research methods, may play a large role in reshaping how we conduct family research. The fascinating findings may transform how we think about those relationships.

Three major intellectual strategies used here fascinated me in particular. First was the central tactic of developing and exploring a typology of relationships. As early as her predoctoral work, Professor Fitzpatrick was clearly intrigued with the intellectually rich formulations about differing types of families that were then emerging from the clinical literature. Her original intellectual base consisted of the influential concepts of Kantor and Lehr. What intrigued her most was that families could be distinguished by their intrinsic or idiosyncratic ideologies: their unique values, perspectives, and aspirations and the specific relationships and interaction patterns that sustained these idiosyncratic and collective visions. The central idea here was that relationships could be distinguished by their enduring patterns, not simply by whether they were smooth or troubled. Indeed, the core concept is that relationships of different kinds may achieve for their participants deep and broad satisfactions, but by very different social processes.

As the reader will soon see, Professor Fitzpatrick delineates a typology of marriage through the use of a carefully crafted and thoroughly tested self-report device that questions each spouse in two broad areas. First, spouses are queried on their personal ideals for relationships, particularly their belief in conventional, gender-specific roles and the value of spontaneity and change. Second, they are asked to describe their actual marriage, particularly their patterns of interdependence and autonomy. Because each spouse fills out this questionnaire separately, there is an opportunity for disagreement. Thus where couples agree on both values and marital descriptions they can be categorized into three pure types; couples who do not agree are classed as "mixed." The entire substance of this research program is to gauge the power of this typology as a scientific tool. As the reader will soon see, this elegant typology has indeed permitted an extraordinary search for the subtle and complex organizational patterns that distinguish among various forms of marital relationships.

The typology alone would scarely deserve notice in the field of family studies, which is now among the most rapidly productive and growing of all the areas of social science research. As Professor Fitzpatrick notes in her first chapter, we already have many typologies of relationships, including marriages; some of them are conceptually intriguing. What distinguishes the current typology of marriages from all others is the breathtaking variety of conceptually and empirically sound methods for exploring its ramifications: assessments of satisfaction of relationships and of gender concepts; direct observations of control, conflict, and disclosure processes; and modes by which emotions are conveyed and understood by marital partners, to name only a few. A large number of carefully conducted studies—some in the laboratory and others in the field—expose the full implications of this typology. There are two impressive features of this work. First, it uses many different methods for assessing marital processes. Second, it explores mechanisms by which relationships are regulated that operate at very different levels of complexity. As an example of the latter, gender concepts are enduring and complex cognitions about behavior that is appropriate for men and for women; these conceptions are central to the mechanisms by which individuals of both sexes regulate their own behavior and their responses to same- and other-sex strangers and intimates. In sharp contrast is the phenomenon of immediate social responsiveness: the extent to which one marital partner recognizes, for example, positive feelings in the other and responds immediately with positive feelings of his or her own. The regulation of relationship behavior by gender concepts clearly involves planning, self-monitoring, and self-correction that occurs across the span of days, months, and even years. In contrast, immediate social responsiveness requires processes of attention, cognition, self-monitoring, and self-correction that must be deployed instantly, often before larger and more complex cognitive processes can apprehend what is happening. Yet processes at both levels, as Professor Fitzpatrick's impressive data convey, are clearly integral to specifying and understanding differences in marriages.

The vast armada of empirical methods organized by Professor Fitzpatrick in the exploration of this typology represents yet a third overarching scientific tactic: the strategic integration of disciplines. Family science, of course, is especially suited for interdisciplinary work. It is not a basic science of its own, in the sense that psychology or sociology is. Contemporary family science in fact arose at the juncture of three separate disciplines. Some investigators—mainly developmentalists—came up from psychology to explore the family context of development across the life span. Some sociologists came down to the family by recognizing that direct study of interaction behavior would help explain not only the effect of larger variables on social structure but also the development and maintenance of those structures. Clinicians recognized that work with the whole family could often enhance the effectiveness of their work dramatically. With this book Professor Fitzpatrick adds a fourth discipline to this mix: communication studies. The family field is largely ignorant of the pertinence of this creative and productive field for family studies. Professor Fitzpatrick introduces us to two major components of this field: First are its concepts and methods for studying intimate relationships, including methods for measuring the communication of emotions and self-disclosure; second are its approaches to studying mass communication. For example, Professor Fitzpatrick presents us with an ingenious study of television as a tool for understanding both popular conceptions of marriages and how various forms of marriage relationships shape the processing of those concepts by marital partners.

In addition to these fascinating scientific strategies, three emerging sets of findings and their implications are, to me, not only enthralling but promise a major revision in our thinking about marriage. The first and most important findings concern the status of the typology itself. No careful reader will complete this book without the conviction that something of great importance has been discovered here. At the outset, the typologies are an interesting device, empirically derived to be sure, but also shaped by the rich intuitions of the investigative team. By the end of the book this typology has acquired, in Edwin Boring's felicitous phrase, "thinghood." What is the nature of this thing? The data strongly argue for the major premise of Professor Fitzpatrick and her group: Marriages can be regarded as separate minicultures. Indeed, an anthropological perspective—if not anthropological methods—may emerge as the most fruitful stance toward the differences among marriages that have been discovered.

This conclusion overlaps that of my own work on families of adolescents, in which the entire nuclear family is treated as the social unit of interest. It also overlaps the conclusions reached by Professors Steven Wolin and Linda Bennett in our group at George Washington University. I have centered my attention on a form of ideology or perspective that distinguishes among family minicultures. I have termed this the "family paradigm." Wolin and Bennett have explored those whole-family processes that maintain the uniqueness of family cultures across time and across generations. They have centered their attention on special forms of repetitive and richly symbolic family behavior, which, following Bossard and Boll, they have called "family rituals." It is quite possible that these three research teams—Fitzpatrick's, Wolin and Bennett's, and my own—have offered the strongest empirical data in support of this concept of family miniculture.

The scientific results reported in this book advance this basic concept in two ways. First, as I have already indicated, Professor Fitzpatrick's fastidious studies of interaction process illuminate a whole new array of social regulatory mechanisms that sustain these minicultures. Moreover, as the reality of the typologies emerges, we are given clues of central importance about how these minicultures develop. Let me tarry a moment on this second point.

It seems to me that the data suggest at least three different mechanisms by which marital minicultures arise. First, the traditional marital type appears to be built around concepts of social process in marriage that are part of the general American culture and are reinforced by its mass media. This suggests that this form of marital miniculture is built through a process of absorbing relational imagery from the immediately surrounding culture. Professor Fitzpatrick's data make it abundantly clear that this process of marital assembly eases the way for marital partners. They take advantage of this prefabrication of their own values. Their expectations of each other become clear early and remain clear sustained not just by their own efforts but, in all likelihood, by a readily accessible set of guidelines from the surrounding culture. They achieve high levels of marital satisfaction with minimal levels of relational work, particularly affect monitoring and conflict resolution.

The independent marital type makes and remakes its own miniculture. It relies relatively little on prevailing standards and conceptions of marriage. Its partners continually renegotiate their expectations of one another; if they achieve high levels of satisfaction it is only through the hard work of careful attention to each others' feelings and a continuing process of confrontation and conflict resolution. As Professor Fitzpatrick points out, with a touch of irony, it is only for marriages of this type that the therapeutic stereotype of enhancing communication effectiveness would seem appropriate.

The separates, in contrast to the first two marital types, appear in a state of premature closure in the evolution of their miniculture, although they can achieve adequate and even high levels of satisfaction. Initially, they seem to draw heavily on prevailing cultural imagery, but, by processes we can only guess at, cannot derive a fully satisfactory template for their own relationships from this imagery in the wider culture. Perhaps as evidence of this incomplete process of absorption they also embrace a diametricallly opposed philosophy emphasizing spontaneity and change. They cannot develop significant levels of interdependence and indeed develop potentially destabilizing asymmetries in their relationships; for example, the wives are more attentive to husbands' feelings than husbands are to those of the wives. Moreover, separates withdraw from potential conflict situations by dampening the negative affect and withdrawing from conversational opportunities. Here relational ability and satisfaction are maintained by the couple's ability to maintain this foreclosed position, the maintenance by each spouse of separate social worlds.

A second major finding emerging in these data is that of strong suggestions of central regulatory principles shaping marital relationships. Perhaps one way of grasping the possibilities here is to imagine a difference between top-down and bottom-up regulation. The repeated finding of the importance of marital ideologies as correlates of a broad range of self-percepts and interaction patterns suggests that ideology itself is a regulator of social interaction; because this is an instance of a more complex structure regulating more minute, moment-to-moment events, this may be regarded as a top-down form of control. This is hardly a novel idea, but the data here are particulary persuasive in two ways. First, they appear to show how broad a range of couple behavior may be regulated by these ideologies: from conflict resolution, self-disclosure, and control patterns to the recognition and management of feelings. Second, particularly in Chapter 9, a very specific mechanism is suggested by the data for how ideologies may exert control: by shaping more immediate, short-term perceptual filters in each partner. These filters in turn may regulate how self and spouse behavior is perceived and how memories about the relationship are formulated. To explore the latter process, Professor Fitzpatrick reports pilot data from a particularly imaginative study of how couples remember their first encounter.

There are fewer though equally intriguing hints of a bottom-up control mechanism as well. Drawing on Berscheid's influential analysis of emotions in intimate relationships, Professor Fitzpatrick draws our attention to interdependence itself as a regulatory principle. The central concept here is that affect is produced when routine sequences of behavior are interrupted. Intimate relationships involve individuals meshing their own sequences with those of their partners; this meshing is a reformulation of the concept of interdependence. The process of such meshing entails the risk of interruption and the emergence of strong affect, either positive or negative. Professor Fitzpatrick summarizes her data to argue that separates for example, do not easily tolerate such a risk and indeed her data show that affect is regularly damped in the exchanges between partners in these marriages. This analytic perspective suggests that it may be more than ideology that keeps these partners in separate social worlds. It may also be the capacity of these partners to tolerate strong affect or the capacity to regulate the physiological arousal that often accompanies it. This capacity to regulate or tolerate affect and arousal, if it does shape the form of marital relationship, would be an important bottom-up regulatory principle. With the introduction of psychophysiological measures into marital research by Gottman and his colleagues, the importance of this regulatory principle can be explored in great detail.

A third finding of immense interest emerges in the final chapter. Here Professor Fitzpatrick provides the first data I know of suggesting that all of us have stable and coherent schemata for perceiving marital relationships that can be activated by very simple instructional sets. What is particularly remarkable is the suggestion that we all have the *same* schemata and *any* of these schemata can be activated in *any* of us under appropriate circumstances. Here the data are from only preliminary investigation, but their implications are enormous, suggesting that the typology of marriages reflects in part a typology of cognitive schemata that all of us acquire in the process of development. We can use any of these schemata to process our perceptions of marital interaction: those of our own marriages, our parents' marriages, and the marital interaction of perfect strangers. If this is true, where do these schemata come from? And how do prospective marital partners select from among them the regnant schema to guide the evolution of their own relationship?

Perhaps it is well to end this preface on a questioning note. It is the function of a good scientific story to raise questions, not to answer them. What you will read is one of the best available; and it is my hope that the questions it raises will serve as a major stimulus to our field.

—*David Reiss*, M.D.
Washington, D.C.

PROLOGUE: INTRODUCING THE COUPLES

This book is about communication between husbands and wives. It demonstrates that there are different types of marriages, styles of communication, and patterns of happiness. What individual spouses mean by communication and what they mean by marital satisfaction can be remarkably different. Couples always choose their own ways of living within the limits set up by the mores of their era. A complete view of all the intimate daily interaction of a couple's emotions, characters, tastes, and so forth is beyond the reach of outsiders but the relations between husbands and wives do fall into a few recurring, discrete patterns. All young lovers feel that "no one has ever felt this way before." Poets and novelists are interested in probing the unique aspects of such feelings and emotions; social scientists, on the other hand, concentrate on the fact that "all" (a statistical majority, in other words) young lovers tend to feel this way.

Couples vary in their values about marriage, in their communication with one another, and in the level of happiness they garner from their relationship. These dimensions form the core of a classification scheme of marriage. The descriptions of marriage are based on statistical and mathematical models, and in this chapter we translate the statistical evidence into verbal pictures. Throughout the decade of research upon which this book is based, people often have wondered if the descriptions of marriage are merely summaries of differences in social class or other demographic factors. Statistics show that the descriptions that follow are equally valid across a number of sociological and demographic dimensions; the patterns of interaction in a marriage are not related, in any obvious way, to the couple's place in the social structure—for example, on their income, their age, the number of children, religion, the number of years they've been married, or whether the wife has a career outside the home. Because spouses believe in stability and predictability, and tend to express emotion to one another in a very controlled manner, does not necessarily mean that they are retired. Because the wife is the chief executive officer of a major American corporation does not mean that she eschews responsibility for housework or dominates her husband. The point is that marital interaction is not well described by the social class of the interactants. If understanding patterns of marital interaction were this simple, I could describe marital interaction in a pamphlet, not a book.

As a preview of the theory and research presented in this book, I would like to introduce you to five different couples. You probably know of couples who fit the following descriptions—your friends, your parents, your favorite TV family, or maybe even yourself. Although you will know some couples who fit a type perfectly, some will fit with minor variations yet variations small enough that these couples are not classified into another type. The descriptions are of general tendencies and not behaviors that always happen. And, a couple's type of marriage may be subject to change through time.

COUPLE 1: TOM AND JENNIFER

Tom and Jennifer have the same philosophy of life; they believe that their marriage is very important and that both should sacrifice some personal independence for the good of the marriage. They believe in stability; they stress the importance of being able to predict each other and their life together. Marriage provides them with a stable, committed relationship that helps to tie them into their community. Tom and Jennifer spend a lot of time together, working on their home and in leisure pursuits. They make time for each other during the day by keeping a regular daily schedule and eating their meals together. They avoid conflict in general and say that when they do disagree, they try to argue only over very important issues. Part of their philosophical agreement about life involves the nature of male/female roles; Tom sees himself as analytical, assertive, and dominant in the marriage, and Jennifer sees herself as warm, expressive, and nurturing. They are good at predicting one another's moods and feelings.

Because they share the same values and have a commitment to conventional male and female roles, Tom and Jennifer do not engage in power struggles in their conversation. Norms and conventions that they follow have already established that Tom is the head of the household and controls decisions in certain spheres of influence. Jennifer, too, has her spheres of influence—the home and the children. But when they do engage in power struggles, they tend to exchange orders rather than to negotiate. In general, they sweep discord under the rug, but this is a fairly effective strategy for Tom and Jennifer because they have very few conflicts.

Tom and Jennifer feel that they can express their innermost thoughts with each other. Tom believes that he can express his anxieties and vulnerabilities to Jennifer and that he's willing to listen to her when she wants to talk. Their actual disclosure patterns to one another are muted, and they actually disclose more positive than negative feelings—matters that are hardly risky to reveal. However, when Tom and Jennifer talk, they're very responsive to each other; they lean toward each other, smile, talk a lot, interrupt each other, and finish each other's sentences.

Tom and Jennifer present themselves to others as a couple; their conversation is peppered with the word "we" ("We think this," "We do this," and so on). When they talk about their marriage, certain themes emerge. They see communication and verbal openness, being in love, and displaying affection, and sharing time, activities, and interests as very important in marriage. They downplay distinct individual traits, habits, or skills because they reject the idea that marriage is a product of separate identities or roles. Tom and Jennifer are somewhat stoic; they both think some problems are just inherent in marriage, and they're willing to moderate their expectations of marital happiness. They believe that sometimes relationships are beyond their direct personal control.

Tom and Jennifer think of their marriage as being extremely well-adjusted. They say they're very happy, they've never thought about divorce, and they agree on all major marital and family issues.

I call Tom and Jennifer *Traditionals*.

COUPLE 2: SCOTT AND MISSY

Scott and Missy have the same philosophy of life; they believe that love and marriage primarily exist for the psychological gratification that the relationship gives to spouses. They believe that a marriage should be based on the satisfaction that each partner derives from the relationship. This couple stresses the importance of having a good time and believes that in this quickly changing world it is vital that each individual has a strong sense of self that is not lost just because that person is married. For this couple, the most freedom in marriage stems from allowing each partner some privacy and independence. Scott and Missy try to spend a lot of time together, but they do not keep regular daily schedules and they both have outside friends and interests.

Scott and Missy thrive on conflict; neither is afraid of openly expressing their views. Part of their philosophical agreement about life involves the nature of male/female roles; they both believe in egalitarianism. Both Scott and Missy tend to see themselves as androgynous or capable of combining masculine and feminine characteristics in their personality. In other words, Scott sees himself as both assertive and nurturing whereas Missy is analytical and expressive. Because they are deviating from the conventional norms about male/female roles that have existed for centuries, naturally Scott and Missy are more likely to engage in conflict, bargaining, and negotiation. They are venturing where few couples have gone before, redefining and renegotiating roles, rules, and norms for marriage. Scott and Missy both believe that they can disclose their innermost thoughts, feelings, and anxieties to one another, but each wants the other to open up even more. They disclose both positive and negative feelings about each other. They are very responsive to one another in conversations, picking up on each other's topics. They tend not to finish each other's sentences; rather, they tend to interrupt with questions. When Scott and Missy talk about their marriage, certain themes emerge; they often blame their marital problems on environmental influences, on elements of their current situation that are beyond their control.

Scott and Missy talk about their separate identities and roles, as well as each person's individual interests; they rarely refer to themselves as a couple by using the word "we." They don't automatically presume to understand each other; they are reasonably maritally adjusted because they "agree to disagree," to work through problems as they arise.

I call Scott and Missy *Independents*.

COUPLE 3: FRANK AND ELEANOR

Frank and Eleanor have the same philosophy of life, and the same ambivalence about that philosophy. They want to believe that marriage is so important that both should sacrifice independence for the sake of the marriage, but they are unsure of these values and ambivalent about how beneficial such values have been for them. Frank and Eleanor live together, but their bond is one of frozen isolation. Togetherness is a matter of habit and convenience, and not a sign of a real desire to be in each other's company.

Frank and Eleanor's marriage provides them with a stable relationship that ties them into the community yet includes little personal closeness. They try not to spend very much time together, either working around the house or pursuing leisure activities. Their major points of contact occur at mealtimes or other regularly scheduled daily events. Frank and Eleanor will go to great lengths to avoid conflict. A strong bond between them is their commitment to conventional male and female roles; each has a sense of the duties and obligations connected with being a husband or wife, and each tries to live up to those obligations. Frank sees himself as analytical, assertive, and dominant, but Eleanor is unsure of her femininity. Neither does very well at predicting how the other sees himself or herself.

Even though they are committed to hiding negative feelings and expressing only positive sentiments, both Frank and Eleanor sometimes confront one another in a type of verbal guerrilla warfare. One spouse might take a verbal "pot shot" at the other, but the attacked partner ignores it and refuses to confront the negative remark; this negativity is equally likely to come from the husband or the wife.

Frank and Eleanor feel that they cannot express their innermost thoughts to one another, and they do not. They don't open up to one another or to outsiders. They are extremely careful in their conversations with one another. They tend not to interrupt each other, and generally they don't talk very much with one another.

When Frank and Eleanor talk about their marriage, they talk about having separate time, activities, and interests, and about each of them having distinct personalities. They see their marriage as the product of factors that are outside of their control, factors that are part of normal stages of life. Frank and Eleanor tell their friends that their marriage is happier than most marriages, and it is. The major source of satisfaction for Frank and Eleanor is that they agree on major issues in married life and they rarely talk about divorce or separation.

I call Frank and Eleanor *Separates.*

COUPLE 4: JIM AND TAMMY

Jim and Tammy have the same philosophy of life, although Jim—unlike Tammy—is sometimes ambivalent about that philosophy. Both believe marriage is very important, and each sacrifices some independence for the good of the marriage. Jim agrees with some of Tammy's traditional emphasis on stability and predictability, but he sometimes feels trapped in the marriage. Jim doesn't value sharing and companionship as much as Tammy does, and he tries to avoid conflict or open disagreement. Both of them have extremely strong commitments to conventional gender roles. Tammy sees herself as remarkably feminine and as the perfect counterpart to Jim's masculine, assertive personality. Both view the marriage as one uniting a "strong, silent male" to a "warm, nurturing female." They see each other as very different but complementary. Tammy is exceptionally good at predicting how Jim sees himself; although he is emotionally remote, she is good at drawing him back into the marriage.

Jim and Tammy give in to each other when either feels strongly about an issue. When Jim makes a snide remark, Tammy really tries to deal with the situation; she may not confront him, but she tries to get him to disclose his feelings. Unlike most couples, when either Jim or Tammy tries to get his or her own way, both feel comfortable using the relationship as a reason that the other should give in; for example, one might say, "You should go see a doctor. We won't have much of a marriage if one of us gets sick."

Jim and Tammy don't openly express their anxieties to each other, but often they don't have to; they can use gender stereotypes to predict how the other is thinking or feeling. And often, they're right. On the other hand, they rarely refer to themselves as a couple by using the word "we."

Jim and Tammy agree about many of the major issues that come up in marriage and family life. According to them, their ability to show affection and to engage in sexual relations is a major source of marital satisfaction. Since Jim is a separate and Tammy is a traditional, I call Jim and Tammy *Separate/Traditionals.*

COUPLE 5: ERIC AND MARIE

Eric and Marie do not share the same philosophy of life; Eric believes in stability and predictability, and Marie believes in personal growth and individual psychological gratification. Because Marie also believes that couples do not have to share complete, total agreement on all issues, she accepts Eric's traditionalism, although she sometimes quarrels with him about it. Eric, on the other hand, has a tendency to distort Marie's values to fit into a more traditional mold; he thinks she's more traditional than she is. Both enjoy spending time together and are capable of having a lot of fun, although Marie tends to value privacy and independence more than Eric does. When they do engage in conflict, Eric tries to keep the conflict muted, but Marie always expresses what she's really thinking and feeling. Part of their philosophical disagreement about life involves the nature of male/female roles. Eric sees himself as very masculine and in general believes men and women should follow conventional roles. Marie is more egalitarian and thinks people should follow their own individual preferences. Marie thinks of herself as feminine but also analytical and capable of leading.

Because this couple is trying to negotiate an acceptable level of closeness and distance in the marriage, their conversations often show signs of a power struggle and these power struggles continue for fairly long periods. Neither side is willing to "give in or give up." They both feel they can express their innermost thoughts and feelings, but Marie would like Eric to open up even more. Like the Separates, Frank and Eleanor, Eric and Marie talk about distinct traits, habits, and skills.

Unlike the Separates, however, when Eric and Marie discuss their first meeting, they remember it fondly and describe one another in very positive terms. They think of their marriage as being extremely well-adjusted. Sometimes Marie thinks about divorce or separation, but Eric says he never does. Despite their disagreements, they are very affectionate and companionable. Eric is a traditional and Marie is an independent: I call Eric and Marie *Traditional/Independents*.

SUMMARY

Eric and Marie, and Jim and Tammy, are examples of the Mixed marriage type; the husband and the wife differ in how they view the marriage. His marriage is different from her marriage. But couples like Jim and Tammy—the Separate/Traditionals—often can be clearly differentiated from the rest of the Mixed couple types because they tend to act differently. Except for Separate/Traditionals, Mixed couples resolve conflict, conduct casual conversations, and manage their daily lives in a very similar manner. The fact that spouses disagree over important dimensions of marriage, such as ideology and interdependence, directly affects their communication behavior.

CONCLUSION

This book provides the research base for the assertions I have made about marriage in a postindustrial society.

In Part I, I explore the conceptual background to the development of an empirical typology of marriage. In this section, I show statistically that there are different, yet patterned, ways for husbands and wives to relate to one another. Here, I systematically categorize marriage and validate those categories.

In Part II, I deal with two fundamental concepts in the study of marriage—power and conflict. A major reason for close social bonds is to give people reasons to coordinate actions and conciliate their diverging interests. This part demonstrates how couples in various types of marriages attempt to dominate or to submit to their spouse, resolve problems, and gain compliance.

In Part III, I discuss the verbal and nonverbal ways couples respond to one another and show their involvement with one another. Couples in various types of marriages express different ranges, intensities, and types of feelings, both verbally and nonverbally. In Part IV, I discuss how spouses, as well as people in the culture at large, think about marriage and how such psychological realities affect the encoding and decoding of messages to the spouse and about marriage.

In the Epilogue, I discuss directions for future research and theory development.

ACKNOWLEDGMENTS

I am extremely grateful for the support that I have received from the National Institute of Mental Health (1 RO1 MH40813), the National Institutes of Health, Biomedical Research Division (1983-1984, UW 141207), the generous support of the University of Wisconsin's Alumni Research Foundation (1979-1980, UW 100571; UW 110985: 1981-1982, UW 120893: 1982-1983, UW 130455: 1983-1984, UW 140367: 1986-1987, UW 871251: 1987-1988, UW 880922), the Graduate Schools of the University of Wisconsin—Milwaukee and Temple University. Without this support, the work described in this book would not have been possible.

My father quoted Mark Twain as saying that the only people who could use the editorial plural were "editors, kings and people with tape worms." Although I fall, luckily, into none of these three categories, I have violated his dictum throughout this book. Over the years, I have had a number of excellent teachers, colleagues, and students who have worked with me in the development and refinement of this marital typology. Arthur Bochner, Herbert Simons, and Michael Burgoon taught me about the importance of rigor and the relationship between theory and data. Robert Doolittle taught me about balancing teaching and research and about managing research groups. These lessons are reinforced daily in the Department of Communication Arts and in the Center for Communication Research at the University of Wisconsin. I am fortunate to work with a group of colleagues who are not easily impressed and who demonstrate excellence in both research and in teaching.

Julie Indvik and I began working together when she was a beginning graduate student and I was a beginning faculty member. We learned together and I am grateful for her friendship. Kathryn Dindia has been extremely helpful in a number of ways during the writing of this book as has Patricia Noller. Robin Williamson, who decided to undertake a complex dissertation on power in marriage, and Isabelle Bauman, who supervised two complex research projects this year, demonstrated a level of competence and dedication far beyond that of many graduate students.

Ann Sapa, Diane Badzinksi, Leslie Vance, Patricia Best, Hal Witteman, Marion Friestad, Barbara Wilson, Susan Fallis, Becky Amdahl, and many other graduate students have diligently served as experimenters, data analysts, and coders on many different projects. I am grateful for the assistance of my tireless crew of undergraduate assistants led by Marie Lindaas who have spent countless hours telephoning couples, setting up appointments, and coding marital interaction.

Ellen Porath, a first-class editor, helped me to begin writing this book and taught me a great deal about clarity in communication. Four scholars have carefully read this manuscript and been extremely helpful in clarifying my thinking and my writing. All are scholars of interpersonal communication who know how to give effective and appropriate feedback. Mark Knapp, an extremely fine writer, is a wonderful editor who knows what to say and when to say it. I can assure Debbie Weider-Hatfield and Diane Badzinski, who have never met, that they have a good deal in common. Both dislike sloppy thinking and are able to catch inconsistencies, ambiguities, and jargon.

Al Sillars has contributed his considerable research ability and analytical talent to studies of power and conflict among couples in the various types of marriages. He has closely read this manuscript and made a number of valuable suggestions and improvements. David Reiss whose work on family paradigms has inspired my thinking for a number of years has graciously consented to write an introduction to this volume. The mistakes that remain are mine in spite of the concerted efforts of these scholars.

I am grateful to the thousands of couples throughout the country who have graciously participated in this research. Basic marital research brings no direct benefit to the couples who participate in the research process. Their hope, and mine as well, was that these studies would contribute to a growing body of knowledge about communication between husbands and wives.

Finally, I would like to thank my husband, Roman Kyweluk, and my family and friends, for their good-natured endurance of my endless monologues on the subject of communication in personal relationships.

I

AN OVERVIEW OF MARITAL INTERACTION

1

Marital Interaction

What Do We Know?

Between 90% and 95% of all Americans get married at least once. In fact, marriage is so popular that even when people get divorced, most remarry within five years. Statistically, few people marry more than twice (Carter & Glick, 1978). Understanding marriage in modern society requires an understanding of the communication that goes on between husbands and wives. For many years, scholars tried to find predictors of marital success or failure by looking at social/demographic factors such as income, education, age at marriage, and the age difference between husband and wife. But social scientists now believe that these factors are far less important than the communication that occurs between partners. For example, it is not the lack of money that causes marital problems, but rather how the couples communicate and negotiate with each other about their economic difficulties. Throughout this book, I will stress that there are many different communication patterns associated with happy and unhappy marriages.

In this chapter, I lay the groundwork for the development of the marital typology by overviewing the major themes and trends in the study of marriage. By both participants and outsiders, marriages are judged as "successful" or "unsuccessful." The bases for that judgment change across societies and historical time periods. Because of the centrality of the concept of marital success in the current research on, and theories of, marital interaction, I begin this chapter with a discussion of the basic theoretical and methodological issues necessary to understand marital success in industrialized society. After a discussion of marital success and marital satisfaction, I turn to a description of the basic models devised to study communication in successful and unsuccessful marriages. Finally, I introduce the concept of a marital typology that posits that marriage is not a monolithic institution. Marital processes differ in systematic ways according to the type of marriage spouses have established.

MARITAL SUCCESS IN POSTINDUSTRIAL SOCIETY

People in twentieth-century Western society often use romantic love and personal attraction as criteria in choosing spouses. In past eras, marriage was an economic relationship designed to strengthen family ties and reinforce social class lines (Duby, 1983). The development of romantic love and personal attraction as bases for marriage is one of the many reasons why satisfaction with the marriage has become important in predicting whether a husband and wife will stay married. Once a person introduces personal evaluations and choice into the decision to marry, then it follows that the success of the marriage per se becomes defined according to a person's own criteria and standards (Shorter, 1975).

Measuring Marital Success

Researchers measure marital success according to marital "stability" and marital "satisfaction." Marital stability is defined as whether or not a given marriage is intact. The measurement of stability is relatively straightforward; one can be classified as married, divorced, separated, or never married. Satisfaction, however, refers to how a husband and wife describe and evaluate the quality of their marriage. Marital satisfaction is a subjective evaluation of a marital relationship as good, happy, or satisfying (Lewis & Spanier, 1979). There are a number of names for the concept of marital satisfaction: happiness, quality, adjustment, lack of distress, and integration. In this book, I use these concepts inter-changeably.

In general, marital satisfaction questionnaires include items on the amount of conflict, degree of agreement, shared activities, self-ratings of happiness, perceived permanence of the marriage, and evaluations of marital quality. Table 1.1 includes representative items from Snyder's (1981) Marital Satisfaction Inventory, in which husbands and wives

TABLE 1.1
Representative Items from Snyder's Marital Satisfaction Inventory

Affective Communication

"My spouse can usually tell what kind of day I've had without even asking."
"My spouse and I frequently sit down and talk about pleasant things that happened during the day."

Problem-Solving Communication

"My spouse has no difficulty accepting criticism."
"My spouse rarely nags me."

Time Together

"My spouse likes to share his or her leisure time with me."
"Our daily life is full of interesting things to do together."

Finances

"Serious financial concerns are not likely to destroy our marriage."
"My spouse and I rarely argue about money."

Sex

"My spouse rarely refuses intercourse when I desire it."
"My spouse seems to enjoy sex as much as I do."

Role Orientation

"The husband should be the head of the family."
"The major role of the wife should be that of housekeeper."

Family History

"I had a very happy home life."
"My parents had very few quarrels."

Children

"Having children has increased the happiness of our marriage."
"For the most part, our children are well-behaved."

Child Rearing

"My spouse and I rarely disagree on when or how to punish the children."
"My spouse and I decide together what rules to set for our children."

Global Satisfaction

"I have never thought of my spouse or me as needing marital counseling."
"I'm quite happily married."

Conventionalization

"There's never a moment when I did not feel 'head-over-heels' in love with my mate."
"I have never regretted my marriage, not even for a moment."

SOURCE: Adopted from Snyder (1981).

NOTE: The major predictors of marital happiness on this scale are good affective and problem-solving communication. The Marital Satisfaction Inventory Manual can be purchased from Western Psychological Services, 12031 Wilshire Blvd., Los Angeles, CA 90025.

report their subjective experiences and appraisals of their marriage by answering "true" or "false" to each of the 280 items.[1]

Not only have questionnaires been completed by individual husbands and wives, but ratings of a couple's happiness are sometimes sought from other family members (Kolb & Strauss, 1974), assessed by interviewers (Birchler, Weiss, & Vincent, 1975; Haynes, Chavez, & Samuel, 1984), or measured by whether a couple has applied for marital therapy (Snyder, 1981). The most common marital-happiness measures involve asking a husband and wife to fill out a questionnaire about their marriage. If marital quality, or happiness, is defined as an individual's evaluation or description of aspects of the marriage, self-reports yield important information on the "insider's" point of view.

The most frequently used scale for assessing marital satisfaction is Spanier's (1976) Dyadic Adjustment Scale (DAS). This scale was carefully constructed from the major marital satisfaction indices used in this century. The care that the author took in the construction of the scale, in the acknowledgment of previous research and theory, and in a concern for validity and reliability is exemplary. The DAS has four components: consensus, cohesion, expressions of affection, and satisfaction. *Consensus* deals with the couple's perception of how much agreement they share on 15 important marital issues, including philosophy of life and child rearing. *Cohesion* refers to how often a couple can work together on a project or have a good time together. *Expressions of affection* deals with whether a couple ever has disagreed about sex or other displays of affection. *Satisfaction* includes an estimate of how often spouses have serious disagreements in the marriage, and also how committed each person is to remaining in the marriage.

Methodological Caveats

The major marital satisfaction measures are either descriptive or evaluative. These different approaches to measuring marital satisfaction have their advantages and disadvantages and involve trade-offs in the kind of information garnered about a given marriage. The Spanier scale consists of descriptive questions about a marriage. Descriptive questions focus on the frequency of activities (such as kissing, sex, and confiding). The problem with descriptive questions is that the researcher makes many assumptions about what makes a marriage happy (Trost, 1985). For example, Spanier (1976) assumes that quarreling, leaving the house after an argument, and being too tired for sex are detrimental to marital satisfaction. On the other hand, he sees having a stimulating exchange of ideas, working together on a project, and confiding in one another as being good for marital satisfaction. As you will see throughout this book, these factors do not necessarily work in the same manner for all couples. Some couples find conflict less threatening than do other couples. Think of two husbands who are experiencing a moderate degree of conflict with their wives. To one man, this may mean that the marriage is in serious trouble; the other man may view it as a positive sign that he and his wife are trying to work out their difficulties.

A further problem in Spanier's test is that it lacks a good balance of items across different areas. Items about the level of agreement on marital issues are overrepresented, whereas items about affection between spouses are underrepresented. This lack of balance becomes especially problematic when an individual's answers are summed to come up with an overall dyadic adjustment score. A person who agrees with the spouse on 15 issues related to marriage, yet scores low on the few questions concerning affection and cohesion, will probably have a higher dyadic adjustment score than a person who disagrees with a spouse on a number of issues, yet has high levels of affection and cohesion.

An alternative marital satisfaction measure is Norton's (1983) Quality Marriage Index (QMI), which consists of evaluative questions. On this measure, marital satisfaction is operationally defined with one scale that measures happiness with the relationship as a whole. The QMI is a series of evaluative questions that ask about an individual's perception of the marriage along a continuum from "good" to "bad." In asking only evaluative questions, as Norton does, the researcher runs the risk of having participants give only socially desirable (or conventional) responses. If you ask people to estimate the happiness of their marriage, 95% will say their marriage is happier than "average" (Fitzpatrick, 1987b; Gurin, Veroff, & Feld, 1960; Terman, 1938). Obviously, this is not possible and this distortion makes it difficult to measure the relationship between marital happiness and any other factor. Although people seem to be unwilling to admit they are "unhappily married," in so many words, they will discuss the specific stresses and strains of their marriage.

Although debate continues on the definition of marital satisfaction, the fact remains that the correlations among the scales used to measure these various concepts are very high (Dindia, 1986; Lewis & Spanier 1979), suggesting that the scales are measuring "nearly" the same thing. Dindia (1986), for example, found correlations between the QMI, the DAS, and the Locke and Wallace (1959) scales ranging from .79 to .87. Despite the fact that the correlations among the scales for a given individual are high, the correlations between spouse ratings of the marriage are less robust. Spouses tend to disagree on their level of marital satisfaction.

In his classic study comparing the adjustment scores of husbands and wives, Locke (1951) chastised earlier researchers for the way they conducted their research. Previous researchers (e.g., Burgess & Cottrell, 1939) found a correlation of .88 between husband and wife satisfaction. Locke (1951) argued that this occurred because spouses completed the questionnaires without supervision and probably consulted one another. When Locke carefully controlled experimental procedures for completing the questionnaires, he found a correlation of .36 between husband and wife satisfaction. During the past 30 years of research on marriage, scientists have found a consistently low correlation between husbands' and wives' assessments of marital quality. Such results led Bernard (1972) to argue that "his" marriage is not the same as "her" marriage.

The lack of agreement on marital satisfaction between husbands and wives has implications for the design of marital communication studies. In a typical study in the area of marital communication (e.g., Ting-Toomey, 1983), a husband and wife independently complete a scale about some aspect of their marital quality. The classic Locke-Wallace (1959) inventory considers a score above 100 as "happily married," and a score of less than 100 as "unhappily married." Husbands and wives who disagree on whether they are happily married (e.g., the husband scores above 110 and the wife scores below 90), or who both score in the middle range of the marital happiness scale, usually are thrown out of the study (or lumped together into a middle group). Therefore, *studies tend to focus on couples who agree that they are either happily or unhappily married.*

Communication Correlates
of Marital Success

Many of the studies relating communication and marital success have used self-report measures of each concept and correlated them. There is a growing emphasis, however, on examining actual communication behaviors between couples in conflict and casual interaction. Couples who agree that they are happily or unhappily married are unusual in that the level of agreement on marital happiness is low in general. Even though these couples are unusual, people who agree that they are very happily married communicate with one another in a radically different manner than do other couples (Fitzpatrick & Badzinski, 1985). In contrast with

TABLE 1.2
Communication Dimensions of the Happy Marriage

Happy couples exhibit

—more positive nonverbal cues
—more agreement and approval
—a higher ratio of agreement to disagreement
—attempts to avoid conflict
—supportive behaviors
—compromises
—consistency in their use of nonverbal cues
—less criticism of each other
—a higher ratio of pleasing to displeasing behaviors

SOURCE: Fitzpatrick & Badzinski (1984, p. 698). Reprinted by permission.

unhappily married people, happily married people say they can resolve their problems and express their emotions to one another. The happily married people believe they communicate well with each other and feel that they are very accurate in interpreting each other's nonverbal communication. When researchers compare the actual communication behaviors of those who agree they are happily married to their reports about communication, these reports agree. Table 1.2 gives examples of actual behaviors that happily married couples use in the laboratory.

Theoretically, marital communication studies may be showing us that level of agreement on the dynamics of marriage is related to ability to report correctly on the patterns and interaction sequences in the relationship. When we find couples who both report a high level of marital happiness, and agree about that experience, we may be tapping the degree of shared reality experienced by a couple. Thus we are not measuring what we think we are measuring (i.e., marital satisfaction) but we are measuring the development of intersubjectivity between married partners.[2]

A recent development in the marital interaction area is to take the marital patterns and sequences observed in laboratory settings and attempt to turn them into questionnaires that determine whether happily and unhappily married couples can report their own communication behaviors (Christensen, 1987; Eggeman, Moxley, & Schumm, 1985). These efforts represent a way to take objective measures into an insider perspective. These new questionnaires are significantly more specific than are previous communication questionnaires. For example, Eggeman et al. (1985) assess spouses' perceptions of three sequential stages of marital conflict (i.e., agenda building, arguing, negotiation), identified by Gottman (1979).[3]

As in the behavioral data, distressed couples clearly differentiated themselves from happy couples in the negotiation phase. Distressed couples say they find it difficult to agree upon a solution whereas happy couples find solutions that are mutually satisfactory.

The practical advantages of using couples' self-reports of their interaction patterns are obvious. Since it takes about 28 hours to categorize 1 hour of marital interaction (Gottman, 1979), if couples can report about complex patterns of marital interaction, such reports would be extremely useful. Despite the obvious advantages, and recent advances in having couples report their interaction patterns, other evidence indicates that the unhappily married are especially unreliable as observers of events in their own marriages (Christensen & Nies, 1980; Elwood & Jacobson, 1982; Jacobson & Moore, 1981). The relationship between level of marital distress, and agreement about that distress, may differentially affect the spouses' ability to report about their interaction. The development of a high degree of shared intersubjectivity may lead to similar reports about marital patterns.

A question that has intrigued scholars concerns whether the unhappily married fail to communicate effectively with their spouses simply because they do not know how. When couples are brought into laboratories and asked to "fake" good marital communication, happily and unhappily married couples can communicate equally well (Vincent, Friedman, Nugent, & Messerly, 1979; but see, Cohen & Christensen, 1980). Also, when unhappily married couples are asked to communicate effectively with people other than their spouses, they appear to have little trouble (Noller, 1984). Unhappily married couples have the skills to communicate effectively, but for a variety of reasons, they choose not to use those skills in their marriage. Consequently, the unhappily married are said to have a "performance deficit" in marital communication, and not a "skills deficit" (Gottman, 1979).

Summary

Marital satisfaction is central to marital success. Scholars debate the very best way to measure this important concept although most now agree that communication is strongly related to marital happiness. Three major controversies dominate the literature. The first controversy turns on the advantages and disadvantages of measuring satisfaction with descriptive versus evaluative questions. The second controversy involves the meaning of agreement versus disagreement between couples on their level of marital satisfaction. The third controversy deals with what the relationship is, both conceptually and methodologically, between self-reports and behaviors.

Yet even as that debate continues, a clear picture emerges that "happily" married couples communicate in a remarkably different way than the "unhappily" married couples. In the next section, we will look at some theories that researchers have proposed to explain the communication differences between the happily and unhappily married.

THEORIES AND MODELS OF MARITAL COMMUNICATION

This section discusses three models of communication in marriage: coorientational, interactional, and typological. These models take into account the "insider" and "outsider" perspectives on relationships (Olson, 1977). Both insider and outsider perspectives can involve subjective and objective types of data. The insider perspective includes what the wife and husband say about the marriage—for example, how they describe their own communication patterns or estimate how happy or unhappy they are with the relationship. Subjective data from the insider point of view are self-reports assessments; whereas objective data from the insider point of view has a couple systematically monitor their own behavior. The outsider perspective involves anyone outside the relationship; it could be the researcher, the couple's children, their friends, or associates. Subjective data in this perspective includes clinical insights whereas objective data involve communication coding schemes.

Both the insider and outsider perspectives are important as are different types of data from both perspectives. On the one hand, couples are not always aware of how they behave with each other; on the other hand, outsiders may misconstrue the meaning of certain marital messages (e.g., Gottman, Notarius, Markman, Bank, Yoppi, & Rubin, 1976). The best models of marital interaction include both insider and outsider perspectives on the marriage; when the two perspectives conflict, or the data derived from both perspectives disagree, these models seek underlying theoretical reasons for divergence and convergence.

Coorientation Models

"Coorientation models" remind us that there are a number of different perspectives on any topic of conversation in a marriage (McLeod & Chaffee, 1972). These models measure whether individuals agree, whether they are accurate about this agreement, and whether they know (understand) that they are accurate or inaccurate. Agreement is measured from the outsider's perspective; a husband and wife are asked their opinions about issues, but it is the researcher (the outsider) who compares their answers to see if the couple agree or disagree. There are two types of accuracy, which also might be called "awareness of agreement." "Coorientational accuracy" is concerned with the ability of one spouse to predict the opinions of the other spouse. "Communication accuracy" involves the ability of a spouse to interpret the other spouse's messages as they were intended (Mehrabian, 1972). Communication accuracy may be the reason that coorientational accuracy exists. Knudson, Sommers, and Golding (1980) measured the interpersonal perceptions of couples as they watched a videotape of one of their own disagreements. Couples who resolved their interpersonal conflicts by openly discussing the disagreement, rather than by avoiding the issue, increased their accuracy in perceptions of their spouse's feelings and thoughts. Sillars and Scott (1983) reviewed evidence on the question of the accuracy of interpersonal perceptions in close relationships and suggested a number of conditions under which accuracy in perception in intimate relationships might falter. For example, spouses are likely to be accurate concerning perceptions where the referent is concrete, easily coded, and stable, whereas spouses are likely to be inaccurate under conditions where the referent is abstract, subtle, and interactional.

For example, imagine a couple, Howard and Jane, and an "issue"— whether or not to have a child. Howard wants to have a baby as soon as possible, Jane wants to wait five years. Jane thinks Howard wants to have a baby five years from now. Howard thinks Jane also wants to wait.

Using the model to analyze this situation, we can see that Howard and Jane do not agree on when to have a family; Howard wants one now, and Jane wants to wait. Jane is coorientationally inaccurate; she incorrectly believes he wants to wait. But Howard accurately perceives Jane's position. They could have a conversation about this topic, in which Howard expressed his opinion and Jane might or might not accurately interpret his message.

Coorientation models are concerned with explaining how intersubjectivity is developed in communication between people. These models remind us to focus on agreement in communication, accuracy of communication, and awareness of communication. From this attention to the structural properties of human communication emerges a concern for the channels that couples rely on to communicate accurately.

Spouses in unhappy marriages disagree with each other on a variety of marital issues (Spanier, 1976). Communicatively, unhappy couples appear to be inaccurate in interpreting each other's messages and to be unaware of this at any given time. Noller (1984) demonstrates that the inaccuracy arises because unhappy wives incorrectly use the vocal channel (tone of voice, paralinguistic cues such as pitch and speech rate) in decoding the messages of their husbands. In contrast, the more accurate happy wives rely on the visual channel (facial expression, etc.). Unhappy husbands rely on the visual channel to understand their wives (and are inaccurate), whereas happy husbands use the vocal channel to better advantage. In her review of the nonverbal communication literature, Hall (1984, p. 140) argues that, in general, men and women seem to be nonverbal modality specialists: women specialize in visual communication and behavior, men in vocal. Thus, in the happy marriages, greater accuracy occurs when spouses rely on the channel they are better at decoding, regardless of the channel the opposite-sex spouse is "better at," and prefers, using.

Critique and recommendation. The coorientational model was originally developed to conceptualize and measure agreement, accuracy, and awareness. Hence the model never discussed what kinds of message exchanges would lead to particular outcomes. The research must be expanded to linking these coorientational states to various channel and message types. In the next section, we turn to models that place communication at the very center of the domain of inquiry.

Interaction Perspectives

"Interaction perspectives" examine the patterns and sequences of marital communication. Measuring how often a behavior occurs is not always as important as measuring the likelihood that one behavior will trigger another. These models of marital communication seek answers to the question, "How can the intricate system connecting a husband and wife be described, analyzed, and explained?" A complete description of this intricate system requires attention to the content, intensity, pattern, and social context in which the interaction occurs (Hinde, 1979). Content could include topics, but usually it does not. More often it means

TABLE 1.3
The KPI Dimensions and Codes

Dimensions	Examples of Categories
Self-disclosure	Expression of feelings and wishes
Positive solution	Constructive proposals; compromises
Acceptance of the other	Paraphrase, open question, feedback
Agreement	Assent, accept responsibility
Metacommunication	Clarification request
Problem description	Neutral question
Criticism	Global negative, specific negative
Negative solution	Negative solution
Justification	Excuse, deny responsibility
Disagreement	Yes-but, blocking

SOURCE: Adapted from the Kategoriensystem fur Partner-Schaftliche Interactions (KPI). See Hahlweg et al. (1984).

NOTE: This scheme has 26 behavioral content codes and three nonverbal codes. The content codes are divided into the ten dimensions listed above.

measuring verbal and nonverbal behaviors. To measure these behaviors, the researcher establishes a coding scheme, which is a method of interpreting behavior based on what the researcher thinks is important (Bakeman & Gottman, 1986). The success of interaction studies (usually outsider/objective measures linked to insider/subjective measures) depends on those distinctions that become enshrined in the coding scheme. What the researcher is saying, in essence, is, "This is what I think is important in human communication." Table 1.3 presents an example of an important verbal content-interpretation scheme used to study marital communication.

One might feel, however, that most of the meaning in marital communication is in the nonverbal communication. Let's say we believe the voice is important in predicting the emotion that a communicator is experiencing. We might look at certain voice types for specific emotional predictions. Table 1.4 uses two dimensions of the voice in combination to predict the emotional state of the communicator.

One also might look at the intensity of the interaction—the pacing, the tempo, and "activity level" of the conversation—by focusing on such

TABLE 1.4
Voice Type Predictions for Various Emotional States

Emotional State	Vocal Tension	Vocal Power
Happiness	relaxed	slightly full
Elation	medium tense	medium full
Disgust	slightly tense	slightly full
Contempt	slightly tense	medium full
Sadness	lax	thin
Grief	tense	thin
Anxiety	slightly tense	thin
Fear	extremely tense	very thin
Rage	very tense	extremely full
Shame	slightly tense	thin

SOURCE: Adopted from Scherer (1986, p. 157).
NOTE: A third dimension, which helps to discriminate two other emotions, is missing from this adaption.

nonverbal cues as pauses, the speed of speaking, the number and type of gestures, and the tone of voice. One also could look for verbal cues of intensity, which could include the use of obscenity or word choices that indicate strong positive or negative feelings about the object of discussion. For example, most people would agree that the statement, "It was devastating to me," is more intense than the statement, "It upset me."

And one might look at patterns of communication—the likelihood that one behavior will follow another. For example, take two couples. Each couple disagreed five times during the conversation. A simple frequency count would suggest that the two couples have the same type of communication. But if one looked at the patterns of their communication, one might come to a different conclusion. One might find out that every time one husband disagreed with his wife, she gave in. But every time the second husband disagreed, his wife changed the subject. Examining the pattern of interactions, even at this simple level, gives us a different picture of the marriage.

Finally, a complete interaction description would include the social context in which the interaction occurs. A husband and wife may change their communication depending on whether they are in public, in front of the children, in a laboratory situation with researchers, or alone on a beach in the Caribbean. Social context also could include the historical context in which something occurs; one cannot use the same standards to compare communication between a medieval knight and his lady with a conversation between a Madison Avenue advertising executive and her husband. Social context is especially important to researchers because it can affect the intensity of the communication between a wife and her husband. This means a couple who argue mildly before a researcher in a lab (Witteman & Fitzpatrick, 1986) will argue more intensely when the research interview takes place in their home (Williamson & Fitzpatrick, 1986), and argue most vehemently of all when the researcher leaves their home and allows them to tape record their own conversations (Sillars, Pike, Jones, & Redmon, 1983). Both the researcher and the physical environment of the home create a different social context for marital interaction.

Models of message exchange. Researchers have proposed seven major theories or models to explain marital interaction patterns. The first five of these models place the exchange of messages at the core of the model. The last two models give communication a secondary, although important, emphasis; the major emphasis is on how communication behavior affects physiological processes. Let's look at the first five:

(1) *Behavior exchange model.* This model (Jacobson, 1984) is based on the assumption that individuals evaluate their relationships in terms of costs and rewards, in the interest of keeping a high ratio of rewards to costs. The core of this model involves comparing the number of "positive exchanges" to the number of "negative exchanges" in a marriage. For example, a positive exchange would be joking, agreeing, and compromising. Negative exchanges would include nagging, criticizing, or complaining. The greater the ratio of positive to negative exchanges, the happier the marriage is presumed to be. An extremely high number of positive experiences can compensate for a high number of negative experiences. For example, a man and woman may argue often and have little money, but such negative exchanges are offset by having a higher number of positive exchanges, such as good times, a satisfying sex life, and mutual understanding. The ratio is important, but couples in unhappy marriages also seem to be more sensitive to negative exchanges. They notice and remember the bad times more than happily married couples do.

(2) *Behavior competency model.* This model (Markman, 1984) argues that marital unhappiness occurs when spouses do not know how to

express feelings with each other, how to argue constructively, and how to develop ways of coping with normal life stresses. It includes a "sleeper effect"; that is, inability to argue constructively during courtship does not appear to affect a couple's satisfaction with the relationship at the time, but it does predict unhappiness with the partner and the marriage five years later. The behavior competency model is a hopeful model of human communication. This model views communication as a skill, such as playing tennis, and therefore communication can be learned. Regardless of one's current level of competence, one can always improve. But to play a game such as tennis requires a certain minimal level of achievement, just as a certain minimal level of communication skill is necessary for a happy marriage. At a minimum, couples must be able to negotiate conflict and express their feelings (Snyder, 1979). A skills perspective also suggests that even an excellent communicator has room for improvement.

(3) *Social learning model.* This model (Weiss, 1981) stresses social reinforcement and the quid pro quo. Reinforcement refers to the delivery of a reward that strengthens a particular behavior. The reinforcement is social when it consists of feedback from a spouse, in this case. Examples include attention, approval, indifference, and hostility. Positive reinforcement occurs when one spouse administers a pleasant stimulus after the other spouse has performed a particular behavior. The wise wife smiles at the husband who has done the dishes, she does not chide him for not doing them more often.

Negative reinforcement is not the same as punishment; rather, it occurs with the removal of an unpleasant stimulus after the behavior has been performed. A husband complains every evening for a week that his wife never takes the car to the car wash; finally, she has the car washed. If he immediately stops complaining, he has reinforced her car-washing behavior and she probably will continue to wash the car. But she has positively reinforced his nagging. Although this example focuses on verbal communication, a good deal of positive and negative reinforcement occurs at the nonverbal level between wives and husbands.

(4) *Relational control model.* Communication offers information at the content level (looking at what was said) and the relationship level (looking at the nature of the relationship between the speaker and the other person, from the point of view of the speaker). This model (Rogers & Farace, 1975), applied to marital interaction, codes messages as attempts to assert or relinquish control. The messages of husbands and wives are then paired in order to understand the nature of control in their relationship. A message to assert control, paired with a message that

relinquishes control, is considered "complementary." A message to assert or relinquish control, paired with a message with a similar intent, is considered "symmetrical." In other terminology, symmetrical couples can be considered egalitarian. A recent review of the relationship between marital satisfaction and power comes to the conclusion that husband-dominant and egalitarian marriages are happy ones, whereas wife-dominant marriages are unhappy (Gray-Little & Burks, 1983).

(5) *Structural model of marital interaction.* There are four major hypotheses in this model of marital communication (Gottman, 1979). The first hypothesis deals with structure and pattern in communication, and argues that unhappily married couples are significantly more rigid and inflexible in their communication patterns than are happy couples. The second hypothesis suggests that unhappily married couples express significantly more negativity in both verbal and nonverbal communication with one another than do happy couples. The third hypothesis suggests that although there are no significant differences in the reciprocity of positive messages by happy and unhappy couples, unhappy couples are significantly more likely to reciprocate negative messages than are happy couples. Thus, in all types of marriages, a compliment begets a compliment, yet a sarcastic remark begets a sarcastic remark only among the unhappily married. The fourth hypothesis suggests that unhappy marriages are marked by asymmetry in predictability; in other words, one spouse dominates the other spouse. For example, when the dominant spouse calls for compliance, compliance is more likely than when the less-dominant spouse calls for it. The asymmetry is in the amount of predictability gained in knowing the behavior of the dominant compared with the less-dominant spouse. If the husband is the dominant member, we would be able to predict the behavior of his wife based on his behavior, but we would not be able to predict his behavior based on her behavior.

Gottman (1979) has tested and supported these four hypotheses with a series of verbal and nonverbal observational techniques and sophisticated statistical analyses. Researchers in the United States (Fitzpatrick, 1987c; Ting-Toomey, 1983) and Europe (Schaap, 1982) have replicated most of the sequential interaction patterns observed by Gottman (1979).

Arousal and marital communication. Although all of the models deal with communication, these last two models relate the messages exchanged between marital partners to the partners' underlying emotional state. The major theories of emotion include three basic components (Candland, 1977): verbal reports, behavior, and physiological measures. With verbal reports, one asks people what emotion they are experiencing. With behavior, one closely examines people's facial expressions or vocal tones. And with physiological tests, one measures heart rate or blood velocity.

Physiological arousal (autonomic nervous system arousal) is signaled by increases in blood pressure, heartbeat, pulse, and perspiration. We become physiologically aroused when we are threatened, in what some scientists call the "fight or flight" syndrome. Biologically, this arousal prepares us to stay and fight the enemy, or to run away. Psychologically, this arousal orients us to pay closer attention to what is happening. The degree of arousal, the frequency of arousal, and how long it takes to calm down again are important aspects of how physiological arousal relates to emotion. Frequent, extreme physiological arousal is associated with a number of life-threatening, stress-related diseases (Gottman & Levenson, 1987).

The next two theories emphasize how communication affects physiological responses between spouses.

(6) *Interdependence theory.* A necessary condition for the experience of emotion is the presence of physiological arousal (Berscheid, 1983). Physiological arousal is said to occur when an individual is interrupted in the completion of an organized behavioral sequence. After the interruption occurs and alternate routes to complete the sequence are blocked, then emotion is experienced. The positivity or negativity of the experienced emotion depends on the context in which the interruption occurs. Positive emotions result if the interruption is seen as benign or controllable, if it leads to the accomplishment of a goal sooner than expected, or if it removes something previously disruptive. Because interruptions are usually uncontrollable, however, most of them lead to negative emotions.

The concept of interdependence is central to understanding what the individual experiences as interrupting. Couples develop a series of organized behavioral sequences that necessitate the spouse as a partner in the action in order to achieve successful completion. The sequences that require the spouse for completion are called "interchain" sequences (e.g., lovemaking, marital conversations). Individuals also have "intrachain" sequences, or personal, ongoing, goal-directed activities that need to be completed once they have begun. The greater the range and diversity of interchain sequences, the more interdependent the marriage. On a day-to-day basis, extremely interdependent couples may not experience strong positive or negative emotions as a result of their interaction.

Berscheid (1983) views interchain causal connections as necessary, but not sufficient, conditions for emotion to occur. Autonomic arousal and emotion occur when some interchain connection interrupts the completion of an individual's intrachain sequence. To illustrate, a highly organized intrachain sequence may involve a wife regaling her colleagues with the story about her recent corporate takeover. The story may be well-rehearsed and often told, and one element of the story carefully builds on another. Usually during this performance, her husband interjects a comment in the middle of the story, "Don't forget to tell them about the lawyer for the Securities and Exchange Commission." This is an organized behavioral sequence for the couple, in which his comment interchains with her intrachain sequence (the story) and serves to help her to complete her narrative successfully. No emotion would be expected to occur as a consequence of this event. Suppose, however, that this wife tells her story and her husband, for the first time, interjects, "Tell them how the next day the *Wall Street Journal* claimed you paid too much for the stock." This statement represents an interruption because it stops or slows the completion of her story. This interruption is physiologically arousing and probably will lead to negative emotion toward her husband. If the husband of this tycoon had commented on a favorable *Business Week* report, the experience also would have been interrupting. This interruption, however, probably would have been interpreted as positive because the interchain connection actually facilitated her narrative.

Curiously, some couples are so well-meshed and so unlikely to interrupt each other that on a day-to-day basis they are unlikely to experience much emotion, positive or negative, even though the marriage is a very close one. Other couples have few common goals and neither help nor hinder each other in attaining those goals; they also experience little emotion in the marriage on a day-to-day basis, but these couples have a very distant relationship.

This theory explains a number of marital paradoxes. It accounts for those couples who have a good deal of conflict and hostility in their marriages but maintain a high enough level of satisfaction to remain married. These couples experience a greater range and diversity of emotions than do their more quiescent counterparts. The theory also explains why spouses who believe their marriage is emotionally dead may experience extreme distress upon actual separation from each other (Hunt & Hunt, 1977). Divorcing individuals often experience strong and conflicting emotions toward their spouses, and a seemingly inexplicable revival of sexual feeling for the disliked spouse (Kressel & Deutsch, 1977; Weiss, 1975). Marriages may seem boring to the participants because they are so well-meshed; however, such relationships often become emotionally very intense when the couples separate.

(7) *Physiological theory of marital interaction.* This theory of marital communication posits fundamental biological differences between males and females. These differences control the exchange of messages between spouses, particularly in tense situations. Husbands are physiologically aroused more easily during confrontations than are their wives, and are slower to calm down afterward (Gottman & Levenson, 1987; Levenson & Gottman, 1983). This effect is stronger for unhappily married husbands. Extreme physiological arousal is very punishing to the distressed husband and causes him, eventually, to withdraw from the marital relationship. Ultimately, this withdrawal can lead to the emotional collapse of the marriage. Women do not experience the same strong physiological reaction as do males. In many unhappy marriages, the husband is not sensitive to subtle, nonverbal displays of his wife's feelings (Gottman, 1979; Noller, 1984), perhaps because he experiences physical stress when confronted by his wife's negative emotions.

This theory is very controversial and is undergoing testing and refinement. It is extremely physiologically arousing to many feminists because of the political implications of these findings. Therapeutically, the theory suggests that distressed husbands should be taught biofeedback to help them control their extreme physiological arousal during confrontations with their wives. Pragmatically, this theory implies that proponents of "total womanhood" are correct in suggesting that wives should subordinate themselves and express only positive messages toward their husbands.

Critique and recommendation. Each of these seven interaction models argues for the importance of studying communication behaviors from the outsider's perspective by focusing on direct verbal and nonverbal message exchanges between husbands and wives. All of these models also attend to the insider's view of the marriage by relating interaction patterns to the individual's subjective perceptions of marital happiness and distress. Each model has added important information about the way couples communicate with each other in happy and unhappy marriages.

These interaction models have very complex views of communication, but very simplistic views of the variety of types of relationships possible. The major characteristic used to identify types of marriages is the degree of satisfaction or dissatisfaction experienced by the partners. Identifying couples based on satisfaction tends to capture couples at opposite ends of the continuum and to discard the majority of couples who display only moderate levels of satisfaction or who disagree on their level of marital satisfaction. The communication behaviors exhibited may be due to the extreme groups of couples used to test the interaction models.

TABLE 1.5
Possible Cognitions of Unhappily and Happily Married Wives

Husband's critical remark: "You don't take any interest in me. I'm sick of it."

Wife's Thoughts in Unhappy Marriages:

"How dare he say that to me? Who does he think he is?"
"This is ridiculous."
"I can't take this anymore."

Wife's Thoughts in Happy Marriages:

"Maybe he's had a bad day. Perhaps I can help him." (Displacement of the problem onto the other.)
"He's in a bad mood. Maybe I should leave him alone for a while. Perhaps I'll go bake a cake." (Self-distraction.)
"This is an unpleasant situation, but we've managed more difficult ones." (Self-reinforcement.)
"I can't take this comment seriously. He's just a little annoyed." (Devaluation of the other.)
"It's normal to have fights in a marriage. It would be unreasonable to expect harmony all the time." (Accepting the given state as normal.)

SOURCE: Adopted from Revenstorf (1984, p. 327).

Scientists are beginning to discuss alternatives to simply considering marital happiness or distress. Additional insider information is needed. Many of the behaviorally oriented theorists in this area (e.g., Hahlweg & Jacobson, 1984), however, have recently argued that we need to include in the models some attention to the cognitions of married couples beyond a mere assessment of their satisfaction or dissatisfaction.

Take a critical remark from a husband: "You don't pay any attention to me. I'm sick of it." Often in unhappy marriages, the remark will prompt a number of thoughts on the part of the wife, and all of these thoughts could increase the unpleasantness between the partners. In happy marriages, such thoughts would be remarkably different. Thus a comment by one spouse may be positively or negatively transformed in the mind of the other spouse. Table 1.5 presents some possibilities of how the comments of one spouse can be interpreted differently by the other spouse.

Three trends in the behavioral research on couples show that it is important to understand the cognitive and perceptual biases that discriminate nondistressed and distressed couples (Jacobson, 1984). First, unhappy couples react more extremely to negative messages than do happy couples. Distressed spouses appear to be hypersensitive, on a subjective, emotional level, to their partner's immediate behavior. Not only does negative behavior occur more frequently in distressed marriages, but also when this behavior occurs, it has a deleterious effect on daily ratings of marital satisfaction (Jacobson, Follette, & McDonald, 1982). In contrast, happier couples appear to have devised some mechanism to deal with negative spousal behaviors.

Second, distressed couples reciprocate negative behaviors to a significantly greater degree than do nondistressed couples, indicating a tendency toward escalation. Distressed couples maintain long cycles of negative interaction, which become more and more intense as the conversation continues (Gottman, 1979). Such cycles suggest different weighting systems that couples in marriages of various levels of distress may be operating.

Third, individuals in unhappy marriages are far more likely to disagree with both outsider and spouse perspectives on their relationship than are happy couples. In particular, distressed husbands and wives tend to underestimate the frequency of a spouse's positive behaviors (Jacobson & Moore, 1981).

All of these points, taken together, suggest that persons in happy and unhappy marriages have very different views about how to assign meaning to the messages of their spouses. To understand what couples are thinking as they communicate, we need more information than simply an evaluation of the happiness or unhappiness of the marriages. One way to go beyond the happy/unhappy marital distinction is to consider a number of different dimensions to describe marriage. To understand the variety of approaches that individuals can take to marriage, scholars in the marital and family area have proposed "typologies" of marriages. Typologies can potentially integrate theory, research, and clinical practice with couples and families (Olson, 1981). In the next section, we discuss a few of the major approaches to categorizing marriage.

Typological Models

In every field of inquiry, typologies help scholars bring order to the phenomena that they study. Proponents of typological models of marriage argue that within any given sample of couples, there are a few basic types of marriages. A typology places in the same category marriages that share a number of the same attributes. Nearly a century ago, one writer noted the difference between what he called "despotic" and "democratic" marriages (Willcox, 1892).

More recently, scholars have categorized marriages as either "institutional" or "companionate" (Burgess & Locke, 1948). An *institutional marriage* emphasizes the value of laws, mores, and authority; the husband is granted the role of disciplinarian, breadwinner, economic coordinator, and decision maker. The wife is the homemaker and the child rearer, and is normally subordinate to her husband in other areas of family life. The behavior of people in institutional marriages is controlled by forces outside the marriage: society, religion, what other people will think, and the like. Partners in such marriages do not display strong feelings toward one another and spend little time together.

A *companionate marriage* emphasizes the values of mutual affection, common interests, and consensus. Although husbands in these marriages are seen as breadwinners, they participate actively in socializing the children and in some home tasks. The wife may work outside the home or do volunteer service, but she still tends to be primarily responsible for homemaking and child rearing. The behavior of people in companionate marriages, however, is controlled by forces inside the marriage: affection and mutual compatibility of the partners (Bell, 1979).

The problem with this continuum of marriages is that it focuses on only one or two dimensions of marriage, and pays little attention to the complexity of relationships in modern society. This typology is useful in considering the changes the family has undergone through history. The continuum is better used to analyze differences among societies and cultures than it is to understand what is going on currently within our society. Other researchers have used this idea to develop a more complex view of marriage in our society.

Sex and the significant Americans. Recent research indicates that institutional and companionate marriages can have subcategories. In the early 1960s, Cuber and Harroff (1965) conducted extensive interviews with more than 400 upper-middle-class Americans. These researchers developed a classification of marriage based on marriages that had lasted at least 10 years between husbands and wives who claimed they had never considered divorce or separation. This definition reduced the original sample to 211 people. The researchers identified three types of institutional marriage and two types of companionate marriage. The typology delineated the patterns by which these people lived together, found sexual expression, reared children, and made their way in the outside world.

The three subtypes of the institutional category include conflict-habituated, devitalized, and passive-congenial couples.

Conflict-habituated couples fight often but rarely settle anything. The tension, although high, is controlled. Their incompatibility is pervasive, and an atmosphere of tension permeates the marriage. As the husband in one conflict-habituated marriage put it:

> We have fought from the time we were in high school together. As I look back at it, I can't remember specific quarrels; it's more like a running guerrilla fight with intermediate periods, sometimes quite long, of pretty good fun. (p. 45)

Devitalized couples once had a very close relationship, but have grown apart since the early days of their marriage. Most of their time is spent in behavior related to "duty": entertaining together, spending time with the children, and pursuing community activities. As the wife in a devitalized marriage said:

> I'll admit that I do yearn for the old days when sex was a big thing and going out was fun and I hung on to everything he said about his work and his ideas as if they were coming from a genius or something. But then you get the children and other responsibilities. . . . You have to adjust to these things and we both try to gracefully. (p. 48)

The *passive-congenials* rarely argue. They share common interests, and they emphasize their civic and professional responsibilities, property, children, and their reputations. A passive congenial couple put it this way:

> I don't know why everyone seems to make so much about men and women and marriage. . . . I think it's the proper way to live. It's convenient, orderly, and solves a lot of problems. But there are other things in life. (p. 51)

There are two types of companionate marriages: the vitals and the totals.

The *vitals* are intensely bound together psychologically in important life matters. An activity is uninteresting to one spouse if the other spouse is not a part of it. One such husband said:

> The things we do together aren't fun intrinsically—the ecstasy comes from being together in the doing. Take her out of the picture and I wouldn't give a damn for the boat, the lake, or any of the fun that goes on out there. (p. 55)

The *totals* are similar to the vitals, but different in extreme; they share everything. Privacy is a foreign idea to these couples. As one wife put it:

It's not so much that I only want to help him; it's more that I want to do those things anyway.... I really don't know what I do for him and what I do for me. (p. 59)

This typology, although extremely interesting, did not offer any clear way to measure how an individual marriage could be put into one of the five basic types. The researchers derived the typology by intuition and provided no clear procedures for classifying couples.

Types and patterns of marital satisfaction. Seeking an alternative to an intuitively derived typology, Snyder and Smith (1986) had 178 couples complete Snyder's Marital Satisfaction Inventory (1981). Individuals' responses on the MSI were scored on the 11 profile subscales. Cluster analyses of husbands' and wives' profiles revealed five types of marriages.

Type I marriages are relatively nondistressed. These individuals have low scores on all of the profile scales that assess relationship distress, although both males and females report moderate discontent with their children and the stresses of child rearing. Both husbands and wives report greater flexibility in the sharing of traditional marital and parental roles. These wives tend to have had unhappy childhoods, or parents with distressed marriages. In addition, husbands in these marriages are more likely to complain about their sexual relationship with their wives.

Type II marriages are very similar to Type I marriages in their lack of distress, but they differ in that people in Type II marriages deny having even minor marital difficulties. People here claim they have a "perfect marriage" and a "perfect mate" and deny ever considering an alternative to marriage to their particular spouse. Such high scores might be achieved by some individuals during periods of unusual marital harmony, but even people with strong positive feelings toward the marriage and a spouse would not score as high as couples in this type do. This marital type reflects a naive, uncritical appraisal of the relationship.

In *Type III* marriages, although group profiles for both sexes reflect moderate levels of marital distress, specific areas of contention differ. Males in this type report little chronic disharmony in their marriages but admit moderate discontent with the manner in which marital disagreements are resolved, as well as moderate conflict over finances and child rearing. Women report similar levels of distress in these areas, but describe additional stresses. These women describe dissatisfaction with the amount of affection and understanding provided by their husbands, with the quality and quantity of leisure time they spend with their husbands, with their relationships with their children; they see their children as interfering with their marriages and their personal fulfillment.

Type IV and *Type V* husbands and wives show extensive marital distress on all of the scales pertaining to any aspect of the marital relationship. The main difference between the types is that Type IV husbands and wives are satisfied in interactions with their children and spouses about their parental roles. Type V people are unhappy in that area, too.

Because there are five types into which an individual may fall, there are 25 possible marital groupings. When Snyder and Smith (1986) compared husbands' and wives' types, 52% of the individuals agreed with their spouses on their marital type. In total, 48% fall into 20 other possible groupings.

The advantage of this typology of marriage is that it demonstrates the inadvisability of relying on global measures of marital distress as the sole criterion for forming comparison groups to study marital communication. In the Snyder and Smith (1986) study, couples who were not in therapy at that time had low scores on global indices of marital distress but exhibited moderate or high distress in specific areas of marital interaction. This investigation shows that there are a number of different ways to be satisfied or dissatisfied in marriage.

The problem with this characterization is that it yields too many different types of marriages. Granted that this difficulty is a technical problem and not a theoretical weakness but it does make using the system unwieldy. These 25 self-reported marital types are not unambiguously related to specific behavioral patterns of communication.

A marital-conflict typology. Olson (1981) used communication behaviors to categorize couples.[4] He examined the behaviors of 396 couples across three dimensions of interaction: task leadership, conflict, and affect. The three dimensions are categorized into high, medium, and low. Logically, this leads to 27 different types of marriages. Analyzing how couples communicate using the Inventory of Marital Conflict, however, indicated that only 9 of the 27 logical possibilities appear. There are five types of husband-led couples. The *disengaged* are those with low conflict and low affect; the *engaged* have moderate conflict and high affect; the *confrontative* have high conflict and moderate affect; the *conflicted* have high conflict and high affect; and the *cooperative* have moderate conflict and moderate affect.

There are three basic patterns of wife-led couples. There are *disengaged* and *confrontative* wife-led couples and a type called *congenial*, which involves low conflict and moderate affect. When the wife is in the dominant position in the marriage, there are no engaged, cooperative, or extremely conflicted marital types.

Finally, only one pattern of shared leadership in couples emerges when interaction is used as the categorization scheme. This is *cooperative*. Thus shared leadership in a marriage correlates with moderate conflict and moderate affect between partners.

This is an extremely interesting typology that captures the relationships among important dimensions of marital interaction. Unfortunately, other than the original work proposing these types of marriages, little else is known about these couples. Olson has not reported follow-up validational studies. Also, the categorization of marriages based on small samples of communication behavior that are collected under laboratory conditions may limit the types' eventual applicability. The interaction differences of a couple may not be stable across topics and time. A typology of marriage must be anchored within a network of constructs that could be used to predict communication style differences in various contexts.

Critique and recommendation. I present these three typologies to give the reader a flavor of what has been done recently to categorize marriages. Typologies based on intuitive dimensions of marital functioning abound, as do those based on interaction data (see Fitzpatrick, 1976, 1977, for a summary). The tradition of categorizing marriages has been an active one because scholars believe that categorizations will eventually lead to a better understanding of communication patterns in marriage. Category schemes require clear descriptions of important dimensions of marriage. Description is a fundamental goal of science. Most of the previous typological descriptions of marriage fall short of fulfilling that fundamental goal because these typologies have been intuitively derived, have lacked specific procedures for classification, have unknown replicability, and fail to provide types that are mutually exclusive and exhaustive.

A good description of marriage has to be exhaustive, mutually exclusive, clearly able to classify couples, and related to other important constructs. Exhaustiveness means all the dimensions that might be important in describing couples have to be included.

Mutual exclusivity means each couple can be assigned to one, and only one, couple type. The classification procedures have to be clear enough to assign a given couple unambiguously to a specific category. Finally, the typology must be related to other constructs of interest. As we have seen, the typologies we have covered so far do not meet all of these criteria.

Summary

I have discussed the three major conceptual approaches to studying communication between husbands and wives. Each approach tries to examine how the messages exchanged by spouses affect the overall status of the marriage. The coorientation models emphasize the importance of accuracy and agreement between spouses. The interaction models emphasize structure and pattern in marital communication. The typological models emphasize that there are different recurring organizational patterns to classify marriages.

The three approaches are like the panels of a triptych; they can stand alone but, taken together, form a more compelling picture.

CONCLUSION

In this chapter, I have observed that scientists define and study marital satisfaction, or the qualitative assessment of a marriage by the partners, in the interest of understanding why some marriages stay together and why some fall apart. Because communication is considered central to the achievement of a satisfying marriage, we introduced the major models that have been used to explain interaction in marriage: coorientational, interactional, and typological. The coorientational model isolates the inputs and outputs of exchanges between people, but it ignores the exchanges themselves. Interactional models capture the complexity of human communication, but ignore the complexity of relationships. Typologies focus on the complexity of human relationships, but give less attention to communication processes and outcomes.

In the chapters that follow, I borrow some of the insights from each of these basic models of human communication to describe relationships in postindustrial society. Throughout the rest of this book, I draw upon the work summarized in this chapter to design studies and devise hypotheses about the nature of communication between husbands and wives. In the next chapter, I discuss important dimensions of marriage and show how they have been used to describe marital types.

NOTES

1. The role orientation items from this scale tap male dominance. This illustrates a problem with the measures generally. The scales often confuse satisfaction with the predictors of satisfaction (i.e., traditionalism).

2. The question remains as to whether the extremely unhappy have also developed a high degree of intersubjectivity. I believe that they have. The development of intersubjectivity may be obscured by the fact that in the practice of research, we can be sure that the "happily married" couples are both happy and in agreement about that happiness,

whereas the "unhappily married" may include couples with a high degree of intersubjectivity and those with a low degree of intersubjectivity.

3. In the first stage, agenda building, the objective is to discuss the issues as each person perceives them (e.g., When you and your mate are beginning to discuss a disagreement over an important issue, how often do you both begin to understand each other's feelings reasonably quickly?).

In the second phase, arguing, the goal is for each partner to argue for his or her point of view and to understand the areas of disagreement between them (e.g., After you and your mate have been discussing a disagreement over an important issue for a while, how often are you able to identify clearly the specific things about which you disagree?).

In the third phase, negotiation, the objective is to achieve a mutually satisfactory compromise (e.g., About the time you and your mate feel you are close to a solution to your disagreement over an important issue, how often are you able to completely resolve it with some sort of compromise that is OK with both of you?). The report (Eggeman et al., 1985) reproduces the entire scale.

4. This marital typology should not be confused with Olson's work on a family typology that uses a self-report instrument (i.e., FACES) to categorize families along the dimensions of cohesion and adaptability.

2

Marital Types
Classifying Marriages

In the first chapter, I discussed the advantages and disadvantages of the three current, predominant models of marital communication. I argued that the coorientational models place too little emphasis on the messages themselves, that the interaction models tend to oversimplify the discussion of types of marriages, and that the typological approaches oversimplify the nature of the interaction process. It is the premise of this book that the scientific study of interpersonal relationships has suffered from a lack of a descriptive phase (Hinde, 1979). Admittedly, theorists have discussed with great subtlety (Knapp, 1978; McCall, McCall, Denzin, Suttles, & Kurth, 1970) the nature, functions and outcomes of a wide variety of nonmarital relationships (friendships, friendly relationships, social relationships, acquaintanceships, working relationships, and so forth). But in many ways, social scientists approach marital relationships in the manner of 1940s movies, in which marriage was the denouement; as the music welled up and the credits began to roll, the couple walked off into the sunset and "lived happily ever after." Some theorists consider that couples might also live unhappily ever after, but that was the extent of it.

Only the clinicians (e.g., Lederer & Jackson, 1968), however, present the insight that marriages can exist across a broad spectrum and different marital arrangements can be satisfying to the partners. Clinical insights suggest that "satisfaction" is better construed as an outcome of marital processes, rather than as a description of those processes. The qualitative aspects of marital relationships that lead to various levels of satisfaction or distress for a couple vary enormously. These variations are neither extremely individual nor highly random. To describe these variations, one needs procedures for classifying marriages, assigning couples to marital types, and validating those types in terms of other variables of interest.

In this chapter, I introduce an empirical (data-based, in contrast to conceptual) approach to the classification of marriages. This empirical approach relies on conceptually important dimensions that couples use to describe their relationships. I have derived these concepts from a careful reading of the major clinical and ethnomethodological studies conducted over the past 25 years. A questionnaire called the Relational Dimensions Instrument (RDI) measures these concepts. Based on this measurement technique, I placed marriages into three distinct categories. From these categories, I constructed the marital types.

APPROACHES TO CLASSIFICATION

Discrete recurrent patterns of marital interaction exist and can be isolated. Variations in marital relationships occur for gender-linked differences, as well as for the structure and patterning of different aspects of interaction within relationships. How do we account for between-couple differences? One answer to this question has been the development of marital classification systems. In this section, I introduce two major approaches that have been taken to classifying marriage: the logical approach and the empirical, polythetic model.

Logical Models of Classification

In a classical typological procedure, the researcher takes two variables that he or she thinks are important in describing a social phenomenon, and divides both into "high" and "low" categories. The researcher then looks for instances in the population that fit into each of the four cells. For example, Levinger (1965) argued that relationships can best be described by two major dimensions that can be directly related to patterns of communication in marriage. The first dimension includes the boundaries, or restraining forces, that act as barriers to the dissolution of the relationship. The second dimension includes the attractions or internal forces that drive people toward one another. This typology was one of the first to recognize the orthogonality (independence) of stability and satisfaction as relationship forces. Levinger (1965) constructed a fourfold table. The *full-shell* marriage is high on satisfaction and stability. Such couples rarely think about divorce or separation, and get along quite well. These couples have an open and expressive communication pattern similar to the conflict engagement style noted by Raush, Barry, Hertel, and Swain (1974). The *empty-shell* marriage involves low satisfaction, but high stability. Although these couples are not very happy in their marriage, they have never seriously considered divorce or separation. These couples do not discuss their problems or experiences, and communication is kept to a minimum. Hostility is high in these marriages, but conflict is restricted to small issues. *Half-shell* marriages are those in which couples are very happy with one another but find it difficult to continue living together steadily. There is little conflict in these relationships. Few married couples fit this pattern, but one might find cohabiting couples here. These couples periodically share the same household, and tend to separate and reunite, separate again and subsequently reunite over time. *No-shell* marriages involve low stability and low satisfaction. These couples are unhappy and find it extremely difficult to continue living together; these types of couples are usually separated or divorced. If we sampled married couples, by definition we would not find any no-shell couples because they are no longer married to one another.

This approach treats the dimensions of marriage—stability and satisfaction—as orthogonal (i.e., independent). As I demonstrated in the first chapter, however, the relationship between marital satisfaction and marital stability is not orthogonal, as Levinger (1965) argued. External barriers holding marriages together do not exert the force that they once did (Berscheid & Campbell, 1981). These two variables are not independent of one another because in today's society couples require more satisfaction in order to remain in married relationships than did husbands and wives in earlier times. Consequently, in actual samples of married couples, we would find few examples of three of the four types of marriages posited in this 25-year-old typology. These two factors alone then do not reveal as much about marriage as they appear to on first glance. We need alternative descriptive approaches that can categorize marriages on more than these two dimensions.

Empirical Models

An alternative to the logical model is an empirical, polythetic classification scheme similar to that used by botanists to categorize plants (Sneath & Sokal, 1973). Such schemes do not start with the assumption that variables are orthogonal to one another, but assume that the interrelationships among the variables used to categorize a phenomenon are of central theoretical importance. One uses the values on a number of different variables, and the interrelationships among these variables, to categorize.

In a polythetic approach to classification, the logical model that we described in the previous section is replaced by a statistical model in which types are represented in a subpopulation. If a particular type does not occur with any statistical frequency in a population, then it is not part of the classification scheme. For example, as we have seen, although no-shell marriages (unstable and unhappy couples) are a logical possibility in thinking about marriage, these marriages do not occur because these couples are divorced or separated. Therefore, this type would not occur in an empirical classification scheme. The polythetic model replaces the "high" or "low" orientation of the classic, monothetic model with a procedure in which the dimensions of the typology are located on a continuous scale with many dimensions. This procedure permits more subtle distinctions among types and does a better job of capturing differences among actual marriages. The empirical, polythetic classi- fication scheme focuses on couples defined jointly along multidimensional criteria rather than on one or two variables.

A polythetic classification scheme places individuals in the same type when they share a large number of characteristics, even though individuals may not be identical on every dimension. Because a polythetic model does not define "empirically null" types—types that occur in theory but not in real samples—the polythetic model is said to be more parsimonious than classical methods. A model is parsimonious when it uses the minimum number of concepts necessary to explain the most data.

The variables that define the dimensions of a typology must be of central theoretical importance. The empirical model of the classification of plants, animals, individuals, societies, or cultures demands that the measures on which a typology is based be objective, repeatable, and explicit. Theoreticians have suggested a number of conceptually impor- tant dimensions of marriage, but without suggestions as to how other researchers or therapists might categorize the couples in a different sample. In one of the typological schemes mentioned in the first chapter (Cuber & Harroff, 1965), a number of difficulties arise in attempting to use that typology to categorize a new sample of couples. For example, "passive-congenial" couples would be difficult to separate from "devi- talized" couples because the current behavior of both types is very similar; although both couple types now are married for institutional reasons, devitalized couples, unlike passive-congenials, at one time had a companionable relationship. Memories of a past, once close, relationship undoubtedly affect the communication style in the devitalized marriage. Researchers need a reliable procedure to discriminate between these two psychologically very different marriages.

Summary

In this section, we have contrasted two approaches to classifying marriage: the logical model and the empirical, polythetic classification scheme. We argued that the empirical model was a better one because it allowed an interaction between the conceptual dimensions of interest and the measurement of those dimensions.

Unfortunately, the classifications of marriage generated from both logical and empirical, polythetic models of marriage have problems. The types of marriage based on a logical model lack comprehensiveness because they focus on only one or two dimensions. Typologies developed through speculation by the researcher (usually following the logical model) have limited utility because they offer other researchers no reliable way to categorize couples. For typologies that are empirically based, those types generated from interaction data categorize couples on limited samples of their behavior, collected in artificial laboratory situations; little is known about marital types other than the means of classification. Also, the empirically based researcher tends neither to develop explicit typologies nor to report follow-up validational efforts.

AN EMPIRICAL, POLYTHETIC CLASSIFICATION SCHEME OF MARRIAGE

The primary goal of an empirical typology is to construct an orderly and repeatable scheme for classification and description. The first step in developing an empirical typology is to construct a series of measures that can tap significant dimensions of relationships. Having developed these measures, the researcher must detect in some empirical manner the existence of subgroups of people on those dimensions. In detecting these subgroups, the researcher should make no initial assumptions concerning the subgroups' nature, number, size, or discriminating aspects. All of these aspects should emerge from an examination of the data. The goal of the empirical, polythetic classification scheme is to uncover types of marriages at distinct points on many conceptually important dimensions.

The Basic Dimensions

What are the basic dimensions of married life? In a major qualitative study of the family, Kantor and Lehr (1975) argue that couples establish patterns of interaction through the ways they use their space, time, and energy (the "access dimensions") to realize the basic goals of marriage of affect, power, and meaning (the "target dimensions").

The use of space, time, and energy may facilitate or prohibit the achievement of one's interpersonal goals. The first goal is "affect," or achieving that sense of loving and being loved by someone in the world. The second goal is "power," or having the freedom to decide what one wants and the ability to achieve it. The third goal is "meaning," or developing a philosophical framework that helps explain reality and define one's identity. Table 2.1 includes representative questions concerning access (i.e., time, space, and energy) and target (i.e., affect, power, and meaning) dimensions.

For example, if one cannot organize one's work to be able to spend time with a spouse, this can have a direct effect on the achievement of a sense of closeness in the marriage. The corporate executive who spends her week on the road and her weekends locked in her study completing reports may find that her marriage is less intimate. One's organization of space and time may affect the distribution of power in marriage. The husband who misses the birth of his first child because it conflicts with his annual hunting vacation may return home to find that his wife has named the child after her father, whom he dislikes. Furthermore, all of these access dimensions can interact with each other and have an effect on the target dimensions.

Although many writers other than Kantor and Lehr (1975) discussed the target dimensions in terms of interpersonal behavior (Bochner, Kaminski, & Fitzpatrick, 1977; Burgoon & Hale, 1984; Indvik & Fitzpatrick, 1986), few other scholars developed in such detail the role of access dimensions in a study of family life. Kantor and Lehr (1975) delineated the commonplaces of everyday life, and the role that space, time, and energy play in promoting or inhibiting communication. Social psychologists now acknowledge the importance of the temporal qualities of relationships (e.g., Werner & Haggard, 1985), such qualities as pacing, cycles, rhythm, continuity, flow, timing, and sequences. Social psychologists also discuss the physical and psychological use of space to promote or inhibit communication (e.g., Altman, 1975). Few social psychologists analyze the role of energy in relationships.

Recently, Argyle (1986) suggested that there are three main sources of happiness for the individual in modern Western society. The pro-

TABLE 2.1
Representative Questions About Access
and Target Dimensions of Marital Life

Access Dimensions

Space

Do you feel comfortable inviting guests into your home without your spouse's permission?

Do you feel it's important to have some private space in your home where it's possible to be alone?

Time

Do you like to talk about past events in your marriage?

Do you like to keep a regular daily schedule?

Energy

Do you invest a lot of energy in your marriage?

Does your marriage seem more exciting than that of most couples?

Target Dimensions

Affect

Do you often tell your spouse how much you care about him or her?

Do you openly express affection for your spouse in public?

Power

Do you often try to influence your spouse on a course of action?

Do you make all the major decisions?

Meaning

Is the meaning and purpose of life clear to you?

Do you believe marriage should not interfere with each person's pursuit of his or her own potential?

SOURCE: Fitzpatrick (1976).

totypically happy person in Western civilization has a satisfying marriage and family life, work that allows some autonomy, and a philosophy (not necessarily religious) about the meaning of life and one's role in it.

Kantor and Lehr (1975) suggested, however, that the meaning and purpose ascribed to life differed among family groups. Reiss (1981) demonstrated that each family develops its own shared, distinctive explanation of its environment and evolves principles to govern its people and events. Families have "family paradigms," or unique sets of shared constructs, expectations, and fantasies about their social world. Families demonstrate different ideological orientations through their characteristic attitudes toward the social environment. These attitudes are manifested in the unique patterns of problem-solving communication that the family develops.

Love and marriage in modern Western society can be seen in terms of two contrasting ideological orientations (Bellah, Madsen, Sullivan, Swidler, & Tipton, 1985). The first is considered the *therapeutic* orientation, which views love and marriage primarily in terms of the psychological gratifications given to individuals. The alternative is the *traditional* orientation, which sees love and marriage as providing people with stable, committed relationships that tie them to a larger society. These conceptions of love and marriage are ideological opposites, suggesting very different bases for marriage in modern society. Couples may share the same ideological orientation to marriage or, as we will see, can have opposing values that can lead to tension, stress, and sometimes even creativity between the married partners. These ideological conceptions of relationships are far more encompassing than the typical discussion that relies only on gender roles and gender specialization as ways to contrast marriages (Peplau, 1983; Scanzoni & Scanzoni, 1976).

In addition to a general ideological orientation to personal relationships as providing either personal gratifications or a sense of community, the issue of interdependence is central to the study of marriage and relationships. Interdependence is the central defining feature of close relationships (Kelley et al., 1983). Spouses are interdependent when (1) they have frequent impact on one another, (2) the degree of impact per occurrence of any given activity is strong, (3) the impact involves diverse kinds of activities for each person, and (4) all of these properties characterize the interconnected activity for a relatively long duration. This means that not all marriages can necessarily be defined as "close relationships."

All relationships exhibit some form of interdependence, but an ongoing tension in marriage is the degree of interdependence versus the degree of autonomy (Bochner, 1983). Couples negotiate implicitly or explicitly the frequency, strength, diversity, and duration of their impact on one another over various activities in the marriage. Couples seek to develop and maintain both a sense of connection and togetherness, and a sense of personal autonomy and independence. Healthy families are said to maintain a reasonable degree of connectedness and cohesion as a family, while also keeping clear boundaries among individuals (Olson, 1981). Extreme togetherness, marked by excessive mutual involvement and too much emotional fusion (Minuchin, 1974), is as much of a problem in family life as is extreme separateness, marked by a lack of concern and disengagement with little emotional connection (Bowen, 1961).

Two patterns of interaction are related to extreme amounts of closeness or distance (Wynne, Ryckoff, Day, & Hirsch, 1958). In the pattern of "pseudomutuality," family members are so concerned about fitting together that they have problems seeing each other as individuals. In the opposite pattern of "pseudohostility," family members are extremely alienated from each other at a surface level, masking the need for intimacy. Many ethnic, cultural, and social class differences, however, have to be taken into account before deciding if the family is too cohesive or distant (McGoldrick, 1982).

In the next section, I discuss the development of a questionnaire, the Relational Dimensions Instrument, designed to measure the major dimensions of marital life. I start with these dimensions not because they are the only dimensions on which marriages can vary, but because these dimensions are the ones that I expect to relate most directly to communication behaviors between spouses.

The Relational Dimensions Instrument

The major component of an empirical typology is the development of measurement criteria. How did we measure the basic dimensions of relational life? We developed a preliminary questionnaire including an initial pool of more than 200 items. These items were based on a careful content analysis of about one-half dozen major studies of the family (Fitzpatrick, 1976). Each item corresponded either to an access (energy, space, time) or a target (affect, power, meaning) dimension. That is, we devised a number of specific questions, asking individuals to assess how they organized their time, space, and energy, and also how they showed affection, displayed power, and achieved meaning in their married lives.

Additionally, 25 of the initial items were specifically designed to assess a person's stand on the importance of autonomy and interdependence in a relationship.

A small set of couples, as well as several experts familiar with the theoretical work, examined the initial set of 200 items for clarity and consistency. These people eliminated redundant and unclear items, leaving 184 items. It is important to start with such a large number of items to assure adequate sampling of the dimensions of interest. In the early phases of the research (Fitzpatrick, 1976; Fitzpatrick & Indvik, 1979), 1,448 married individuals completed the questionnaire, subsequently named the Relational Dimensions Instrument (RDI). Statistical analyses (factor and item analyses) of the responses reduced the 184-item scale to a reliable 77-item instrument. In other words, when couples completed the 184-item questionnaire, only 77 items were systematically related to one another in sensible ways, and the remaining 107 items were superfluous for the purposes of this research.

There could be a number of reasons for these items' lack of significance. Some of the 107 questions could have been poorly phrased. Some of them could have isolated important concepts in married life, but perhaps there were too few questions on those concepts to define another separate factor. Some of the questions could have been making individuals estimate aspects of their married life that they found difficult or impossible to discuss. Some aspects of interpersonal relationships simply cannot be measured with questionnaires.

The dimensions that we started with (space, time, energy, affect, power, meaning, and autonomy/interdependence) are analytical categories that appear to be highly related in the minds of married couples. Hence statistical solutions weight many of these analytical categories on the same dimension, or factor, rather than on separate dimensions. This means, for example, that a particular use of space is so highly correlated with a particular level of affect in a marriage that these two items will show up as the same factor, rather than as separate space and affect factors. In addition to the mixing of access and target dimensions across the subscales of the RDI, it is interesting to note that few of the energy items emerged on the final version of the scale. It may be that the concept of energy in relationships is too abstract to be assessed by self-reports.

Witteman (1985) used confirmatory factor analysis (Joreskog, 1969) to explore the interrelationships among the access dimensions, using the data from Fitzpatrick (1976) and Fitzpatrick and Indvik (1979). First, he selected the items on the RDI that measured space, time, and energy—20 space, nine time, and five energy items. Second, using the means, standard deviations, and internal consistency of the items, he reduced this set to four items per access dimension. These twelve items are listed in Table 2.2.

TABLE 2.2
Access Items in the Confirmatory Factor Analysis

Space Items

(1) I feel free to interrupt my spouse/mate when s/he is concentrating on something if s/he is in my presence.
(2) We share many of our personal belongings with one another.
(3) I feel free to invite guests home without informing my spouse/mate.
(4) I open my spouse's personal mail without asking permission.

Time Items

(1) We serve the main meal at the same time every day.
(2) Events in our house/apartment occur without any regularity.
(3) In our house, we keep a fairly regular daily time schedule.
(4) We eat our meals (i.e., the ones at home) at the same time every day, at least during the week.

Energy Items

(1) We seek new friends and outside experiences.
(2) I think that we joke around and have more fun than most couples.
(3) There seem to be many minor crises in our life.
(4) Our life together seems more exciting than that of most couples.

SOURCE: Witteman (1985).

Witteman (1985) tested a number of different mathematical models to explore the relationships among space, time, and energy. He was particularly interested in determining whether energy could be measured as a stable dimension of marital life apart from estimates of space and time. Furthermore, by using two separate samples, he could examine the stability of these concepts. Basically, he found that whereas space and time are independent factors in marriage, energy differentially influences space and time in the two samples. Estimates of energy are situationally dependent and best described in terms of space and time. Witteman's (1985) work gives some support for the conceptual study of the access dimensions. This study also suggests that allowing the energy items to remain (as these items load on other factors) is acceptable, both conceptually and statistically.

The factor and item analyses on the original questions of the RDI identified eight factors, or subscales: Sharing, Ideology of Traditionalism, Ideology of Uncertainty and Change, Assertiveness, Temporal Regularity, Conflict Avoidance, Undifferentiated Space, and Autonomy. Table 2.3 shows representative items from the RDI.

Factor One reflects all six of the dimensions stipulated by Kantor and Lehr (1975). Of the 23 items loading on this factor, 10 are concerned with affect, whereas the remaining 13 span the other five dimensions. The affect pattern typified by this factor suggests a continual and mutual exchange of thoughts between the relational partners. A high score on this factor would suggest an open sharing of love and caring, and the tendency to communicate a wide range and intensity of feelings. There is a sharing of both task and leisure activities, as well as a considerable degree of mutual empathy. Finally, these relational partners not only visit with friends but also seek new friends and experiences. Given the high frequency of interaction between this couple as well as between the couple and the outside world, this factor is called *Sharing*.

Factor Two contains items from five of the original six dimensions of Kantor and Lehr (1975). Of the 11 items that define this factor, 7 were originally conceived as meaning items. These items suggest a strong commitment to tradition and to conventional values and institutions. This factor stresses traditional customs: A woman should take her husband's name when she marries, infidelity is always inexcusable, and the wedding ceremony is important. Those who score high on this factor appear certain about the meaning and the purpose of life, in general, as well as the rules that should govern child rearing and family behavior. The lifestyle of these relational partners is consistent with Bott's (1971) finding that the more traditional the couple, the more closed their networks. In a closed network, all of a couple's friends know one another. This factor is labeled the *Ideology of Traditionalism*.

The six items that correlate with Factor Three also predominantly reflect the meaning dimension. In contrast with the second factor, however, this pattern emphasizes an openness to uncertainty. Indeed, the ideal relationship, from this point of view, is marked by the novel, the spontaneous, or the humorous. The individuals who score high on this factor seem open to change. They believe that each person should develop his or her own potential and that relationships should not constrain an individual in any way. For these reasons, this factor is considered the *Ideology of Uncertainty and Change*.

Factor Four contains six items that were originally constructed to reflect the power dimension of a relationship. Four of these items tap an interpersonal persuasion, inducement, or combativeness aspect of a relationship. However, the other two items are concerned with the separate cooking and eating of meals and with open arguing before

TABLE 2.3
Representative Statements
from the Relational Dimensions Instrument

___

IDEOLOGY

Ideology of Traditionalism

A woman should take her husband's last name when she marries.

Our wedding ceremony was (will be) very important to us.

Our society as we see it needs to regain faith in the law and in our institutions.

Ideology of Uncertainty and Change

In marriage/close relationships, there should be no constraints or restrictions on individual freedom.

The ideal relationship is one marked by novelty, humor, and spontaneity.

In a relationship, each individual should be permitted to establish the daily rhythm and time schedule that suits him or her best.

INTERDEPENDENCE

Sharing

We tell each other how much we love or care about each other.

My spouse/mate reassures and comforts me when I am feeling low.

I think that we joke and have more fun than most couples.

Autonomy

I have my own private workspace (study, workshop, utility room, and so on).

My spouse has his or her own private workspace (study, workshop, utility room, and so on).

I think it is important for one to have some private space that is all his or her own and separate from one's mate.

Undifferentiated Space

I feel free to interrupt my spouse/mate when he or she is concentrating on something if he or she is in my presence.

I open my spouse/mate's personal mail without asking permission.

I feel free to invite guests home without informing my spouse/mate.

Temporal Regularity

We eat our meals (i.e., the ones at home) at the same time every day.

In our house, we keep a fairly regular daily time schedule.

We serve the main meal at the same time every day.

COMMUNICATION

Conflict Avoidance

If I can avoid arguing about some problems, they will disappear.

In our relationship, we feel that it is better to avoid conflicts than to engage in them.

It is better to hide one's true feelings in order to avoid hurting your spouse/mate.

Assertiveness

My spouse/mate *forces* me to do things that I do not want to do.

We are likely to argue in front of friends or in public places.

My spouse/mate tries to persuade me to do something that I do not want to do.

___

friends or in public, and therefore broaden the factor to one of assertiveness toward the relational partner. Thus the best name for this factor is *Assertiveness*.

Factor Five consists of three items that are clearly associated with the time dimension. These items suggest a strict scheduling of household events. For this reason, the factor is called *Temporal Regularity*.

The four items that load on Factor Six reflect the affect dimension. These items suggest the avoidance of arguments and disputes between partners, as well as the importance of sharing good feelings, but not bad feelings. This analysis suggests that *Conflict Avoidance* is an appropriate name for this factor. Support for this factor label comes from the work of Raush and his associates (1974), who discovered two distinct patterns of conflict management—avoidance and engagement—in the couples they observed. This factor probably taps the self-report component of that behavioral pattern.

The five items that correlate with Factor Seven were originally conceived of as spatial items. These items seem to indicate few constraints on territorial boundaries. The spouses feel free to open each other's personal mail, to interrupt one another when concentrating, and to share many of their personal belongings with impunity. Respondents with high scores on this factor believe guests should feel free to enter any room in their homes. They also believe guests may be brought home without asking for the partner's permission. The spatial freedom of those who score high on this factor comes at the expense of privacy. Given this openness between the partners, as well as their openness to guests, this factor is called *Undifferentiated Space*.

Factor Eight consists of six items that are predominantly concerned with space. In contrast to the spatial fusion of the seventh factor, however, these six items signify a spatial fission. Spouses take separate vacations, and each has his or her own private space. Private space is highly valued by those who agree with these items. Finally, the fact that such couples can go for long periods without spending much time together suggests that this factor can be named *Autonomy*.

A second-order factor analysis (Rummel, 1970) indicated that these eight factors, or subscales, represent three major conceptual dimensions of relational life.[1] The first dimension is *conventional/nonconventional ideology*. The beliefs, standards, and values that individuals hold concerning their relationship and family are a major factor guiding not only interactions with a spouse but also the judgments individuals make about these interactions and their outcomes. Values concerning relationships can range from those stressing the importance of stability and

TABLE 2.4
Alpha Reliabilities of the Relational Dimensions Instrument

	N = 900 Sample 1 64 Items		N = 136 Sample 2 64 Items	N = 448 Sample 3 77 Items	
Ideology					
Traditionalism	.76	(11)	.77	.80	(11)
Uncertainty	.49	(6)	.64	.60	(8)
Interdependence					
Sharing	.88	(23)	.88	.88	(23)
Temporal Regularity	.83	(3)	.81	.82	(5)
Undifferentiated Space	.44	(5)	.42	.52	(8)
Autonomy	.63	(6)	.62	.46	(6)
Conflict					
Conflict Avoidance	.45	(4)	.45	.60	(10)
Assertiveness	.65	(6)	.64	.65	(6)

NOTE: The alpha reliabilities reflect the internal consistency of each subscale.

predictability to those emphasizing the importance of change and uncertainty. A recent study by a group of social psychologists and philosophers (Bellah et al., 1985) who surveyed middle-class Americans' satisfactions and dissatisfactions with life in general found the same two ideological dimensions. Bellah and his colleagues (1985) called their dimensions *traditional* and *therapeutic*, and argued that these dimensions discriminated people's approaches not only to private life (love, marriage, and the family), but also to work, to public, political, or community service, and to religion.

The second dimension is *interdependence/autonomy*. Theoretically, the closer the relationship, the more interdependent it is (Kelley et al., 1983). A problem in human relationships is how to achieve a satisfying degree of connectedness. Each spouse tries to cast the relationship in a form that satisfies the ways in which he or she wants to be together, yet needs to be apart. To figure out how connected spouses are, one has to look at the amount of sharing and companionship in the marriage as well as at the couple's organization of time and space. The more interdependent the couple, the higher the level of companionship, the more time they spend together, and the more they organize their space to promote togetherness and interaction.

The third dimension is *conflict engagement/avoidance*. Inevitably, individuals in ongoing relationships have disagreements. The ways they resolve these differences, however, range from totally avoiding conflict to actively engaging in it. Couples vary as to their willingness to engage in conflict and their degree of assertiveness with one another.

In developing a measure, the question of scale reliability is important. In the initial sample of 900 individuals, the first factor analysis yielded a 64-item measure. The overall reliability of that measure, using coefficient alpha (Nunnally, 1967), was .71 (The second sample, of 136 people, using the same number of items, had approximately the same reliabilities.) In the third sample of 448 individuals, we increased the number of items on some of the less-reliable subscales in order to improve the coefficient alpha. The overall reliability of the scale did not greatly improve.

The Relational Definitions

The statistical methods that we have used so far in developing this empirical, polythetic classification scheme have concentrated on exploring the relationships among the variables. The statistical methods used in this second step are concerned with exploring the relationships among individuals; this technique is a form of cluster analysis (i.e., linear typal analysis). After the cluster analysis, the types are defined by a discriminant analysis, again using the eight subscale scores on the RDI. Such a procedure allows a researcher to find and name the patterns that individuals use to describe their marriages.

In the initial phase of the research, the number of unique marital definitions was unknown. The number and the specific characteristics of the marital definitions emerged from an examination of the responses that people made to the basic dimensions. We examined a variety of different solutions that would provide the best fit for the number of relational definitions. The linear typal analysis suggested that the three-cluster solution provided the best explanation of the data because it yielded the most unambiguous assignment of people to marital definitions. In the Appendix we provide a complete description of a cluster analysis program and solution, as well as a complete version of the Relational Dimensions Instrument.

For each sample drawn throughout this program of research, the typal loadings were examined to assess the goodness of fit of the three-cluster solution and to assign subjects to a definition. Not only must each group be relatively homogeneous with respect to the eight factors, but also each individual should clearly resemble one, and only one, cluster. The criteria used to assign the subjects to clusters were a primary loading above .30 and a secondary loading at least .10 smaller than the primary loading. For example, Subject 1 had a loading of .54 on the first type, .01 on the second type, and .10 on the third type. Subject 2, the wife of Subject 1, had a

TABLE 2.5
Means on the Relational Dimension Instrument
Across Five Samples

	Trad	Indep	Sep
		Relational Definition	
Ideological Views			
Ideology of Traditionalism	4.97[a]	3.93[b]	4.88[a]
Ideology of Uncertainty	3.52[a]	4.35[b]	4.19[b]
Autonomy/Interdependence			
Sharing	5.01[a]	4.73[b]	4.07[c]
Autonomy	3.20[b]	4.39[a]	4.40[a]
Undifferentiated Space	4.44[a]	4.41[a]	3.88[b]
Temporal Regularity	4.71[a]	3.23[b]	4.41[a]
Conflict			
Conflict Avoidance	3.94[b]	3.60[b]	4.54[a]
Assertiveness	2.80[b]	3.54[a]	3.27[a]

NOTE: Means with different superscripts across relational definitions differ from each other at the .10 level by the Scheffe procedure. Relational Dimensions Instrument ratings are on a 7-point scale. N = 1,672.

loading of .64 on the first type, .29 on the second type, and −.31 on the third type. Clearly, both subjects have Type 1 marriages. At this point, we know only that both the husband and wife have clearly emerged on the Type 1 marriage cluster; we do not as yet know what to call that cluster. In a separate analysis, we must examine the profiles of each cluster to determine what these types are.

Across the various samples, only 8% failed to meet the primary and secondary loading criteria. In cases of these complex loadings, individuals were assigned to the cluster with the highest loading. Olson (1981) also found about 8% of his couples could not be clearly typed by their behavioral styles. To verify the classification of individuals to clusters, discriminant analysis was also used to assign individuals to clusters. This independent classification was compared to that produced by the linear typal analysis. An examination of the results of these analyses across samples indicated that never less than 94%, and usually 97%, of the cases were assigned to the identical group by both procedures. These discriminant analyses also suggest that the three-cluster solution is appropriate.

According to their scores on the RDI, three discrete relational definitions, or ways to describe the marital relationship, were identified. These definitions are traditional, independent, and separate. Table 2.5

summarizes the responses to the RDI of five different samples totaling 1,672 individuals.

Traditionals hold conventional ideological values about relationships. These conventional values place more emphasis on stability in a relationship than on spontaneity. A conventional orientation stresses traditional community customs; these include the custom that a woman should take her husband's last name when she marries, and the belief that infidelity is always inexcusable. Traditionals exhibit interdependence in their marriages. The interdependence of a traditional marriage is marked by a high degree of sharing and companionship in the marriage. This companionship is strongly reinforced by the traditional's use of time and space. A regular daily time schedule and low level of support for autonomous physical space in the home facilitates companionship. Traditionals also report that although they are not assertive, they tend not to avoid conflict with their spouses.

Independents hold fairly nonconventional values about relational and family life. At the opposite end of an ideological continuum from a traditional orientation, an independent believes that relationships should not constrain an individual's freedom in any way. The independent maintains a high level of companionship and sharing in marriage, but it is qualitatively different from that of a traditional. Although he or she tries to stay psychologically close to a spouse, an independent maintains separate physical spaces to control accessibility. In addition, an independent has a difficult time maintaining a regular daily time schedule. Independents report some assertiveness in their relationships with their spouses and tend not to avoid conflicts.

Separates seem to hold two opposing ideological views on relationships at the same time. Whereas a separate is as conventional in marital and family issues as a traditional, he or she simultaneously supports the values upheld by independents and stresses individual freedom over relationship maintenance. Supporting two opposing sets of values suggests that the separates are ambivalent about their relational values. They may espouse one set publicly while believing another privately. The separates have significantly less companionship and sharing in their marriage. They attempt to keep a psychological distance in their relationship to the spouse and they try to maintain some autonomy through their use of space. The major way that a separate indicates interdependence in the marriage is by keeping a regular daily schedule. Separates, although they report some attempts at persuasion and assertiveness toward the spouse, indicate that they avoid open marital conflicts.

TABLE 2.6
Schematic Representation of the Relational Typology

	Conventional Ideology		Unconventional Ideology	
	High Conflict	Low Conflict	High Conflict	Low Conflict
High Interdependence	Traditional		Independent	
Low Interdependence		Separate		

NOTE: The empty cells define empirically null types in a currently married population. In other relationship forms, such as dating couples, it may be possible to uncover individuals who are unconventional ideologically, high in interdependence, and low in conflict.

In most classical typological schemata, the three major conceptual dimensions of ideology, interdependence, and conflict would be divided into high and low values, and eight possible relational definitions would be hypothesized. When the theorist takes an empirical approach and examines samples of married couples, only three of the eight logically possible definitions occur: traditional, independent, and separate. The remaining cells define empirically null types. Table 2.6 is a schematic representation of the relational typology.

In samples of married individuals, no relational definition emerges in which high conflict occurs with low levels of interdependence, regardless of the ideological orientation of the individual. Those scholars interested in studying relationship development might want to use this schema to predict which couples among a dating sample will not progress toward marriage. Alternatively, those married couples who fit into the empty cells would be expected to progress toward divorce.

Summary

This empirical, polythetic classification scheme of marriage begins with the delineation of important conceptual areas to be studied in reference to marriage and family life.

An instrument, called the Relational Dimensions Instrument, measures the delineated facets, and through a series of statistical analyses, the RDI is shown to have eight factors. Two factors measure ideology, four measure interdependence, and the remaining two measure conflict. When the eight scores on the RDI are cluster analyzed, three basic relational definitions emerge: traditional, independent, and separate. In the next section, we turn to the third step in the development of this typology,

TABLE 2.7
Proportions of Pure and Mixed Couple Types
Distributed Across 700 Couples

| | | Wife Type | |
Husband Type	Traditional	Independent	Separate
Traditional	.20	.07	.07
Independent	.06	.22	.09
Separate	.07	.06	.17

NOTE: The samples from which this table is derived are reported in full in Fitz-patrick (1976), Fitzpartick and Indvik (1982), Best (1979), and Vance (1981).

which involves comparing the relational definitions of husbands and wives.

MARITAL TYPES

By comparing the husband's and wife's perspectives on their marriage, couple types are identified. Throughout this program of research, great care is taken when the scales are administered to ensure no collaboration between husbands and wives on their answers. Consequently, when spouses are placed in different clusters, it means that they disagree on important dimensions of the marriage. From the three individual relational definitions, nine relational types can be logically constructed. The Pure types are those in which the husband and wife independently agree on a definition of their relationship. Husbands and wives who share the same ideological views of relationships, who experience the same level of autonomy and interdependence in their marriage, and share the same view of conflict expression, end up in the same cluster. These couples are Traditional, Independent, or Separate.

Spouses who disagree on major aspects of these basic dimensions end up in different clusters. These couples are categorized in one of the six Mixed types (e.g., independent husband married to a traditional wife) in which the husband and wife describe their relationship differently. The major Mixed type uncovered in the early research is the Separate/ Traditional, in which the husband defines the marriage as separate whereas his wife defines the same relationship as traditional. By convention, relational definitions are not capitalized although couple type designations are. In addition, in discussing Mixed couples, the definition of the husband precedes that of the wife. A Separate/Independent couple consequently is one in which the husband defines the relationship as separate while his wife sees the relationship as independent.

Of the 700 couples who completed the Relational Dimensions Instrument in the early phases of the research, 60% were unambiguously classified into one of the three Pure types. In other words, 60% of the husbands and wives agree on the basic definitions of their marriage. Parallel to this finding is that of Bernard (1972), who suggests that often the husband's description of a marriage is significantly different from that of his wife. "His" marriage is significantly different from "her" marriage in 40% of the couples who have completed the RDI. The distribution of the couple types across five samples appears in Table 2.7.

Of the 700 couples represented in Table 2.7, 20% are Traditionals, 22% are Independents, and 17% are Separates. Approximately 30% of the remaining Mixed marriages involve a separate partner or one who is emotionally divorced from the marriage. Contrary to the assumption that it is more likely for the husband to be estranged in a marriage and unable to communicate with his spouse, there are as many wives as husbands categorized as separates.

Although it appeared in the early stages of the research that Separate/Traditional couples were the most frequently occurring Mixed type, this finding has not held up across the samples. In the total sample, no Mixed type occurs with any greater frequency than the others.

Sampling of Marital Types

Four sampling strategies were used in the research reported in this book. The first was convenience sampling. Questionnaires were distributed in political and social groups, in hospitals, schools, factories, and offices. This strategy was used in the early stages of the research in order to isolate the major patterns in the data and to develop a reliable scale (Fitzpatrick, 1976, 1977; Fitzpatrick & Best, 1979).

The second strategy used was a stratified sampling technique. Neighborhoods within a standard metropolitan statistical area were categorized according to seven demographic criteria such as income and type of housing. Fourteen neighborhoods were randomly selected and their statistical profiles were checked against what was known about the entire metropolitan area. These profiles were found to be representative of the stratification of that metropolitan area. A street directory was then used to select households randomly for interviews (Fitzpatrick & Indvik, 1982).

The third sampling strategy involved the random selection of married couples from lists provided by organizations such as political groups, churches, and university housing offices (Fitzpatrick & Dindia, 1986a; Williamson & Fitzpatrick, 1985; Witteman & Fitzpatrick, 1986).

TABLE 2.8

PARTICIPANTS NEEDED
FOR *MARITAL COMMUNICATION STUDY*

Volunteer participants are needed for a study of marital communication. Participants will be screened first in a brief telephone interview. Both husbands and wives will be asked to come to the Center for Communication Research at the University of Wisconsin-Madison. The session will last approximately *two* hours. A payment of $20.00 per couple will be offered. If you are married and interested in participating in this study:
PLEASE CALL
263-3699 or 263-9644
Between 8:30 a.m. – 4 p.m. Monday–Friday
University of Wisconsin
Center for Communication Research

NOTE: This advertisement appeared weekly in Madison's newspapers.

The fourth sampling strategy involved using university news releases describing the research and the general reasons for studying marital communication. The purpose of the news releases was to establish credibility in the community that the research was legitimate. These releases tied in to the second part of this sampling strategy—two months' worth of weekly advertisements in the local newspapers, asking for volunteers for a study of communication in marriage (Fitzpatrick, 1987a; Fitzpatrick & Noller, 1987). Table 2.8 includes a copy of the newspaper advertisement.

What kind of couple volunteers to participate in a study of marital communication? Marital researchers acknowledge either explicitly or implicitly in the procedures they follow that unhappily married couples are difficult to recruit for research. This difficulty is the reason why most marital researchers contact clinicians and therapists for referrals of the distressed couples to the research laboratory. It is not uncommon for researchers to advertise specifically for distressed couples. In addition to the unhappily married, the upper classes are significantly less likely to be included in marital and family studies.

In one recent study (Fitzpatrick & Dindia, 1986a), we looked at couples who agreed to participate in research spanning three different experimental sessions over a one-month period, and compared those couples with couples who agreed to answer the Locke-Wallace marital satisfaction questionnaire. We found no significant differences on any of our demographic measures or in marital satisfaction between the sample who completed the questionnaire and the sample who volunteered for the three-week laboratory experience. There may be few differences between those who volunteer to answer a questionnaire and those who agree to more elaborate procedures. Of course, we still need more information on those who refuse to participate in research on marital and family processes.

We cannot generalize to the population at large from these samples because they are not all random samples of couples. Indeed, it is difficult to generate a random sample of couples because it takes only one partner's refusal to participate in the research to invalidate the data as couple data. Although we cannot say with assurance that 20% of the married population have Traditional marriages, we can examine some demographic indicators from the stratified random sample to see if the couple types describe marriages at different points in the life cycle of the family.

In the stratified sample of 224 couples, there were no significant differences among the couple types on any of the demographic indicators used in the research. Couple types did not differ on number of years married, on whether or not the husband or wife was married before, on number of children, on religion of either spouse, or on level of schooling, employment, or income. There was no significant relationship between this set of demographic variables and the type of marriage that a couple had evolved. The variance in couple type cannot be explained by a couple's place in the social structure.[2]

Marital Types and Other Research

We have seen that the dimensions on which the typology is based are conceptually important aspects of married life from a variety of different theoretical perspectives. The actual definitions of marriage uncovered in this research represent patterns of marital interaction discussed in other recent research. The similarity in some of the work across these disparate areas is striking. In both conceptual discussions of possible marital types (e.g., Peplau, 1983) and in empirical investigations of marriages and families at various stages in the family life cycle, types of marriages emerge that resemble the Traditional, Independent, and Separate prototypes. Three independent lines of investigation of marriage at three different times—courtship (Huston, Surra, Fitzgerald, & Cate, 1981), marriage (Fitzpatrick, 1984), and divorce (Kressel, Jaffe, Tuchman, Watson, & Deutsch, 1980)—yield remarkably similar results. From early in courtship, some couples seem to start their relationships as "Separates," emotionally and psychologically less involved with one another than other couples are. These Separate couples, who emerge in cross-sectional studies of marriage, tend not to communicate very much with one another and rarely engage in serious conflicts. Such a type of couple appears again in divorce mediation. From early in courtship, it appears that some couples do not develop the numerous interconnected sequences of interaction that Berscheid (1983) links to the experience of strong emotion in close relationships. Our current cross-sectional data cannot tell us whether the couples who begin in this fashion are the ones who end this way. Undoubtedly, the process of relational growth and disintegration takes markedly different paths for different couples.

Reiss (1981) has developed a family typology that is grounded in one of the few programs of systematic experimental research on family problem solving. Initially, this typology was part of a larger effort to discover the variables that discriminate pathological from nonpathological families. Reiss offers evidence, however, that these categories are also applicable to normal groups. This typology assumes that each family develops its own shared and distinctive orientation toward its environment and manifests a unique pattern of problem solving.

In Reiss's (1981) typology of family problem-solving styles, one family type is referred to as "environment-sensitive," because of that type's mastery orientation toward the environment. The environment-sensitive family resembles the Independents in that both fall on the midpoint between the extremes of high cohesion and high autonomy. Another family type, which Reiss calls the "consensus-sensitive" family, shares with the Traditional prototype an emphasis on harmony. The consensus-sensitive family is too concerned with maintaining family cohesion to consider extensively problems originating in the environment. A third family type, labeled "interpersonal-distance sensitive," is reminiscent of the Separates because of their mutual emphasis on individual autonomy over togetherness. This family type is too fragmented to coordinate discussion of environmental problems.

Peplau (1983) theorizes that marriages can be divided on two basic dimensions. The first concerns the power relations between the sexes; that is, the extent to which the husband controls the wife. The second dimension concerns the extent of role specialization between the spouses. This includes both activities internal to the couple, such as communication and household tasks, and activities external to the couple, such as participation in the work force. In her Traditional couple, the husband dominates the wife and they exhibit considerable male-female role specialization. Her hypothesized "traditional" marriage is actually far closer to the pure Separate or the Separate/Traditional type in the Fitzpatrick model. In Peplau's "modern marriage," male dominance is muted and role specialization is less extensive. This couple type is very similar to Fitzpatrick's Traditional marriage. Finally, Peplau's "egalitarian" marriage pattern, which rejects the basic tenets of male dominance and role specialization by gender, is remarkably similar to the Fitzpatrick Independent marital type.

The similarity of the typological perspective and other views on relationships is not limited to those views that expressly describe "types" of marriages. A good deal of similarity exists in the delineation of dimensions of relationships as well. Stephen (1986), for example, has been working within a symbolic exchange perspective that discriminates couples according to their agreement on five dimensions: exclusivity, awareness of problems, importance of talk, importance of reciprocity, and constancy and fun. The names for these dimensions vary yet the content of these factors is very similar to the content of the RDI. The exclusivity dimension is a variant of the ideology of uncertainty and change dimension with particular emphasis on premarital issues. The importance of talk is similar to the conflict avoidance factor of the RDI. The dimensions with which Stephen works differ from the RDI in that they are phrased in a pro-Independent couple manner. Agreement between couples on these dimensions implies that those couples are Independents.

From a number of different theoretical perspectives researchers have pointed to a set of consistent dimensions and types of marriages. Such theoretical convergence suggests that a typological approach to understanding marital communication is promising.

Summary

The marital typology is built on the comparison of the husband and wife perspectives on the marriage. Spouses individually complete the Relational Dimensions Instrument and their answers are submitted to a cluster analysis program where each individual is defined as either a traditional, independent, or separate. Subsequently, the responses of husbands and wives are compared. Couples can be assigned to either a Pure or a Mixed type. In general, about 60% of the couples are categorized as one of the Pure types and 40% as one of the Mixed types. In this section, we discussed the sampling strategies utilized and the relationship of these marital types to other work on marital and family interaction.

CONCLUSION

In this chapter, I have discussed the conceptual background to the development of the Relational Dimensions Instrument. Starting with more than 180 items designed to assess important dimensions of married life, I developed a scale called the Relational Dimensions Instrument. Couples who participated in the research led us to believe that ideology, interdependence, and conflict were basic, important aspects of marriage. Based on the responses of husbands and wives to the RDI, three types of marriages can be defined. The first is the traditional marriage, which supports conventional ideas about marriage and family life, values interdependence between partners, and favors restricting open conflicts to serious issues only. The second is the independent marriage, which supports nonconventional ideas about marriage and family life, values autonomy as well as interdependence between partners, and favors open conflict to resolve major as well as minor differences. The third is the separate marriage, which supports conventional ideas about marriage and family life but shows ambivalence about these values. This marriage devalues interdependence and avoids open conflict. Comparing husband and wife perspectives, I formed couple types.

This chapter covered the complexities of the cluster analysis procedures and looked at sampling methods. Furthermore, it demonstrated the relationship between the couple types and similar categories uncovered in other programs of research.

I have shown that marriages can be classified in one of three basic ways, that husbands and wives can be compared as to how they categorize their relationships, and that such classifications are not merely psychological manifestations of demographic differences. These facts are useless unless the scheme allows a researcher to discriminate these types on a number of different attributes of relationships. In the next chapter, I present the results of the initial investigations on the relationship between the couple types and other attributes of marriage.

NOTES

1. In the second-order factor analysis, the two ideology measures load on the first factor; the sharing, temporal regularity, undifferentiated space, and autonomy factors load on the second factor; and conflict avoidance and assertiveness load on the third factor.

2. Although I have found no significant demographic differences in the major random sample of couple types, any given sample drawn by a researcher may demonstrate demographic differences. Differences may exist between urban and rural couples or between younger and older married people (see, for example, Burgraff & Sillars, 1986).

3

Validating the Types

Gender Roles and
Marital Happiness

In the previous chapter, we presented an empirical typology of marriage. Typologies are elegant but have little utility unless the marital types can be systematically related to other attributes. It might be possible, for example, to uncover types of marriages and to categorize them reliably, yet have chosen dimensions that do not predict other aspects of marriage. Or, it may be that it is not the types, per se, but rather the individual's relational definition that best predicts the attribute of interest.

In this chapter, we demonstrate that the typology can predict other aspects of marital functioning. We also show that it is the couple type, and not an individual's definition of the marriage, that predicts these variables. The requirement that couple type and not individual relational definition is related to the dependent variable is an especially hard test of the validity of the typology because the data that we report here are taken from individual self-reports. This validation test requires that measures relate to measures from both spouses while simultaneously not relating to the individual relational definition of a husband or wife. The fact that a person is a separate is not expected to predict the dependent variables without knowing how that person's spouse views the marriage.

In the early validation efforts, my colleagues and I were interested in how husbands' and wives' perceptions of their ideological orientations, interdependence, and expressivity related to gender attitudes and dyadic adjustment. Our first set of studies concerned the gender attitudes and the gender stereotyping of couples in the various types. The typology's ideological dimension can predict relatively clearly the gender attitudes of husbands and wives. People who espouse traditional orientations to marriage and family values are expected to have more conventional attitudes toward male and female roles than people who do not hold such traditional views. Furthermore, we expected more gender stereotyping of the spouse in marriages in which both spouses held traditional orientations to the family than in marriages in which both were less traditional.

The second major validation effort centered on dyadic adjustment. Dyadic adjustment, or some measure of contentment with the marriage, is the most frequently studied dependent variable in marital literature. It is important to validate the marital types in reference to their levels of dyadic adjustment in order to be able to compare the results from the marital typology studies with results from other research programs.

GENDER AND MARRIAGE

A central biosocial issue in a marriage is how each person interprets the meaning of "maleness" and "femaleness" (Hess & Handel, 1959). As Rossi (1985, p. 161) states:

> Gender differentiation is not simply a function of socialization, capitalist production or patriarchy. It is grounded in a sex dimorphism that serves the fundamental purpose of reproducing the species. Hence, sociological units of analysis such as roles, groups, networks, and classes divert attention from the fact that the subjects of our work are male and female animals with genes, glands, bones, and flesh occupying an ecological niche of a particular kind in a tiny fragment of time.

In this section, we differentiate the couple types according to their gender attitudes and according to both self and spouse gender stereotyping. We began with the question of gender because of its central importance to relationships. It is intriguing to note that in the study of personal relationships in general and marriage in particular, the gender of the participants is frequently ignored in theory and research (Peplau, 1983). At this stage of the research, we wanted to show the clear ties between our measure of marital ideology and concepts that husbands and wives hold about what it means to be male or female.

Gender Attitudes

In our study of gender and marriage, we first examined the *gender attitudes* of husbands and wives. The study of gender attitudes includes attitudes toward men, attitudes toward women, attitudes toward gender subtypes (e.g., women managers, male nurses), and evaluative feelings about sex-role arrangements.

Gender attitudes tap men's and women's evaluative orientations concerning relations between the sexes. The study of gender attitudes is important for at least two reasons (Del Boca, Ashmore, & McManus, 1986). First, attitudes toward men, women, and sex roles are often part of a larger belief system that involves other issues (e.g., abortion) and target groups (e.g., feminists). Second, these attitudes have implications for public policy issues relating to male and female relations. The range of issues that can be subsumed here is large. Issues such as parental leave, men's participation in fatherhood, women's involvement in organizations outside the home, the amount of time spent in household work versus outside commitments, male response to female success in organizations, and so forth are all related to the gender attitudes that individual husbands and wives hold.

In 1977, when we collected the data reported below, the only published national survey of attitudes toward gender was that of Mason, Czajka, and Arber (1976). Using five different samples of women, these researchers analyzed the change in women's sex-role attitudes between 1964 and 1974. Regardless of the sample, considerable shifts in women's sex-role attitudes occurred, but attitudes about the traditional sex-role division of labor in the home continued to be more conventional than did attitudes about the division of labor in the workplace and outside the home in general. Attitudes about family and home changed as much as did attitudes toward work, but attitudes about family and home were simply more conventional to start with. Both sets of attitudes moved in a less traditional and more egalitarian direction. Women from all walks of life were less likely to support traditional gender attitudes, suggesting that these attitudinal shifts are not simply a product of the woman's personal circumstances and position in society. Comparable data for males during this period do not exist.

Based on these data, we predicted less support overall for traditional gender attitudes and more support for male and female equality in this sample. Couples with traditional ideologies on family values are hypothesized, however, also to have more traditional gender-role attitudes than are the less traditional couples. The sample consisted of 448 adults

TABLE 3.1
Wording of Some Gender Attitude Items on Surveys

Egalitarian response (agreement with the following items):

(1) A working mother can establish just as warm and secure a relationship with her children as a mother who does not work.

(2) Parents should encourage just as much independence in their daughters as in their sons.

(3) Men should share the housework, such as doing dishes, cleaning, and so forth, with women.

(4) Men and women should be paid the same money if they do the same work.

(5) Women should be considered as seriously as men for jobs as executives or politicians or even president.

Traditional response (agreement with the following items):

(1) A man can make long-range plans for his life but a woman has to take things as they come.

(2) It is more important for a wife to help her husband's career than to have a career herself.

(3) It is much better for everyone involved if the man is the achiever outside the home and the woman takes care of the home and family.

(4) A preschool child is likely to suffer if his mother works.

(5) Women who do not want at least one child are being selfish.

SOURCE: Mason, Czajka, & Arber (1976). Reprinted by permission.

(224 couples). The sample was drawn using a stratified, random sampling frame. Of the households contacted by the interviewers, 10% were ineligible because no married couples lived at the address, and another 10% refused to participate. The primary function of the interviewers was to prevent collusion between spouses as they completed the questionnaires. Each subject completed the Relational Dimensions Instrument, the Sex Role Orientation Questionnaire and the Bem Sex-Role Inventory for both himself or herself and the spouse. In total, 51 Independent couples, 54 Traditional couples, 17 Separate couples, 17 Separate/ Traditional couples, and 85 Mixed types participated (for a complete description, see Fitzpatrick & Indvik, 1982).

The Sex Role Orientation scale developed by Brogan and Kutner (1976) measured gender attitudes. The questions on this 36-item scale are very similar to those in Table 3.1; the scale was designed to probe the subject's assessment of "correct" male and female behavior patterns rather than "typical" traits, behaviors, or interests of males and females. Three scales emerged from a factor analysis of this instrument. The first

There are a number of problems involved in dealing with data taken from husbands and wives. Statistical inference procedures such as analysis of variance and least squares regression require that the set of data upon which the inference is drawn be independent. The value of one observation, in other words, should not provide information on the value of other observations (note: not variables). The most common sets of dependencies of observations are due to group, sequence, and space (see Kenny & Judd, 1986, for an accessible discussion). Communication researchers should be at the forefront in considering these dependencies *substantively* rather than as statistical errors or noise in the data.

I am primarily concerned in this section with dependencies introduced into data by the fact that samples are derived from intact groups (i.e., married couples). The real question for the working researcher is the following: Does nonindependence due to group (a redundancy in information provided by husbands and wives) interfere with significance testing? The answer is unambiguous: *The effect of within-group correlation can seriously bias the validity of hypothesis testing and the bias can go in two directions.* When the correlation is positive, the bias is toward excessive liberality (tendency to reject the null when it is, in fact, true); and, when the correlation is negative, the bias is toward excessive conservatism (tendency to accept the null when it is, in fact, false). This problem is associated with significance testing and not with estimation procedures. The researcher should not hesitate to lump together husband and wife responses for factor or cluster analysis as long as the technique does not involve an inferential process.

How do we handle the problem of nonindependence of spousal data? A common approach to this problem (other than ignoring it completely) is to throw out the data. Randomly deleting either spouse effectively solves the statistical problem. I am constitutionally incapable of such a solution. Aside from my personal peccadillo, this solution changes the research from one on marriage to something else entirely. In the simple case of husband and wife comparisons, a correlated "t"-test is appropriate. Kraemer and Jacklin (1979) developed a generalization of the matched-pair "t"-test. The test is limited in scope applying to a single dependent variable and a single comparison dimension (e.g., happily versus unhappily married couples on talk time), although Mendoza and Graziano (1982) have extended this approach to multiple dependent variables.

Given the fact that the typology contains multiple levels of an independent variable, and I am often examining multiple dependent variables, I have relied on a number of solutions. These choices were made based on the research questions and the particular data array with which I was working at a given time. First, I have split the sample, and analyzed husband and wife data separately. This has the advantage of clarifying male and female differences yet loses information about marriage. Second, I have used a repeated measures design in which the couple type was a between-subjects factor and the sex (husband-wife) was a within-subjects factor. This solution yields important information about typological and sex differences. It is cumbersome interpretatively in the multivariate case. The researcher can always conduct separate analyses for each dependent variable and hold the alpha level constant, if the relationship among the dependent variables is not of interest (Tukey, 1980). Third, I have used a multivariate round-robin analysis of variance procedure that analyzes the correlations among husband and wife responses, after accounting for other sources of variations. This allows a test of all possible sex combinations and a variety of dependent outcomes. The design does not allow a direct test of couple type and its effect on communication behavior.

A recent solution to this problem is that of Cappella and Palmer (1987). These scholars are working on a regression approach to this problem of nesting dyads (couples) within various levels of factors. The regression approach is more powerful and flexible and can be used with unbalanced designs and so on. Regression approaches also allow the straightforward testing of covariates and other predictors. This solution holds great promise not only for relationship research but for communication research generally.

Figure 3.1 Caveats on couple data.

TABLE 3.2
Gender Attitudes Across the Nine Couple Types

| | Attitudes | | | | | |
| | Conventional | | Female Equality | | Personal | |
Types	H	W	H	W	H	W
Traditional	3.79	4.29	5.52	5.22	4.05	3.87
Separate	3.91	4.71	5.20	4.76	4.04	4.16
Sep/Trad	3.92	4.16	5.06	5.34	4.10	3.92
Trad/Sep	4.47	3.53	4.62	4.97	3.56	4.33
Independent	3.05	3.45	5.92	5.54	5.18	4.82
Ind/Trad	3.86	3.21	5.17	5.82	4.64	4.58
Trad/Ind	3.98	4.02	4.85	5.51	3.82	4.29
Ind/Sep	3.85	3.58	5.62	5.55	4.47	4.61
Sep/Ind	3.90	3.33	5.26	5.91	3.75	4.56

NOTE: The scale values range from 1 to 7. Two MANOVAs with couple type as the independent variable and the three sex-role orientations as the dependent variables were significant, as were the follow-up univariate tests.

factor (alpha = .84) represented a *conventional orientation*, which suggests that men should dominate and control the leadership roles in the society and that women should follow traditional female pursuits. The second factor (alpha = .76) represented *female equality*, which suggests that no restrictions should be placed on females competing with males for jobs, in athletics, in developing independence, and so forth. The third factor (alpha = .80) represented a *personal orientation*, which suggested that the individuals should determine their own behaviors based on their personal preference rather than on role prescriptions defined by one's sex.

Using the individual relational definition as the independent variable and the three gender attitudes as the dependent variables, there were no significant differences for males or for females on the three gender attitudes. In other words, when a male described his marriage as a separate one, this in itself did not predict his attitudes toward gender. The picture changed, however, when couple type is the independent variable.

Clear differences in gender attitudes emerged. Similar to the national survey data, a conventional orientation to gender roles was less strongly supported by females and males than either the female equality or the personal gender orientations. The second pattern was that male-female equality was more likely to be supported.

Aside from these overall trends, couple types differed in the predicted directions in their gender attitudes. The MANOVA, group centroids (multivariate means), and discriminant functions indicated that the Traditionals, Separates, Separate/Traditionals, and Traditional/Separates agreed with conventional orientations and rejected attitudes suggesting individuals should follow personal preferences in deciding which gender attitudes to adopt. The Mixed types were as conventional in their gender orientations as were the couples in which both spouses had traditional family ideologies. Thus even when one spouse adopted a nonconventional ideology of relationships, a conventional orientation to gender roles prevailed for both spouses. The independent spouses in Mixed marriages are caught with conflicting values about family life and marriage and gender roles. The Independents were clearly discriminated from all the other couple types by agreeing less with the conventional orientation and more with both male-female equality and personal orientations to gender roles. Independent couples had the strongest profile on these gender attitudes; these couples are the most strongly opposed to conventional orientations and the most supportive of the egalitarian position.

Within a symbolic interactionist framework, the history of the family within the past two centuries in Western society can be summarized as a series of transformations from an *institutional* to a *companionate* system (Adams, 1986). The marital relationship has gradually moved along a continuum of family systems from one determined primarily by specified duties, obligations, and social pressures impinging upon the couple (i.e., the institutional marriage) to one in which unity develops out of mutual affection and intimate association, albeit along traditional role lines (i.e., the companionate marriage). According to Burgess (Burgess, Locke, & Thomes, 1963), a complete transition to a companionate marital form will occur only when there is true male and female equalitarianism. The modern family has not yet arrived at the companionship-type marriage in the sense of a fully equal partnership between a husband and a wife. The marital system appears to be evolving, however, further along a continuum toward egalitarianism.

Viewing the history of marriage along this single evolutionary continuum, the data presented here support an interpretation that the Independent relationship represents the future of marriage in Western society and an advanced evolutionary form of marriage.

Independents have not made the complete transition to egalitarianism, but they are further along on that continuum than any other couple type. Within this framework, Traditional and Separate marriages represent the usual lag times in the adoption of new social forms; both the Traditionals and the Separates may be seen as representing different points along the institutional-to-companionship continuum of family development. With their lack of support for egalitarianism, yet high levels of companionship,

Traditionals represent a particular form of companionship marriage. Separates, on the other hand, in pairing lack of egalitarianism with less companionship, may represent the vestiges of the institutional form of marriage. Separates may be bound more by external forces such as compliance with predetermined roles, carrying out of tasks, stability, and permanence than are other marital forms.

What of the Mixed types? The movement along this continuum is not expected to proceed smoothly or at the same rate for males and females. The transformation from one system to another takes a great deal of time and is expected to be met with conflicts between ideology and behavior. The Mixed couples represent the ongoing negotiation of the movement along this continuum. This does not suggest that an individual couple will necessarily change their marital type over the course of their marriage but rather that as a group these couples represent the transitional state of marriage in Western society.

Egalitarianism and conventionality may be better understood, however, within a conflict perspective that rejects a single evolutionary continuum. For the majority of couples, this research demonstrates that even the conventional orientation has moved in the direction of egalitarianism. These results do not suggest that the Traditional couples have become less conventional as conventionality means doing what the culture tells you to do. That is, in a matriarchal society, conventional individuals believe in female dominance. Conventionality implies subjugation of individual to group goals so a conventional system may be egalitarian in the service of the group (e.g., Japanese style of decision making by consensus). The Traditional couple is not "male dominated" but rather the decision-making authority is divided along a priori grounds (in home versus out of home) and the egalitarianism that does exist is mutually supported for the good of the marriage. Separates are then "failed" Traditionals in that they are not as likely to sacrifice harmoniously the individual to the group goals.

Conversely, the distinctive characteristic of nontraditional couples and families (i.e., Independents) is the combination of individuality and egalitarianism. In an egalitarian society, conventionality means governing by consensus. Because issues of power and dominance are more salient in a system that emphasizes individuality than in a system that emphasizes group maintenance and harmony, achieving equality is both more emotionally significant and problematic for the Independents. The conflict-perspective implies that marital forms can exist side-by-side in the culture and all of the forms do not gradually move to the Independent pattern.

Gender Attributions About the Self

What gender-related characteristics and traits do husbands and wives use to describe themselves? Wide consensus exists about masculine and feminine traits across groups that differ in age, sex, race, religion, marital status, and education (Broverman, Vogel, Broverman, Clarkson, & Rosenkrantz, 1972). Masculine traits are instrumental and defined by competence, rationality, and assertion, whereas female traits are expressive and hence defined by warmth, expressiveness, and nurturance.

Using the Bem Sex-Role Inventory (Bem, 1974), husbands and wives rated themselves on 20 "masculine" adjectives (e.g., dominant, analytical), and 20 "feminine" adjectives (e.g., likes children, nurturant). Four groupings result from this technique: masculine, feminine, androgynous (possessing high masculinity and high femininity scores), and undifferentiated (possessing neither high masculine nor feminine scores). Assigning either masculine or feminine attributes to oneself (or some combination) involves ascribing socially desirable characteristics to oneself. Thus those who score in the undifferentiated category have stated that neither set of positive traits nor any particular combination of positive masculine and feminine traits applies to them. Males who see themselves as masculine are sex-typed; males who see themselves as feminine are sex-reversed; females who see themselves as feminine are sex-typed; females who see themselves as masculine are sex-reversed.

Collapsing the possible combinations of these psychological gender groupings for couples resulted in the following: both sex-typed (N = 66), both androgynous (N = 38), both undifferentiated (N = 44), one sex-reversed (N = 68), and the rest combinations or an androgynous spouse paired with a sex-typed mate, and so forth (N = 198). In total, 17 couples did not complete this section of the questionnaire, and the majority of those who did not finish were Separates.

Only 36% (74 of 207) of these couples agreed on a psychological gender grouping. We also matched an individual's self-perception score to the perception that he or she had of the spouse. The perception of similarity is greater than the actual similarity. For "perception of agreement on psychological gender," the data are as follows: sex-typed (N = 73), androgynous (N = 58), undifferentiated (N = 57), sex-reversed (N = 68). In total, 51% saw their spouses as similar on psychological gender orientation.

We predicted that Traditionals and Separates would attribute sex-typed traits to themselves whereas Independents would see themselves as androgynous. For husbands, a comparison of the five relational types (three Pure types, plus Separate/Traditional and Mixed types) by psychological gender category was not significant nor was the individual relational definition of the husbands by gender grouping significant. Most of the husbands rate themselves as masculine sex-typed, regardless of their marital type or individual relational definition. The type of marriage a man has established does not seem to affect his view of himself in terms of psychological sex-stereotypic characteristics.

How is it possible that Independent husbands, with their different attitudes toward gender, rate themselves like more Traditional husbands on attributions concerning their own instrumental behaviors? Why are the Independent males not androgynous? There are two explanations. First, the initial egalitarian set of gender attitudes focused on male-female equality and personal preferences. None of the items used to measure these factors implied that males should be more nurturant, open, or expressive. Rather, these attitudes supported the position that women should be more assertive and oriented toward leadership. Thus it is not inconsistent with the egalitarian gender attitudes espoused by Independent husbands to rate themselves as masculine sex-typed. Females may achieve certain prerogatives usually reserved for males without males necessarily changing or giving up their privileges. Second, androgyny has differential consequences for males and females. Our society appears to value the acquisition of male traits by females more than it values the acquisition of female traits by males, although that may be changing (Pleck, 1981).

For women, there were no significant differences by individual relational definition, but a comparison of the five relational types by psychological gender groups was significant (chi-square (8) = 17.43; p < .03). Table 3.3 presents the summary of the wives' psychological gender orientations within each marital type.

Like their husbands, wives see themselves as sex-typed. Only the separate wives in the Mixed types tend to deviate from this generalization. When a separate wife has a traditional or an independent husband, she sees herself as having few positive expressive or instrumental traits: She is undifferentiated. If her husband is a separate, the separate wife may see herself as sex-typed. Perhaps, this wife can see herself as warmer and more nurturant than he is, although such a self-attribution would be difficult for the separate wife who compares herself to a traditional or independent mate.

TABLE 3.3
Wives' Perceptual Sex-Role Orientations by Marital Type

Husband	*Wife*		
	traditional	independent	separate
traditional	sex-typed	sex-typed or androgynous	undifferentiated
independent	sex-typed or undifferentiated	sex-typed or androgynous	undifferentiated
separate	sex-typed	androgynous or sex-typed	sex-typed or undifferentiated

NOTE: Husbands in this sample saw themselves as sex-typed masculine.

Gender Attributions About the Spouse

Spouses are capable of making attributions about their partners' gender-related personality characteristics. Although the content of gender attributions is not limited to personality traits, we have used them to study accuracy because the traits most frequently studied as representative of gender are strongly correlated to interpersonal behavior and communication (Ashmore, Del Boca, & Wohlers, 1986). How accurately can the couples in the various types predict the gender attributions their spouses make about themselves?

The type of accuracy we are studying is coorientational accuracy (see Chapter 8 for communication accuracy). Coorientational accuracy is making correct predictions about a partner. Correct predictions about a partner can come from using a number of data sources (Miller & Steinberg, 1975). The first source is sociological data, such as the spouse's group memberships and the roles he or she plays in those groups. On any given issue, one may think of the spouse as a "typical wife" or a "typical husband" and use stereotypes about women and men in that role to predict a partner's attitudes or cognitions. Sociological data serve as a baseline for interpersonal judgments by establishing expectations for others' behaviors. Members of particular groups are assumed to respond in certain ways in certain situations. Very little human communication could proceed without each party being capable of making sociological predictions about others and about how these others probably respond to certain messages. Only when individuals deviate from these expectations are other data necessary to increase accuracy. Thus stereotyping is useful; it often leads to correct predictions about the cognitions of the other person. Even though a spouse may have a good deal of psychological information about a mate does not mean that he or she needs that information to predict accurately the mate's cognitions or attitudes. Thus spouses can be accurate because they are predicting mates' opinions or attributions on the basis of sociological generalizations: *stereotypic accuracy.*

Among the couples, we predicted that those couples with high traditional values and companionable relationships (i.e., Traditionals and Separate/Traditionals) would use stereotypic information about the spouse correctly. These relational factors would produce more stereotypic accuracy because traditional value orientations establish clear concepts of male and female behaviors and amount of time spent with the spouse allows checking out of the stereotypes about husbands and wives against the spouses' typical behaviors. By the same reasoning, the Independents would not use stereotypic information to achieve coorientational accuracy in making attributions about their spouses. Independent couples develop individualized expectations and not role-based ones.

The second source is psychological data, or those characteristics that distinguish a person from others in his or her group. The better we know another person, the more likely it is that we have information about his or her unique concerns or propensities. Although most men love to watch televised sports, for example, a given wife may come to realize that her husband never watches televised sports events. Spouses can be accurate because they predict the specific responses of marital partners using psychological data: *differential accuracy.*

We predicted that the Independents with their commitment to maintaining some independence within a reasonably close relationship would be more accurate in using differential or unique information about the spouse. These couples would be better able to see the degree to which their spouses deviated from conventional or expected behaviors.

A third source of accuracy is projection in which the spouse correctly attributes self thoughts to the mate. Spouses can be accurate because they correctly assume that mates share their view: *projective accuracy.* Because of the lack of closeness in the Separate relationship, and the restricted nature of the communication in these couples, we hypothesized that the Separates would be the least accurate in predicting the gender attributions of a spouse. Independents, on the other hand, with good

TABLE 3.4

Wackman's Accuracy Measure and Correlations of
Spousal Accuracy Across the Couple Types

	HACC	WACC	Correlation
Traditionals	.56	.58$_b$	.360*
Independents	.48	.55$_b$	.527*
Separates	.43	.42$_c$	.645*
Sep/Trad	.57	.62$_a$	.455
Mixed	.51	.54$_b$	.480*

NOTE: There are no significant differences among husbands in predicting their wives.
Mean accuracy with different subscripts across wives' relational types are significantly
different at the .05 level. Asterisks indicate that the correlation between husbands
and wives scores is significant. The correlation for Independents is significant because
there are 51 Independents, in contrast with 17 Separate/Traditionals.

levels of companionship, yet a nonconventional view of marriage that
supports open conflict and expressivity, should have relatively greater
differential accuracy. Independents were expected to be the most likely to
use psychological data in predicting the spouse and more likely to be
accurate in using that data source. Both Wackman (1969) and Cronbach's
(1955) accuracy measures were used with these data. Wackman's (1969)
measure, a correlation profile measure, partials out each spouse's self-
rating (or assumed similarity). After the correlation profile scores were
computed for each individual, the profile scores for husbands and wives
were correlated and averaged. This average was compared to a random
male and female pairing. The average husband and wife correlation was
significantly larger than that of the random pairing (Fitzpatrick & Indvik,
1979). This analysis indicates that stereotypic accuracy was not the
primary source of accuracy left when projection was removed.

Neither individual relational definition, sex, or number of years
married predicted these accuracy components. Because accuracy scores
for Mixed couple types (for both husband and wife samples) were not
significantly different from one another, the Mixed couple types were
collapsed for analysis.

Table 3.4 presents the means for accuracy for husbands and wives in
each relational type and the correlation within type for husbands and
wives. Although there were no significant differences on this measure of
accuracy for the couple type for husbands, the overall pattern of the
means displayed in the table supports the differential accuracy hypothesis
for couple types. The wives in all relational types tend to be more accurate
than husbands in predicting their spouses' behaviors and attitudes. The
traditional wife in the Separate/Traditional marriage is the most accurate

TABLE 3.5
Cronbach's Accuracy Components for the Couple Types

	Differential		Stereotypic		Projective	
	H	W	H	W	H	W
Traditional	1.96	1.90	.73	.63	.43	.46
Independent	1.99	1.75	.79	.65	.04	.07
Separate	2.29	2.87	1.16	.84	.90	.51
Sep/Trad	1.37	1.45	.77	.50	.37	.09
Mixed	1.81	1.96	.74	.61	.51	.45

NOTE: The lower the score, the more accurate.

of the spouses in predicting her husband, whereas the Separates are the least accurate. Traditionals, Independents, and Mixed couples do equally well in predicting their spouses. In the Traditional marriage, both partners do equally well in predicting the spouse whereas in the Separate marriage, both partners do equally poorly.

Although there are accuracy differences between men and women, there are strong positive correlations within each couple type between partner's accuracy scores. Only the Separate/Traditionals exhibit a nonsignificant husband-wife correlation, although both the husbands and wives in this marriage score high on accuracy.

One difficulty in interpreting the results from the Wackman analysis is that the correlation profile measure combines stereotypic and differential accuracy while removing the projection component. This analytical technique, while providing important general information, does not allow us to test the sources of accuracy in the gender attributions of husbands and wives. Thus we calculated the accuracy scores on these traits by using Cronbach's procedure. As we can see in Table 3.5, the same general pattern of the mean values on accuracy holds.

The Separate/Traditionals are more accurate than the other couples and the Separates are the least accurate. As a couple, the Separate/Traditionals achieve a high degree of accuracy because of the traditional wife in this marriage. The wife uses stereotypic information about the husband correctly and is not likely to project her own views on her spouse. Their sizable projection score indicates that Separates project characteristics onto their spouses and overassume similarity. Independents, Traditionals, and Mixed couples achieve the same level of stereotypic and differential accuracy and use these data to about the same degree. We argued that the Independents can achieve accuracy through the use of a differential strategy. The data indicate, however, that Independent coorientational accuracy comes more from their ability to control projecting (incorrectly) their own personality characteristics and traits onto their attributions of the spouse. Separate/Traditionals appear to use both stereotypic information and unique information about their spouses to predict accurately how these spouses rate themselves on classic masculine and feminine traits. The wives in this couple type are especially good at using information about their husband's unique characteristics to achieve coorientational accuracy. Recall that this wife rates herself as very feminine. When she does project her own gender attributions onto her spouse, she correctly projects.

Faulty stereotypic attributions, lack of understanding of the unique characteristics of the spouse, and a tendency to project one's own attitudes onto the mate are all problems preventing coorientational accuracy for Separates. The Mixed couple types are the best at seeing the uniqueness of their spouses in reference to these gender attributions. Having different attitudes and values on marriage may help to make uniqueness more salient.

Summary

These initial validation studies were extremely successful. We demonstrated that gender attitudes about male and female roles in society, the attributions that husbands and wives make concerning their own gender-related traits and behaviors, and the accuracy of the gender attributions spouses make about one another are systematically related to the type of marriage. Across the sample, all respondents demonstrated less attitudinal agreement with traditional sex-role norms and values. Those with traditional ideologies of family life espoused these value somewhat more strongly but the overall level of support even for these couples was moderate. In terms of self-attributions on gender, marital type is more strongly related to how the wife views herself than to husband attributions. Although sex-typing predominates for all types, for the independent wife, androgyny is equally as likely a possibility as is undifferentiation for the separate wife. How these wives categorize themselves depends on how they see the marriage. Marriage affects wives' *but not husbands'* self-attributions of gender-related traits. Independent and Traditional women's self-attributions are also in line with their gender attitudes. The more conventional one's gender attitude, the more likely that a woman types herself as feminine. This statement does not hold for separate wives who view themselves as undifferentiated. Espousing traditional gender attitudes, yet seeing oneself as not possessing the requisite feminine traits to carry out the roles, suggest that separate wives are under particular strain in their marriages to traditional and independent men.

Both the gender attitudes and the self-attributions are assessed with questionnaires, as is the marital type. Shared method variance may account for some of the significant results. The coorientational accuracy study gives a hopeful picture as this study also demonstrated significant differences in the predicted direction among the couples in the various types. This approach qualifies as a relational approach because it examines the interpenetration of perspectives of the spouses. A comparison of the perspectives in each marital type suggests that different interactional patterns will be uncovered in each of the couple types.

Regardless of data analytic technique employed, the Separates are significantly less accurate in predicting the gender attributions of their spouses. Moreover, wives are more accurate than husbands in predicting their spouses across all three data sources. One explanation of the coorientational accuracy of wives in contrast to husbands—the power differential explanation—is that lower-status people must correctly interpret the cognitions and attitudes of higher-status people. Wives are structurally considered to have less power than husbands and hence are better able to predict their spouses. Such an explanation is, however, highly speculative.

Research is needed on gender in marriage. We know little about sexuality of couples in the various types, clearly an important issue in understanding gender in marital interaction. Of particular interest would be study relating the couple types to the "gender-linked" language effect (Mulac, Lundell, & Bradac, 1986). Couples with traditional ideological orientations toward male and female roles should demonstrate these linguistic characteristics in marital conversations significantly more than those without such an orientation.

MARITAL SATISFACTION
AND THE TYPOLOGY

Marital satisfaction or related concepts, such as adjustment, integration, success, or happiness, is the most widely studied dependent variable in the literature (Hicks & Platt, 1970). Despite our criticisms of marital satisfaction (see Chapter 1), there are three important reasons to examine adjustment in the marital types. First, the construct of adjustment is theoretically significant and has been related to a variety of other processes and outcomes in marriage. To compare the typology to other studies of marriage, it is useful to have information on the adjustment of the various couples.

Second, when studies or programs of research omit the assessment of the level of marital satisfaction experienced by a couple, a vital piece of information is lost. Raush and his associates (1974), in their now-classic study, neglected to ask couples for information about marital distress or happiness (using any psychometrically valid scale). A decade later, Gottman (1979) reanalyzed the data from that earlier experiment and discovered communication patterns in all of Raush's couples that strongly suggest marital distress. Although the Raush group used a random sampling procedure, all couples in the sample appear to have been unhappy in their marriages. Many of the conclusions reached in this study may need to be reevaluated because of the relationship between communication and marital satisfaction.

Third, a contingency model of marital interaction may be the most discriminating (e.g., Sillars et al., 1983). Such a model may be considered a typological model of marital satisfaction. Both the typological information and the level of marital satisfaction need to be taken into account in predicting sequences of marital interaction. Although there are some difficulties with this perspective (e.g., the use of relational definition and not couple type; the difficulty of finding "unhappy" Traditional couples), success has been achieved in fitting models of communication behaviors to individuals who are categorized according to both their relational definition and marital satisfaction.

Measuring Adjustment
in the Couple Types

Dyadic adjustment is viewed as a process whose outcome is defined by the degree of consensus, cohesion, affection, and satisfaction in the marriage (Spanier, 1976). *Consensus* is the extent of agreement that couples believe they have on important issues in their relationship. *Cohesion* refers to how often spouses engage in positive interaction with one another. *Affection* refers to how frequently an individual expresses affection to a spouse and whether affection is a problem in the relationship. *Satisfaction* measures the intensity and number of conflicts experienced in the relationship.

Two major conceptual dimensions of the typology—interdependence and expressivity—lead to hypotheses about the components of dyadic adjustment. Given our Chapter 1 critique of dyadic adjustment, we expect Traditional couples to have higher dyadic adjustment scores than other

TABLE 3.6
Means for the DAS Across the
Pure and the Mixed Couple Types

| | DAS | | | | | | | |
| | Consensus | | Affection | | Satisfaction | | Cohesion | |
	H	W	H	W	H	W	H	W
I	59.59	60.65	12.12	13.00	46.53	47.94	20.59	20.09
S	65.29	62.36	12.86	12.00	47.21	45.79	19.36	18.21
T	67.20	67.20	13.60	13.80	53.70	53.30	24.00	23.20
S/T	62.00	62.56	14.00	13.78	50.33	50.33	20.33	20.11
M	58.40	62.20	12.50	14.00	47.00	46.40	19.50	20.00
F (4, 59)	3.37	1.79	1.33	2.75	4.39	3.33	2.12	2.09
p. <	.02	.14	.27	.04	.003	.02	.09	.09

NOTE: Separate one-way analyses of variance were calculated with couple type as the independent variable and each of the four measures as dependent variables.

couple types because of the bias of the scales. We also predict that because of their high levels of sharing and expressivity, Independents will have higher cohesion scores than will the other couple types except the Traditionals, and lower satisfaction scores than all the other couples. Satisfaction, as the reader recalls, includes items admitting that the couple has conflict in the relationship.

In total, 60 couples completed the Relational Dimensions Instrument (RDI), the Dyadic Adjustment Scale (DAS), and some demographic questions. Couples were in their mid-30s, had been married approximately nine years, and had two children. Overall there were 10 Traditional, 14 Separate, 17 Independent, 9 Separate/Traditional, and 10 Mixed couples.

The marital types differ in their levels of marital adjustment. Across all scales except affection, both spouses in the Traditional marriage indicate that they experience a higher degree of dyadic adjustment than couples in the other types.

To visualize the differences among the couple types on dyadic adjustment, a discriminant function analysis was calculated in order to plot the group centroids. The first (chi-square (12) = 81.03, p < .0001), second (chi-square (6) = 39.17, p < .0001), and the third (chi-square (2) = 14.67, p < .0007) discriminant functions were significant, indicating that the couple types could be separated on three dimensions. The first dimension can be labeled "satisfaction," the second "consensus," and the third "cohesion" (Bochner & Fitzpatrick, 1980). Figure 3.2 shows the Traditionals set apart from the other types by their relatively higher

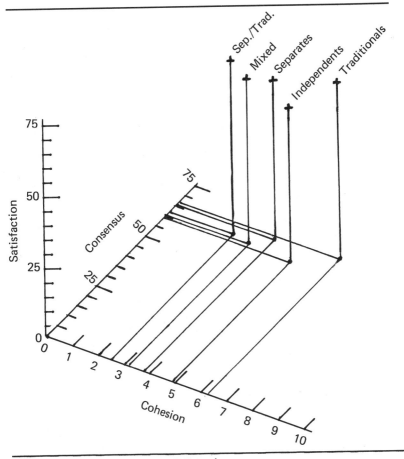

Figure 3.2 Couple types on the DAS dimensions.

satisfaction, consensus, and cohesion in the marriage. The Separate/Traditionals and the Traditionals share the same level of satisfaction in their marriage whereas the Separates are close to the Traditionals on the consensus in their marriage. The Independents, although their satisfaction and consensus may be lower than the Traditionals, are closer to the Traditionals on relational cohesiveness. Although the figure indicates differences among the types, the Pure types cluster more closely to one another than they do to the Mixed types. Agreement on basic relational issues is related to adjustment in marriage.

Table 3.7 presents another set of data on the issue of dyadic adjustment in the couple types. No national norms of the sort developed for the

TABLE 3.7
Summary Statistics for the DAS from Spanier (1976)

	Score	Difference from Total
Spanier (1976)		
Married	114.8	36
Divorced	70.7	80
Fitzpatrick & Best (1979)		
Traditionals	158.0	24
Independents	139.0	43
Separates	122.0	60
Separate/Traditionals	147.0	35
Mixed	124.0	58

NOTE: Both were convenience samples, drawn from outside the university community.

Locke-Wallace test exist for the DAS. Furthermore, the way we scored the DAS differs slightly from the approach used by Spanier (1976). Compare, however, the results from the original Spanier (1976) study and the Fitzpatrick and Best (1979) work. The highest possible score on the Spanier scale is 151, and the divorced sample scores below the midpoint on that scale. The highest possible score on the DAS, with our coding, is 182.[1] Not even the Separates, who have the lowest overall score, come close to the scale midpoint. Whereas the couple types differ in levels of dyadic adjustment, each appears to have worked out a stable relationship form. Separates are not necessarily waiting for divorce.

The typology represents an alternative to defining couples by their level of marital satisfaction or dyadic adjustment. It is an alternative because it allows for couples (i.e., the Independents) who have a good deal of conflict and an openness to dealing with relationship difficulties to be considered as potentially as well adjusted as the couples in a Traditional marital form. Furthermore, we have seen that couples who have a good deal of agreement on basic relationship issues, and some concern for conventionality (i.e., Separates), are above the midpoint on the major scale of dyadic adjustment. The typology is concerned with stable marital patterns.

A Pragmatic Test of Marital Adjustment

Who are the happy couples? Researchers sometimes use "snowball" sampling techniques (a technique that makes demographers blanch). In other words, they ask happy families to refer them to other happy families, or families with disabled children for the names of others, and so forth. We were interested in finding a sample of couples who publicly put forth their own marriages as happy ones. We turned to religion (no, we did not ask God for guidance, we went to church-sponsored marital enrichment courses).

Recently, organized religion in America has decided that something should be done to bolster marriage and the family. In the past few years, a great deal of attention has been paid to the development of programs designed to enrich marital relationships. The focus of many of these programs is on the enhancement of communication skills; many programs are expressly directed at couples who are currently in "good marriages." We have recently published an article that is fairly critical of the Marriage Encounter movement (Witteman & Fitzpatrick, 1987). The focus of that critique is that the movement, although advertised as a communication training program, does not teach communication skills in the ways that most therapeutic and counseling programs have found to be the most effective.

This paper lead us to consider the types of couples actively involved in this movement, particularly those couples who are publicly involved in the Marriage Encounter movement. By examining these couples, we are really examining couples who feel that they have a reasonably good marital relationship—a relationship that they publicly advertise as a good one. Our prediction is that given the ideological orientation of the Marriage Encounter movement that stresses traditional values of marital companionship, interdependence, and unity over autonomy and individuality, very few Independent couples would be actively involved.

We collected two different samples. The first consisted of the entire sample of team leader couples (N = 24) of the Marriage Encounter movement working in a city of approximately 300,000 people. The second was a random sample of couples who had been involved in the movement and advertised this fact in a series of advertisements run over a few months in a number of local newspapers (N = 40). These couples were about 40 years old, had been married for 15 years, had four children, had completed some college, and had incomes over $25,000 annually. In interviews, both sets of couples indicated that they spent much of their social time involved in meetings and follow-up sessions with other couples who had participated in a Marriage Encounter weekend. These two samples did not differ in their level of commitment to their own marriages, on how pleased they had been with their initial encounter experience, or on demographic variables; therefore, the samples were combined for analyses.

There were 29 traditionals, 12 independents, and 23 separates, or 10 Traditional couples, 3 Independent couples, 8 Separate couples, and 11 Mixed couples. We compared the frequency of individual relational definitions and of couple-type designations from this sample with the expected frequencies generated from the random sample of 448 couples (Fitzpatrick & Indvik, 1982). Although there were not more traditionals (or Traditionals) in this sample than expected by chance, there were significantly fewer independents than expected by chance (chi-square (1) = 9.21, p < .01). Surprisingly, there are more separate individuals (chi-square (1) = 9.05, p < .01) and more Separate couples (chi-square (1) = 11.45, p < .01) in Marriage Encounter than expected by chance. Furthermore, there was no significant difference in the amount of agreement on marital definitions between the general population and the Marriage Encounter sample. These couples appear to be no better than the general population in developing a cohesive relational definition.

Church-sponsored programs to improve "good" marriages may attract a variety of couple types initially, although those who remain with the movement may be expected to be those who share the ideological orientation of the program. The fact that Independents are not allied with this program fits the basic premises and assumptions of the typology. The large number of Separates in the program is curious and demands some explanation.

Separates share many values with the Traditionals although these couples are not as close nor as disclosive to one another as are their Traditional counterparts. The level of self-disclosure required of team leaders in running a Marriage Encounter program, however, is minimal. The program does not specify any commitment to expressivity or openness between spouses. Within their traditional value orientations, Separates may be drawn to activities that they can do together, yet that enable them to maintain emotional distance in the marriage. The Separates in this study may represent the happy and adjusted Separates isolated by Sillars and his group. And, these couples may be interested in helping other couples to deal with their marital difficulties through emotional distance and a different ideological commitment. In the Cuber and Harroff (1965, p. 127) study, a clergyman whom they interviewed summed up what might be happening here:

> I'm embarrassed to say this, but I think you suspect it. If there were more solid relationships between the husbands and wives in my congregation, we'd have a hard time keeping this church as organized as it is. . . . Why, half of our lay leadership is available only because there are such vacuums in their personal lives that they need something just to take up the time.

Of course, a church-sponsored enrichment program is not the only couple-oriented avoidance activity. Sports, community activities, and children's programs all can function to help stable couples avoid personal interaction with one another. And, as the data on the dyadic adjustment of the Separates clearly indicates, such a pattern is not distressing to certain couples.

Summary

There may be some variation within the various marital types as to the level of satisfaction experienced by certain individuals. Separates, for example, may be made up of those who are happy and satisfied with the emotionally distant equilibrium in the marriage and another group of those who are distressed at the state of the relationship. In the research of Sillars and his group (e.g., Burgraff & Sillars, 1986), significant communication differences are found for what they characterize as "happy" and "unhappy" Separates. Such a categorization seems reasonable for Separates although few differences occur when the other types are split according to their level of happiness.

Who is the happiest of them all? The unambiguous answer to this question is that Pure-type Traditionals experience the highest levels of dyadic adjustment of all the types of couples in the typology. It is important to note, however, that couples in all of these types score above average in marital happiness or satisfaction. Each of these types may represent functional or workable marriages in that each has achieved a level of marital adjustment that appears to operate without debilitating impasses or blockages. The internal and external stressors that could potentially affect each of the various marital types will differ.

CONCLUSION

The reliable assignment of couples to marital types can predict the gender attitudes of couples, their personal definitions of masculinity and femininity, and their levels of dyadic adjustment. Psychological gender and accuracy, although not associated with husbands' relational types, also were not associated with the individual relational definition of a male. These two variables were significantly associated with marital type, albeit only for wives.

The Traditional relationship is one in which spouses have very conventional approaches to male and female roles and in which they see their personalities as matching these cultural stereotypes. These husbands and wives are accurate in predicting how the spouse sees himself or herself on a variety of attributes. These couples experience the highest degree of dyadic adjustment. The Independent relationship allows liberal orientations to gender issues, although the Independent husband sees himself as relatively masculine sex-typed, whereas his wife is likely to be androgynous. Independent wives are quite accurate at predicting their husbands' behavior and attitudes, yet these husbands do less well in predicting their wives' behavior and attitudes. Their level of dyadic adjustment overall is high, with cohesion as the major source of adjustment. The Separate marriage supports conventional gender attitudes, although the wife in this marriage rates herself as possessing neither positive feminine nor masculine traits. Both husbands and wives in this marriage do poorly in predicting their spouse. The high perceived consensus on issues is the major source of adjustment in this marriage.

The Separate/Traditional couple is the only Mixed type that is consistently discriminated from other couple types. Separate/Traditionals represent a type of marriage—the withdrawn husband and the companionate wife—frequently found by other researchers (e.g., Komarovsky, 1964; Slater, 1970). Separate/Traditionals have the same conventional gender attitudes and rate themselves as the most sex-typed of the couples. These couples are the most accurate in predicting one another, and they experience a high degree of dyadic adjustment.   In general, the Mixed types (other than the Separate/Traditionals), are more similar to one another than they are different. These husbands and wives are more accurate than Separates in predicting how their spouses view themselves, yet less accurate than the Separate/Traditionals. The Mixed types also receive the lowest scores on consensus, indicating that the "Mixed" classification is appropriate.

The marital typology is validated across a number of indices of marital functioning. Given shared method variance, however, it is much easier to predict self-reports from self-reports. In the next two sections of this book, we examine the actual exchange of messages, both verbal and nonverbal, between couples in the various types. In the next section, we discuss power and conflict.

NOTE

1. A factor analysis of the Dyadic Adjustment Scale (DAS) suggested that three items should be moved to different subscales. We scored the Spanier scale starting from 1 rather

than zero. This scoring technique should be taken into account when comparisons are made with other studies. In this study, consensus is measured by 13 items, which range from a high of 6 (Always Agree) to a low of 1 (Always Disagree). The highest possible score is 78, and the alpha reliability on this scale is .85. Cohesion is measured by five items. One question has a high score of 5, whereas the other four have high scores of 6. Thus the highest score possible is 29, and the alpha reliability is .80. Affection is measured by four items. The highest possible score on this scale is a 16, and the alpha reliability is .67. The satisfaction scale has 10 items; the high score on this factor is 59, and alpha is .82.

II

POWER, CONFLICT, AND COMPLIANCE GAINING

4

Who's in Charge

Power Strategies
in Marital Conversations

Power is the ability to produce intended effects on the behavior or the emotions of the spouse (Scanzoni & Szinovacz, 1980). Theorists agree that this ability to produce intended effects can be studied in three separate domains (Olson & Cromwell, 1975). These three domains include the bases of power, or the resources that increase a spouse's ability to exert situational control; the process of marital power, or what occurs in interaction between husbands and wives; and the outcomes of marital power, or whose decision the couple adopts. We are primarily concerned with the process of marital power because we are interested in examining what occurs between husbands and wives during interaction.

To define power as an ability implies that, like many abilities, power is not always exercised (Huston, 1983). Even though a spouse may be able to produce some intended effect on a partner, he or she may choose not to exercise this ability. In many communication situations, power may remain latent. In order to see how power worked in conversations between partners, we choose communication situations most conducive to operation of manifest power processes. We examined conversations in which husbands and wives have at least partially conflicting interests. As one moves up the following continuum of family situations from general family discussions, decision-making interactions, problem-solving interactions, conflict resolution interactions, to crisis management, conflicting interests become more evident in family communication (Olson &

Cromwell, 1975). In other words, although power processes are inherent in all marital and family interactions, the expression of power becomes more problematic, and more notable in the latter instances of the continuum. To measure power in marital interaction, the research reported in this chapter concentrates on conflict between husbands and wives. In the studies in which couples are asked to engage in casual as well as conflict interaction, the casual conversation is used as the baseline.

This chapter examines verbal power strategies through the relational control model. This model, discussed in Chapter 1, specifies that theorists can study communication at the content level (looking at what was said) and at the relationship level (looking at the nature of the relationship between the speaker and the other person). The relational control model's premise is that we define our relationships with others through talk. This model considers "control" to be the power to direct the character of interaction, hence defining the nature of the relationship between the spouses. Both spouses influence the patterns of control that emerge out of interaction.

Merging these two major approaches to the study of relational definitions—the typological and the relational communication perspectives—strengthens both views of relationships. The typological approach defines couples according to a number of dimensions of relationship life. As we saw in the second chapter, when individuals are asked about a number of aspects of their marriage, there is little variability in their discussion of relational power or control (Fitzpatrick, 1977). Although willing to report different ideological conceptions on the nature of marriage (Fitzpatrick, 1977) and on various sex-role orientations (Fitzpatrick & Indvik, 1982), respondents either cannot, or choose not, to extrapolate from these views to a discussion of the distribution of power or control in their marriages.

In the first investigation in the typological series, the majority of the more than 900 respondents reported totally egalitarian patterns of decision making and power distribution in their marriages (Fitzpatrick, 1976). Because there is little variability in self-reports of the nature of power in relationships, the study of power must be approached from other perspectives. The relational communication view offers that perspective. Following Bateson (1938, 1958), this view argues that social scientists need to move away from studying the individual in isolation toward examining the patterns of relationships between individuals. A relational communication view maintains that power is best conceptualized as a dyadic rather than as an individual-level variable, and, as such, is not accurately assessed by individual-level reports. As a dyadic

TABLE 4.1
Sample Conversation

Husband:	"But then I don't remember; what did I say?" (223)
Wife:	"You explained the wrong ways and the right ways and other things." (114)
Husband:	"Oh, yah, I remember that. Let's see . . ." (211)
Wife:	"Over on the East Side they already have a program, so he really already knew the right way." (113)

SOURCE: Adapted from Rogers and Farace (1975).

variable, power must be examined in the stream of interaction (Raush, Grief, & Nugent, 1979). To understand the dynamics of power within the various types of marriages, the interaction patterns of the couples must be analyzed.

In this chapter we report the results of two studies that differentiate the Traditional, Independent, Separate, and various Mixed couple types in their use of relational-control strategies during conflict and during casual interactions.

POWER MOVES IN
MARITAL CONVERSATIONS

To examine power moves in conversation, we utilized two different coding schemes and two different experimental procedures. The first scheme (Rogers & Farace, 1975) considers the "speaking turn" as the unit of analysis. A speaking turn is defined as the uninterrupted talk of one person; it can range from one word to a lengthy monologue. Coders assign each speaking turn a three-digit code. The first digit refers to the speaker as (1) wife, or (2) husband. The second digit designates the grammatical form as (1) assertion, (2) question, (3) talkover, (4) noncomplete, or (5) other. The third digit describes the function of the message, relative to the immediately preceding message, as (1) support, (2) nonsupport, (3) extension, (4) answer, (5) instruction, (6) order, (7) disconfirmation, (8) topic change, (9) initiation/termination, and (10) other. Table 4.1 shows a conversation between a husband and wife, and the appropriate three-digit code for each speaking turn.

Communication researchers analyze the messages from one spouse in terms of how the partner responds. Each speaker can send a message designed to assert control (what researchers call a "one-up" message), a message designed to relinquish control (one-down), or a message that is neutral on the control issue (one-across). For example, in Table 4.1, both of the husband's statements are one-down messages. The wife's first statement is a one-up message, her second statement is a one-across message.

There are 50 possible message types. The grammatical form and function define messages as asserting, giving up, or equalizing control. Relational control cannot be defined by looking at only one message. We must look at the pattern of messages and responses over time. Every message is a stimulus for the next message in the sequence.

The interaction patterns of a relationship can be manifested in one of two basic ways: symmetrical and complementary (Watzlawick, Beavin, & Jackson, 1967). In symmetrical interaction, the husband and the wife offer similar messages designed to control the definition of the relationship (Bateson & Jackson, 1968). There are three basic types of symmetry: *competitive*, characterized by escalation and fighting; *neutralized*, characterized by mutual respect and by not taking a stand on the issue of control; and *submissive*, characterized by mutual coalescence and surrender. In complementary interaction, one spouse seeks control over the definition and the other yields it. The participants' behaviors are compatible but fully differentiated. Examples of complementary interaction patterns are giving and taking instructions, or asserting and agreeing. Table 4.2 gives examples of these nine types of interactions.

The second coding scheme we used suggests that control messages may vary in intensity (Ellis, Fisher, Drecksel, Hoch, & Werbel, 1976). The speaking turn is the unit of analysis, and this scheme, called Rel/Com, has five control modes—two one-up, two one-down, and one one-across.

These five control modes are the following:

(1) *Domineering*—Attempting to restrict the behavioral options of the spouse severely (One-up, strong). This includes challenges, personal nonsupport statements, and so forth.

(2) *Structuring*—Attempting to restrict the behavioral options of the spouse while leaving some options open (One-up, weak). This includes disagreement and idea extension.

(3) *Equivalence*—Attempting mutual identification (One-across). This includes repetition and clarification.

(4) *Deference*—Being willing to relinquish some behavioral options to spouse while retaining some choice (One-down, weak). This includes agreement and information seeking.

TABLE 4.2
Examples of the Nine Types of Interactions

(1) *Competitive symmetry* (one-up/one-up):
Paul: You know I want you to keep the house picked up during the day.
Margie: I want you to help sometimes!

(2) *Complementarity* (one-down/one-up):
Margie: With your help, Paul, I know we can get out of this.
Paul: I do know how to organize things.

(3) *Transition* (one-across/one-up):
Margie: I was thinking of taking sleeping bags.
Paul: No, we don't need them.

(4) *Complementarity* (one-up/one-down):
Paul: Let's get out of town this weekend, so we can work this thing out.
Margie: Okay.

(5) *Submissive symmetry* (one-down/one-down):
Paul: I'm so tired. What are we ever going to do?
Margie: Please don't leave.

(6) *Transition* (one-across-/one-down):
Paul: I was thinking of doing household chores.
Margie: Whatever you want to do.

(7) *Transition* (one-up/one-across):
Paul: I definitely think we should have more kids.
Margie: I remember my parents always wanted more grandkids.

(8) *Transition* (one-down/one-across):
Margie: I'm sorry I don't want to go out very often. What can I do about it?
Paul: I don't know.

(9) *Neutralized symmetry* (one-across/one-across):
Margie: I heard it was snowing in the mountains.
Paul: That's going to make driving a little slower.

NOTE: Each message is seen as an offering of a momentary relational definition, from subtle to more direct presentations.

(5) *Submissiveness*—Relinquishing behavioral options to the spouse while retaining little choice (One-down, strong). This includes extended ideational support and personal support in the question form.

A variety of different types of symmetrical and complementary interaction patterns can be uncovered using this coding scheme since intensity of the control moves is measured. For example, strong competitive symmetry involves the pairing of two strong dominance messages; for example, the statement "You are a lousy lover," is met by the counterstatement, "I'd be a better lover if you weren't so fat."

Multiple Measures
of the Same Construct

Although both of these schemes can yield reliable interaction data, scholars have questioned both the representational and construct validity of these two schemes (Poole, Folger, & Hewes, 1983). Neither control scheme is said to have representational validity; that is, individuals in the same culture as the speakers do not necessarily "see" the communication behaviors isolated by these researchers as control moves. In one study (Folger & Sillars, 1980) examining the representational validity of the Rogers and Farace (1975) scheme, the major variable that respondents choose as measuring relational control was talk time, or how long a speaker held the floor. Thus a representationally valid coding scheme of relational control should include some measure of talk time, in addition to the verbal measures. We agree that speakers can exercise power in conversation by maintaining attention on themselves, by extensive verbal participation, and through the attempted and successful use of interruptions (Hadley & Jacob, 1976; Mishler & Waxler, 1968). We do not, however, report vocal time measures as Chapter 8 covers nonverbal behaviors in the couple types.[1]

The questions raised concerning these coding schemes by those favoring the demonstration of representational validity also lead to a concern for the connection between the message codes and their designation as bids for dominance or submission. Although on face, most would agree that orders and commands by a speaker are bids for dominance, many would question the designation of agreement as a bid for submission. Most other coding schemes consider agreement as a positive affiliative cue between marital partners rather than a verbal move signaling submission (e.g., Gottman, 1979; Weiss & Summers, 1983). There appears to be some confusion between control and affiliation in these coding schemes. Control and affect are the two basic domains of interpersonal behavior (Bochner et al., 1977). These two domains, however, are orthogonal to one another. In other words, it is possible to isolate behaviors that are high on both affiliation and control, low on both affiliation and control, or high on one dimension and low on another. Because of this conceptual confusion, the second study in this chapter reports the data from the Rel/Com system at both level of the actual messages as well as their coded control designations. In this way, the reader will have a clearer picture of what happened in the dialogues and will be able to differentiate control and affect messages.

The second major critique of these coding schemes concerns convergent validity. Both coding schemes are based on the interactional view (Raush et al., 1979). Thus both have a strong theoretical basis. Coding schemes designed to measure the same behaviors and based on the same theoretical perspective should measure the same things. Disconfirmation, topic change, instruction, order, or failure to support a previous utterance are one-up moves or bids for dominance in both control schemes. Unfortunately, there are differences in the schemes. In Rogers and Farace (1975), agreement is always a bid for submission, whereas in Ellis et al. (1976), agreement can be any one of the three control moves. Agreement with extension is structuring, conditional agreement is equivalence, and simple agreement is deference. There are also some differences in coding extensions between the two schemes. Thus the same communication behaviors are considered to fulfill different control functions in these two schemes. Primarily, however, the difference lies in the fact that the Ellis scheme codes for intensity of the control bids whereas the Rogers and Farace system does not. Thus the Ellis scheme tends to distribute message type across the levels of the scheme and thus places some messages in different "categories" than does the Rogers and Farace scheme.

Each of the schemes takes the previous and subsequent message into account in order to assign codes, however, there is a serious unit of analysis problem in comparing these two schemes. The Rogers and Farace system allows the double coding of a speaking turn if the response to the previous message is different from the stimulus. The Ellis scheme chooses the predominant code in any speaking turn. When O'Donnell-Trujillo (1981) coded the same data with both schemes, agreement between the systems on the units was poor. To remedy this problem and to make the data across our two studies comparable, we analyze only the first code in a speaking turn in the first study. This strategy maximizes the comparability of the two studies.

Power Moves in Salient
and Nonsalient Conflict

In the first study, 43 couples were tape recorded in their homes as they discussed two issues, one highly salient and one less salient, on which they disagreed (Best, 1979). In total, 14 couples were categorized as Traditionals, 8 as Independents, 10 as Separates. The remaining 11 were evenly distributed among the Mixed couple types, and these 11 were combined for analysis. Couples' discussion data for the highly salient and the less salient disagreements were coded using the relational communication coding scheme of Rogers and Farace (1975). Two coders rated the message codes for each of the 43 couples. Using percentages of agreement, reliability figures were determined for eight discussion topics (10% of the total) across the four selected dyads. The pair-comparison percentages ranged from 0.64 to 0.94. Average reliability across all 16 pair comparisons was 0.84.

Significant differences among the couple types occurred in both the high- and low-salience conditions. Across all couples, the majority of the interacts used in the conflict discussions were categorized as either complementary or competitively symmetrical. Figure 4.1 shows that regardless of the importance of the disagreement, Independents engaged in more competitively symmetrical exchanges than did the other couple types. Competitively symmetrical exchanges occur when one spouse refuses to give in to the control moves of the other spouse; one-up moves are countered with one-up moves. Regardless of the importance of the issue under discussion, the Separates used proportionally fewer competitively symmetrical exchanges than the other couple types. Separates are far less likely to fight for control of a segment of the conversation.

The issue under discussion affected the Traditionals and the Mixed types in their use of competitively symmetrical exchanges. Traditionals decrease their use of competitive symmetry when the disagreement between them is unimportant, whereas the Mixed couple types marginally increase their use of this exchange pattern when the issue is less salient.

Figure 4.2 indicates that accepting the control moves of the spouse, or complementarity, reflects a different pattern than does competitive symmetry. Across both conditions, Separates used significantly higher proportions of complementary transactions than did the other couple types. The Independents used the same proportion of complementary exchanges in the highly salient disagreement as when the disagreement

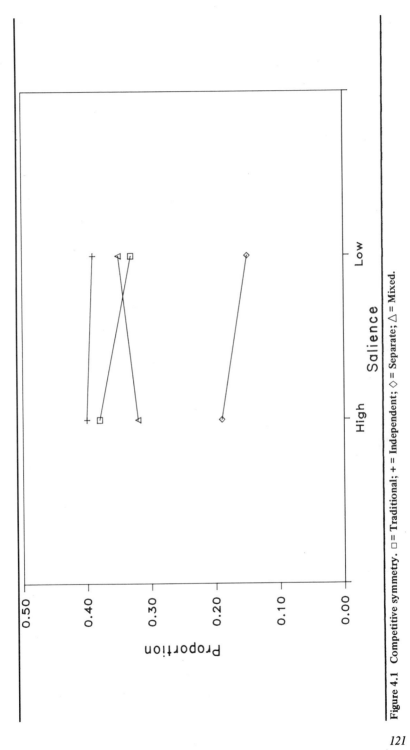

Figure 4.1 Competitive symmetry. □ = Traditional; + = Independent; ◇ = Separate; △ = Mixed.

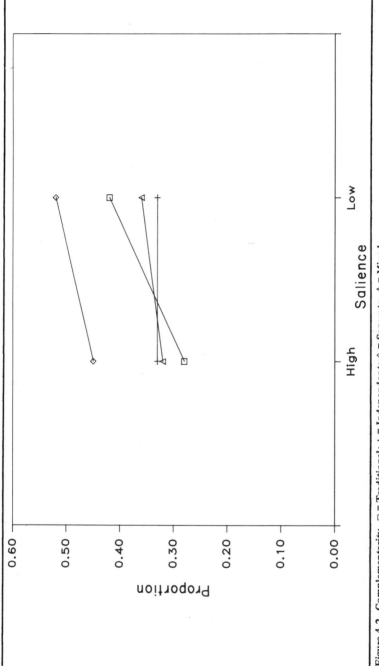

Figure 4.2 Complementarity. □ = Traditional; + = Independent; ◇ = Separate; △ = Mixed.

was of less concern to them, whereas the Traditionals and the Mixed increased their use of complementarity when the issue was less important.

A major premise of the relational communication approach is that messages must be examined as interacts (message pairs). This premise, however, itself needs to be statistically tested with a technique designed to show that there is a high degree of probability that one particular message follows another. The chi-square test proceeded "as if" interacts described the interaction patterns of these couples. One way to examine these data is lag sequential analysis (Bakeman & Gottman, 1986). Lag sequential analysis identifies the conditional probabilities that messages follow (or precede) one another in predictable chains. A behavior is chosen as the criterion and the communication behaviors that predictably follow this criterion are examined. Lag probabilities are tested for statistical significance against the null hypothesis, which states that there are no dependencies among sequential messages with respect to the criterion behavior. The suggestions of Allison and Liker (1982) concerning the modifications of the z-score formula were followed in these analyses. Four criteria suggested by Sackett (1977) and Gottman (1979) were used to determine the significant pattern of control: (1) that the z-score must exceed + or -1.96 and be significant at .05, (2) that the observed frequency of the criterion behavior must compose at least 5% of the data set, (3) that the behaviors with respect to the criterion must occur at least six times at the specified lag, and (4) that 85 instances of behavior must occur to stabilize the z-score. The sequential patterns reported conform to all four criteria.

Unlike the chi-square reported earlier, the data for the two conflict conditions were combined because there were not enough data per couple type to estimate the sequential structure. This means that we can not explore the differences between low-salience and high-salience conflict interaction in these data with this technique. Furthermore, when the lag sequential analysis was computed, there were too few instances of one-across behaviors to calculate their sequential probabilities. As we can see in Table 4.3, all couple types except the Separates engage in competitive symmetrical interacts. In addition, husbands in the Mixed couple types, unlike their wives and unlike all other husbands, consistently respond to a wife's bid for submission with a submissive message.

Two major conclusions can be drawn from this study. First, couples categorized into one of the marital types exhibit significantly different control patterns during conflict interaction. Second, the conversational data of couples exhibits sequential structure, with some specific control

TABLE 4.3
Lag One Sequential Analysis Results of
Relational Control Patterns

	TRAD	IND	SEP	MIXED
Competitive Symmetry				
HUP-WUP	.546*	.537*	.321	.551*
WUP-HUP	.563*	.636*	.362	.550*
Submissive Symmetry				
HDOWN–WDOWN	.208	.341	.356	.276
WDOWN-HDOWN	.158	.187	.235	.316*
Complementarity				
HUP–WDOWN	.357*	.390*	.566*	.375*
WDOWN–HUP	.673*	.640*	.529*	.519*
WUP–HDOWN	.355*	.243*	.596*	.321*
HDOWN–WUP	.573*	.568*	.444*	.474*

NOTE: WUP = Wife one-up; HUP = Husband one-up; WDOWN = Wife one-down; HDOWN = Husband one-down. There were too few instances to check the lags for once-across messages.
*Significant at .05 level.

moves more likely to follow others. The frequency analysis suggested that the saliency of the conflict had a differential effect on the couples in the various types. Unfortunately, the data from the two discussion conditions had to be combined in order to run the lag sequential analysis. To expand upon these results and to probe for specific interaction patterns of control that differentiate the couple types during various kinds of discussions, we conducted the next study.

Power Moves in Conflict and Casual Conversations

A sample of 40 couples was drawn from two different populations for this study. The first sample was randomly selected from a complete list of all married couples belonging to an urban congregation. Only 2 couples of the 22 contacted refused to participate in this study. The second sample was randomly drawn from a list of volunteers associated with a social science department of a large southwestern university. None of the 20 couples in the second sample refused to participate.

All of the couples in the study were married, had lived together about six years, and were in their early 30s. Overall, 75% had at least one child. The educational level of the volunteers was high; more than 50% of the participants said they had finished college or completed advanced graduate or professional training. In this sample of 40 couples, there were 11 Separate couples, 7 Independent couples, and 3 Traditional couples. The 19 remaining fell into the Mixed couple type.

The study was conducted in the participants' homes and couples were audiotaped as they engaged in two discussion tasks. In one task, couples discussed their most recent serious conflict; in the other task, couples discussed a neutral issue. Each discussion lasted 10 minutes and the topics of the discussions were counterbalanced. Transcripts were made of all 80 conversations. Coders were trained in the appropriate use of the system. When the reliabilities of the coders reached 85%, they began coding these marital dialogues. The reliabilities of the coders were checked throughout the coding of the data and not merely at the beginning of the task. This helps to decrease the effect of coder drift in which coders begin to use the codes idiosyncratically. Reliability figures were determined for 10% of the discussions across eight randomly selected conversations. Using percentages of agreement, the average reliability was .89, with the individual pair comparisons ranging from .79 to .94.

The data for the two discussion topics of each couple type were analyzed in two ways. First, a multivariate frequency analysis of the individual message categories was computed for each couple type. Second, sequential analyses were used to examine how each couple type structured its interaction.

Multivariate frequency analysis. Many interactional studies move far beyond the data. Abstract coding schemes and complex statistical procedures blur comparisons among studies. For clarity, we first analyzed the frequency counts of the specific communication behaviors that made up the first level of the relational coding scheme. Verbal behavior categorized as a strong one-up message, for example, includes structuring in the imperative mode, abrupt topic changes, disconfirmation of the previous comment, challenges, justification in response to a challenge, and personal nonsupport. By reporting the data at the first level of the relational coding scheme, we accomplish two goals. First, this analysis allows comparisons among studies that do not move to the level of relationship patterns. Many observational researchers are interested in topic changes and personal rejection statements, and not necessarily in the implications of these messages for power. Second, the analysis is a manipulation check on the data for the two discussion conditions. Following Gottman (1979), we expect the frequency of negative communication behaviors—such as disagreement, personal nonsupport, and challenges—to increase in the conflict conditions compared to the neutral discussions. If this occurs, our communication task manipulation worked.

For the strong "one-up" or dominance category, couple type by discussion task, couple type by communication act, and discussion task by communication act represented the best fit for the model ($L\chi^2 = 31.28$, df = 35, p < .65, $\chi^2 = 38.68$, df = 35, p < .31). Generally, all couple types demonstrated significantly more dominance acts in the conflict condition compared with the neutral communication condition. The use of significantly more strong dominance messages across all couple types in the conflict discussion indicated that the topic manipulation worked as intended. The Independent couples used significantly more dominance behaviors of all kinds than did other couples.

For the deference or weak "one-down" categories, the couple type by discussion task and couple type by communication act represented the best fit to the data ($L\chi^2 = 13.66$, df = 8, p < .90, $\chi^2 = 13.5$, df = 8, p < .96). All couple types except the Independent/Traditionals (independent husband, traditional wife) used a higher proportion of deference acts in the neutral communication condition. This finding strongly indicates that the topic manipulation worked.

For the submission or strong "one-down" categories, the best model for the data is represented by couple type by communication act ($L\chi^2 = 27.35$, df = 16, p < .04; $\chi^2 = 22.71$, df = 16, p < .12). Across conditions, no couple type was likely to use the intense submissive communication category.

The frequency analysis indicates that the neutral condition for all couples is characterized by more agreement, restatement, clarification, and attention to procedure than is the conflict condition. For example, when discussing a neutral topic, the following types of comments were common:

Husband: We need to decide collectively on three books.
Wife: We have six good choices. Now we need to narrow it down to three.

Conflict discussions are characterized by more orders, challenges, justifications, personal nonsupport statements, disagreements, and less information seeking. For example:

Wife: I don't want to go back to work to pay for a truck. It would be bad for the baby.

Husband:	Day care will be good for him.
Wife:	Not now. He's too young.
Husband:	It'll toughen him up.
Wife:	Not now. I need to be with my baby.

Apparently individuals in some marital types moderate their communication depending upon the topic under discussion. In general, the Independents change the frequency of usage of various message types significantly less across topics than do other couple types. The Mixed couple types are more affected by the topic under discussion in their message usage. The coding breakdown also indicates gross differences in the average amount of interaction exchanged across conditions. In the neutral condition, Independents, Traditionals, and Traditional/Independents exchange the largest mean number of interacts, whereas Separates, Separate/Traditionals, and Traditional/Separates exchange far fewer. This combination of emotional distance and traditional ideology leaves a couple with little to discuss. They may not argue, but neither do they talk. During conflict, the largest mean number of interacts are exchanged in Traditional/Independent marriages, although pure Traditionals have the least to say to one another during tense interactions.

Is there a definable power structure in the discussions of couples in the various types? To test for sequential structure, Markov and lag procedures were used. The log-linear results provided information about individual message behaviors and the Markov and lag sequential techniques provide information about the pairs of messages defined according to their control codes.[2]

Markov models. Three assumptions regarding the interaction data were tested: order, stationarity, and homogeneity. The power process in the various couple types is best represented as a stationary, first-order process. This means that the interaction patterns of these couples do not shift substantially over time and that the relational control interact or message pair is the correct unit of analysis. The homogeneity tests may be considered tests of the typology because they demonstrate whether the couples within the various types assert control or signal submission similarly to one another yet differently from other couples.

Three different sets of homogeneity tests were performed on this interaction data in order to test the marital typology's premise that couples categorized into different types of marriages interacted differently. The first was a within-groups homogeneity test to determine whether couples categorized in the same type interacted in the same way. For both conditions, the Likelihood Ratio Value tests indicated that the within-groups homogeneity assumption was satisfied at the .05 level. All eight couple types in both conditions were found to exhibit interaction patterns that were not significantly different from the other couples within their type. This first test gives strong support to the notion that the couples within each type exhibit the same power processes. We wanted an even more stringent test of the typology, so we conducted two more homogeneity tests. The second homogeneity test was a between-groups test designed to see if the power patterns among the eight couple types differed. This test compared the interaction of each couple type with a composite matrix. Only the three Pure types differed from the overall composite matrix. The interaction of the various Mixed couple types was not different from the overall pooled matrix. In other words, Pure couple types interacted in a significantly different manner than did the Mixed types. The data from the Mixed types were combined in the analyses that follow. In this study, Mixed couple types are similar to one another in their exhibition of relational communication patterns during both conflict and casual interaction.

A third homogeneity test was performed. This test pooled the interaction among the Pure types and tested whether the three Pure types differed from the overall Pure type matrix. It was possible, for example, that the real differences were obtained between two major couple types: Pure and Mixed. The results indicated that the three types in both topic conditions were significantly different from the overall pooled interaction matrix of the Pure types.

Based on these three homogeneity tests, it appears that Mixed couple types display the same interaction patterns within condition. The Pure types differ both from one another and from the Mixed types. These homogeneity tests indicate that there are four major couple types: Traditional, Independent, Separate, and Mixed. Because of the Markov results, the lag sequential analysis will test the differences among the Traditional, Independent, Separate, and Mixed type marriages in neutral and conflict conditions. The basic assumption of the typology that couples with different definitions of marriage interact differently is strongly supported for this set of interaction data. These tests also demonstrate the utility of combining the typological and the relational control perspective.[3]

Lag sequential analysis. Lag sequential analysis is a useful statistical tool for identifying conditional relationships among a large number of variables. The method can identify behaviors that precede or follow one another in predictable chains. The categories of the Ellis et al. (1976) coding scheme were chosen as criterion behaviors, that is, dominance, structuring, equivalence, deference, and submission. Because the Markov analysis showed that these data are best represented as a first-order process, only the behaviors significant at lag one for the Pure and Mixed couple types are reported. The rules discussed for the lag sequential analysis in the first study were followed here as well. The associated probabilities and z-scores are reported in parentheses.

Relational communication scholars may be interested to note that of the 15 possible first-order interactions that could have emerged from the use of this coding scheme, only a few statistically significant interaction patterns were found to occur. Strong complementarity, for example, occurs in no couple type. When a strong control move is made by a spouse (dominance), such a move is met with dominance. Attempts to assert control in marriage need to be done with some subtlety or they backfire and probably escalate conflict.

Traditionals. According to the above guidelines, the only sequential string that could be tested for these couples involved structuring as the criterion in the neutral condition. The pattern that emerged was the following: structuring/deference (.40, $z = 3.51$), which is a type of weak complementarity. Because the Markov analysis indicated a first-order process in the data, we note that in the neutral condition, these couples exhibited structuring/submission (.67, $z = 3.13$) and deference/structuring (1.00, $z = 3.93$). The Traditionals did not exhibit the hypothesized neutralized symmetry. Because of the small number of Traditional couples in this study, we did not have enough data to test the presence of neutralized symmetry.

The frequency data indicated that Traditionals exchanged the most interacts in the neutral condition, but the fewest in the conflict condition. Traditionals appear to resolve their salient disagreements quickly. The lag sequential analyses revealed three interaction patterns of complementarity in the neutral condition and reliance on competitive symmetry in the conflict condition. Traditionals change their pattern of interaction depending on the topic of discussion. Complementary in neutral discussions, Traditionals refuse to relinquish control in conflict.

Examples from couples' actual dialogues may help us to understand the statistical findings. In the neutral conditions, for example, Traditional couples do not tend to use challenges and justifications when they attempt to dominate. Instead, Traditionals exchange orders:

Husband: You've got to let me have that encyclopedia.
Wife: You have to get rid of that defensive tone.

During conflict, Traditionals tend to use less agreement than other couples but more information seeking. Clarification in the form of information seeking is of prime importance to the Traditionals.

Husband:	But were we disagreeing about anything?
Wife:	We got mad and were disagreeing about your children.
Husband:	But can we actually call that disagreement significant?
Wife:	Any argument about family relationships is significant.
Husband:	Why do you feel we argued about the children?
Wife:	Because their mother has different values than I do.

Independents. In the neutral condition, the lag sequential analysis yields the following results: (1) dominance/dominance (.46, z = 7.65); (2) structuring/deference (.26, z = 3.51); (3) equivalence/equivalence (.34, z = 4.20); and (4) deference/structuring (.68, z = 4.28). The conflict condition patterns for the Independents were somewhat similar: (1) dominance/dominance (.49, z = 6.20); (2) structuring/deference (.19, z = 1.99); (3) equivalence/equivalence (.25, z = 2.27). Independents demonstrated both competitive and neutralized symmetry and weak complementarity in neutral and conflict discussions. The frequency analysis disclosed that the Independents used more dominance and less information seeking across conditions than any other couple type. The sequential analysis of the Independents revealed across conditions a peculiar mix of strong competitive and neutralized symmetry, tempered with strings of weak complementarity. Independent interaction patterns are suggestive of their relational definition—strong assertiveness and resulting conflict, yet through equivalence arises a sense of mutual regard and interdependence. The Independents demonstrate that they are very expressive with one another. Independent interaction remains stable in that it tends not to be affected by the topic.

Even in a casual conversation, Independents challenge and justify.

Husband:	The dictionary is a useless book. Why would you put down such a ridiculous choice?
Wife:	Untrue. Without a dictionary, you can't expand your knowledge and vocabulary.
Husband:	You think it's more important to speak properly than survive?
Wife:	Survival is only one of our choices. The other is obviously literacy.

During conflict, Independents mix challenges and justifications with orders.

Wife:	You yelled at me.
Husband:	Your smoking bugs me. Your dingy smoke is messing up my car.
Wife:	Greedy s.o.b. It's my car too.

Separates. The lag sequential analysis on the interaction of the Separates yielded the following results for the neutral condition: (1) structuring/deference (.35, z = 3.44); (2) equivalence/equivalence (.39, z = 4.12); and (3) deference/structuring (.80, z = 4.98). The lag analyses of the conflict interaction presented similar findings: (1) structuring/deference (.25, z = 2.16); (2) equivalence/equivalence (.33, z = 3.79); and (3) deference/structuring (.63, z = 3.20). Separates used both weak complementarity and neutralized symmetry in neutral and conflict discussions with their spouses. The topic of the discussion does not appear to affect their patterns of relational control. The frequency data for the Separates revealed that the messages they exchange are not dependent on the discussion topic. In the neutral condition, the Separates displayed a substantial proportion of the midrange structuring, equivalence, and deference behaviors, but no extreme messages of dominance or submission. Conflict elicited similar behaviors. Given the situation, the Separates exchanged as few messages as possible and relied on less intense communication behaviors. The lag sequential analysis suggested that Separates use neutralized symmetry and weak complementarity during both discussions. As their relational definition of emotional distance between partners suggests, the Separates appear adept at avoiding potentially explosive communication patterns.

Here is a Separate conflict exchange. Notice that the attack is more subtle than for the Independents.

Husband:	Before you gave up your totally organic house, nothing grew in here, not even mold.
Wife:	You are irresponsible in your use of chemicals.

Mixed. The significant sequences of the Mixed couple types in the neutral condition are the following: (1) dominance/dominance (.46, z = 19.40); (2) structuring/deference (.29, z = 6.66); (3) equivalence/equivalence (.46, z = 12.33); and (4) deference/structuring (.65, z = 8.62). The conflict condition yielded the following results: (1) dominance/dominance (.48, z = 18.48); (2) structuring/structuring (.52, z = 3.68) or structuring/deference (.21, z = 4.20); (3) equivalence/equivalence (.40, z = 11.26); and (4) deference/structuring (.62, z = 6.20).

The sequential patterns of the Mixed types indicated strong competitive symmetry in both conditions. Even in the neutral condition, a significant amount of struggle for control was present. For example:

Husband: You'd put in a novel. While we're starving you'd read?
Wife: I'd put it in so I wouldn't get bored.

The conflict condition demonstrated an increased strain on the relationship as evidenced by the occurrence of the weak competitive symmetrical form of structuring following structuring.

Among all couples, only those couples composed of a traditional and a separate refrained from personal attack during conflict. These couples appear to stay focused on the issue.

Husband: Why do you say your job is more demanding than mine?
Wife: I not only teach all day but I have band practice every night.
Husband: Why don't you quit your job?
Wife: I have worked too hard to get where I am.

Couple types use unique interaction patterns in keeping with their respective a priori relational definitions. The integration of the typological and interaction approaches gives the investigator a broader view of how the relational definitions relate to actual communication behavior.

The results of this study demonstrate that the various types of couples achieve control in markedly different ways. Couples defined a priori according to their levels of interdependence, their ideological orientations, and their views on conflict employ different control patterns in their marital relationships.

Summary

By reporting multivariate frequency analysis results at the first level of the coding scheme, a clearer picture emerged of what actually happened in these interactions. This style of data reporting illuminates what may prove to be important subcategory differences in message usage in various marriages. Strong one-up or dominance messages take different forms in this coding scheme, and various couple types show dominance toward the spouse in linguistically different ways. In casual conversations, both Independents and Mixed couples use challenges and justifications as attempts to assert control over the spouse, yet Traditionals rely on orders. In casual conversations, spouses with markedly different ideological orientations will challenge and counterchallenge one another verbally when each is attempting to assert control. In contrast, couples with highly similar and conventional orientations exchange orders when either spouse asserts dominance. There is little of the give-and-take in Traditional exchanges that appears in Independent and Mixed relationships.

In all marriages, there is a change from issue attack to personal attack when a conflict occurs. All couples use personal nonsupport statements as linguistic attempts to assert dominance in conflict. *What differs among couples is how a spouse responds to that personal attack*, not the occurrence of the attack in the first place. These results parallel those of Gottman (1979), who finds that in happy marriages, one spouse de-escalates a conflict by not responding in kind to the negative communication acts of his or her partner.

CONCLUSION

The relational typology demonstrates that marriage is not a monolithic institution. Marriages can be differentiated by various ideological orientations, patterns of companionship and sharing, and levels of conflict and assertiveness. Furthermore, the interaction of spouses in these marriages differs according to predominant patterns of control.

A marriage can be defined by the patterns of control measured in the interactions of husbands and wives. Couples who use a predominance of symmetry are symmetrical couples, those who use a predominance of complementarity are complementary couples, and those who balance both patterns are parallel couples (Lederer & Jackson, 1968). Despite the elegance of this idea, it is difficult to categorize marriage solely by the interaction patterns that couples display. Categorizing couples by their predominant interaction patterns requires a systematic sampling not only of actors (married couples) but of interaction behaviors (various verbal and nonverbal behaviors) and contexts (home versus laboratory, conflict versus nonconflict). Basing the definition of an entire relationship on small, unsystematic slices of the interaction of spouses ignores theoretically important aspects of relational life. Concepts such as affect and ideology help theorists develop a fuller understanding of the control patterns observed in couple interactions. The same control patterns observed in interactions will have markedly different meanings for couples in fundamental agreement with one another on a number of family issues versus those couples who fundamentally disagree.

The typology yields insights into interaction-based definitions of marriage. Traditional couples shift from complementarity to symmetry when the discussion turns from casual to conflict. Such a shift, as well as the fact that Traditionals engage in conflict only on issues of importance, indicates that Traditionals may be the parallel couples. Parallel couples are those who do not have a rigid communication style but rather can shift from complementarity to symmetry as the occasion demands (Lederer & Jackson, 1968). Separates who maintain complementary interaction patterns regardless of the nature of the communication may be said to be complementary couples because Separates rigidly refuse to assert control over the definition of the relationship in their marriage.

Both Independent and Mixed couples rely on competitive symmetry whether the issue is one of disagreement or not. Independents are likely to engage in conflict whether or not the issue is a serious one. Both couple types are symmetrical in the sense that they attempt to wrest control from their spouses across interaction topics. Independent and Mixed couples demonstrate symmetrical patterns for different underlying reasons. Independents have relational definitions in which they have agreed to disagree over a number of relationship issues. Both members of this relationship are committed to uncertainty and change, and both struggle to control the definition of the marriage. The Mixed couples disagree on fundamental issues in their relationships yet do not philosophically value such disagreement and dissension. The relational definitions of these couples suggest that there may be two types of symmetrical couples. The first type involves those who demonstrate symmetry as a sign of an underlying philosophical commitment to change, whereas those in the second type exhibit symmetrical patterns because of serious disagreements on the nature of the relationship. In the next chapter, we examine conflict resolution styles in the various couple types.

NOTES

1. Achieving representational validity for a communication coding scheme used primarily to analyze conversations between strangers is relatively painless for the researcher and probably insightful. The culture from which the speaker comes is easy to identify. In examining intimate communication, however, who are members of the culture of the

relationships apart from the intimates themselves? In our case, what is the "culture" of marriage?

The marital typology may represent distinctly different marital cultures. Following this reasoning, couples from a given type could be asked to code the communication of other couples from their same type. We have long been interested in conducting such a study and have devised no procedures to handle the problems of confidentiality and the protection of the privacy and rights of the participants in our studies. We have not completed such a study as yet, but think it is a good idea for future research. Of course, using stimulated recall techniques (Fitzpatrick & Noller, 1987), couples could be asked to code their own communication. The coding judgments of couples in the various types could be compared with those judgments made from the researcher's perspective.

2. The statistically sophisticated reader may be saying to himself or herself that the log-linear models and the Markov and lag sequential models are the "same" model. That is, one could test a number of sequential models using log-linear techniques. The Markov and lag sequential tests are computed to be consistent with other studies examining relational control in the communication literature, even though log-linear techniques could be used to test a number of sequential models.

3. The homogeneity assumption tests whether the interaction data from one couple can be combined with the interaction data from another couple because the structure of the data is essentially the same. The order assumption tests whether the data demonstrates first-order structure. If the data demonstrate second- or third-order structure, the model based on the first-order transitions will not predict accurately. The stationarity assumption tests whether the structure of the interaction data remains the same across time. The Likelihood Ratio Values of Anderson and Goodman (1957) were used to validate the homogeneity and stationarity assumptions, whereas statistical tests based on Kullbeck, Kupperman, and Ku (1962) were used for the order assumption.

5

Marital Conflict

Avoidance, Cooperation,
and Confrontation

Since the needs, desires, and ambitions of people involved in close relationships cannot always be synchronized, some form of conflict is inevitable in close relationships such as marriage. Conflict is the interaction of interdependent people who perceive incompatible goals and interference from each other in achieving those goals (Folger & Poole, 1984; Frost & Wilmot, 1978). Ideally, couples deal with their conflicting interests with some form of negotiation or problem-solving strategy: one spouse states a position, seeks and obtains validation of the position from the partner, and the two engage in a straightforward problem-solving exchange. In this ideal scenario, communication between spouses is free of distortion, and both parties work toward resolution until some acceptable solution is obtained.

Obviously, all couples do not use this idealized style of negotiation and problem solving in discussing all the issues that arise between them. The basic couple types differ in the level of interdependence in their marriage and in how comfortable they are in actively engaging in conflict with their spouses. These relational dimensions are related to the use of direct or indirect, and hostile or friendly, strategies in discussing salient conflict issues with the spouse. Under conditions of disagreement, we are interested in exploring how evasive, confrontational, or cooperative couples are with one another.

In this chapter, the first three data sets analyze the use of avoidance, competition, and cooperation in couples' conflict. Special attention is paid to the multiple functions that conflict avoidance can serve in marriage, to the vocal tones couples use during tense interactions, and to sex differences in confrontation, cooperation, and evasion. In addition, the chapter reports a replication of a classic experiment on problem-solving sequences in marital dialogues.

CONFLICT RESOLUTION
STRATEGIES IN MARITAL TYPES

In any conflict, both parties seek an outcome that they believe the other is unwilling to provide. Each conflict between parties involves a distinctive set of moves, or ways of pursuing the conflict, in order to settle it. A series of moves, or tactics, makes up a strategy of conflict resolution. These strategies can be classified along two major components (Blake & Mouton, 1964; Killmann & Thomas, 1977; Putnam & Wilson, 1982). The first is *assertiveness*, defined as behaviors intended to satisfy one's own concerns. The second is *cooperativeness,* defined as behaviors intended to satisfy the partner's concerns (Pruitt & Rubin, 1986). These two components define four strategies: avoidance, accommodation, collaboration, and competition. The question is: What strategies are couples in the various types more likely to rely on to handle conflicts?

According to the typology, marriages can be discriminated according to the amount of interdependence that a couple experiences. A high degree of interdependence between spouses would be indicated by a balancing of the concerns of each partner whereas significantly less interdependence would suggest a focus on either the concerns of the self or the other. The choice of a conflict-management strategy in the various couple types depends on the balance of concerns in the marriage, and the feasibility of the strategy. The balance of concerns can be estimated from the couple's level of interdependence. Feasibility can be estimated from the couple's general views of expressivity and openness to conflict and negative interaction (Pruitt & Rubin, 1986). Let us now turn to the four basic conflict strategies that emerge and their hypothesized relationships to the couple types.

(1) Conflict *avoidance* is unassertive and uncooperative. Conflict avoidance, or the psychological withdrawal from a conflict, is accomplished by a number of communicative acts designed to move the discussion away from the matter at hand. Speaking abstractly about an

issue, denying that a problem exists, and making jokes are a few examples of how individuals use avoidance. Failing to engage in conversation is the most extreme form of avoidance. Avoidance is used when the speaker has very little concern for his or her own outcomes or those of the partner. We expect Separates to use conflict avoidance more often than do the other couple types because Separates are not as interdependent as the other couple types. Separates are thus predicted to use the blatant forms of conflict avoidance such as denying that anything is wrong.

(2) *Accommodation*, or *yielding*, is unassertive and cooperative. The person gives in to the other at the cost of his or her own concerns (Pruitt & Rubin, 1986). Spouses may lower their aspirations and settle for less than they would have liked. Included here may be some types of verbal compromises. People who adopt this strategy attempt to avoid conflict for the sake of maintaining the relationship. Yielding is used when the speaker thinks it is feasible, is concerned about the other's outcome, and is afraid of conflict (Pruitt & Rubin, 1986). Because of their expressed fear of conflict, Separates are hypothesized to use yielding tactics to a greater degree than the other couples. Because of their willingness to engage in conflict, Independents are expected to resist any attempt on the part of their spouses to yield. When the issues are important, the interdependence of the Traditionals suggests that these couples are unlikely to avoid conflict. When the issue is not a serious one for the Traditionals, they tend to yield to the spouse quickly with compromises.

(3) *Problem solving*, or *collaboration*, is high on assertiveness and cooperation. People who use these strategies pursue an alternative that satisfies the aspirations on both sides. Problem solving is accomplished with messages implying cooperation, validation, or contracting. Emphasizing what they have in common, and accepting responsibility for problems are a few examples of cooperative communication acts. Problem solving occurs when individuals have high concern for their own outcomes and for those of their spouses (Pruitt & Rubin, 1986). The more common ground that a couple share, the more feasible this strategy is: Each side is able to achieve its aims without excessive cost. The Traditionals are expected to use more problem solving than the other couple types use, because they have dual concerns in their interactions and because these couples perceive they have a good deal of agreement on basic marital issues (Fitzpatrick & Best, 1979).

(4) *Competition*, or *contending*, is high in assertiveness and low in cooperation. People using this strategy seek to impose their preferred solution on the other party. This strategy includes those communicative acts that find fault with, or blame, the partner. A form of contending is

compliance gaining. Here, speakers also try to achieve their own ends by using a repertoire of subtle persuasive tactics in order to achieve their own goals. A detailed treatment of compliance gaining is taken up in the next chapter. Contending occurs when spouses are concerned with their own outcomes and consider the disputed issue to be important (Pruitt & Rubin, 1986). In general, Independents are expected to use more contentious tactics than are the other couples because of the Independents' concern for preserving autonomy and individuality in marriage. For this reason, any seemingly trivial issue will be defined as important by Independents; these issues are seen as reflecting on the balance of autonomy and interdependence that couples want to maintain in their marriage. Under certain conditions, every couple uses contentious tactics: Contentious behavior occurs when the issue is important to an individual, when individuals value their own outcome above all others, and when the messages are not expected to damage the view that the individual has of the relationship (not just damage the relationship).

Let us turn to the studies that examine conflict in marriage. These studies may be viewed as tests of the dual concern—concern for one's own outcomes versus concerns for the other's outcomes—model (Pruitt & Rubin, 1986) applied to marital conflicts. Can marital type, which represents the level of interdependence in the marriage, predict the predominant conflict-management strategy chosen by couples?

Communication and
Conflict Management

Conflict is managed through communication. Sillars (1986) has developed and validated (Sillars, Coletti, Parry, & Rogers, 1982) a coding scheme for conflict strategies. There are seven main distinctions that can be made in coding couples' conflict dialogues: (1) denial and equivocation, (2) topic management, (3) noncommittal remarks, (4) irreverent remarks, (5) analytic remarks, (6) confrontative remarks, (7) conciliatory remarks. Denial and equivocation refer to statements that deny conflict or that are evasive and ambiguous. Topic management refers to statements that shift or terminate the topic in an evasive manner. Noncommittal remarks, which represent a neutral style of communication, neither acknowledge, deny, nor evade conflict. Irreverent remarks make light of the conflict in a friendly manner. Analytic remarks provide or seek information about the conflict in a nonconfrontative manner. Confrontative remarks are verbally competitive, individualistic comments such as insults, criticisms, hostile jokes, and imperatives that seek concessions. Conciliatory remarks

TABLE 5.1
Conflict Management Coding Scheme

Avoidance Behaviors

Denial and Equivocation
(1) *Direct denial.* Person explicitly denies a conflict is present.
(2) *Implicit denial.* Statements that imply denial by providing a rationale for a denial statement, although the denial is not explicit.
(3) *Evasive remark.* Failure to acknowledge or deny the presence of a conflict following a statement or inquiry about the conflict by the partner.

Topic Management
(4) *Topic shifts.* A break in the natural flow of discussion that directs the topic focus away from discussion of the issue as it applies to the immediate parties. Do not count topic shifts that occur after the discussion appears to have reached a natural culmination.
(5) *Topic avoidance.* Statements that explicitly terminate the discussion of a conflict issue before it has been fully discussed.

Noncommittal Remarks
(6) *Abstract remarks.* Abstract principles, generalizations, or hypothetical statements. Speaking about the issue on a high level of abstraction. No reference is made to the actual state of affairs between the immediate parties.
(7) *Noncommittal statements.* Statements that neither affirm nor deny the presence of a conflict and that are not evasive replies or topic shifts.
(8) *Noncommittal questions.* Unfocused questions or those that rephrase the questions given by the researcher.
(9) *Procedural remarks.* Procedural statements that supplant discussion of the conflict.

Irreverant Remarks
(10) *Joking.* Nonhostile joking that interrupts or supplements serious consideration of the issue.

Cooperative Behaviors

Analytic Remarks
(1) *Description.* Nonevaluative, nonblaming, factual description of the nature and extent of the problem.
(2) *Qualification.* Discussion explicitly limits the nature and extent of the problem by tying the issue to specific behavioral events.
(3) *Disclosure.* Providing "nonobservable" information; that is, information about thoughts, feelings, intentions, causes of behavior, or past experience relevant to the issue that the partner would not have the opportunity to observe.
(4) *Soliciting disclosure.* Asking specifically for information concerning the other that the person himself or herself would not have the opportunity to observe (i.e., thoughts, feelings, intentions, causes of behavior, experiences).
(5) *Soliciting criticism.* Nonhostile questions soliciting criticism of oneself.

(continued)

TABLE 5.1 Continued

Conciliatory Remarks

(6) *Empathy or support.* Expressing understanding, support, or acceptance of the other person or commenting on the others' positive characteristics or shared interests, goals, and compatibilities.

(7) *Concessions.* Statements that express a willingness to change, show flexibility, make concessions, or consider mutually acceptable solutions to conflict.

(8) *Accepting responsibility.* Statements that attribute some causality for the problem to oneself.

Competitive Behaviors

Confrontative Remarks

(1) *Personal criticism.* Stating or implying a negative evaluation of the partner.

(2) *Rejection.* Rejecting the partner's opinions in a way that implies personal rejection as well as disagreement.

(3) *Hostile imperatives.* Threats, demands, arguments, or other prescriptive statements that implicitly blame the partner and seek change in the partner's behavior.

(4) *Hostile questioning.* Questions that fault or blame the other person.

(5) *Hostile joking or sarcasm.* Joking or teasing that is used to fault the other person.

(6) *Presumptive attribution.* Attributing thoughts, feelings, intentions, and causes to the partner that the partner does not acknowledge. This code is the opposite of "soliciting disclosure."

(7) *Denial of responsibility.* Statements that deny or minimize personal responsibility for the conflict.

SOURCE: Sillars (1986) *Manual for Coding Interpersonal Conflict.* Unpublished manuscript, Department of Interpersonal Communication, University of Montana. Reprinted by permission.

express supportiveness or a desire for reconciliation through compliments or concessions. These seven subcategories can be organized into the three broad classes of conflict behavior: avoidance, cooperation, and competition. As we can see in Table 5.1, a number of specific verbal tactics fall under each major category.

Neophytes to marital communication research often wonder how investigators induce conflict between spouses in laboratory interactions. Before an experiment begins, it is impossible to define the topics a couple should discuss, if the focus of the investigation is on conflict. Between couples, anything can be an important issue of dispute. Sometimes a seemingly trivial issue is the cause of serious conflict because the issue represents an important structural problem between partners: What is at

TABLE 5.2
Marital Issues

- Pressures or problems at work that affect your marriage.
- Criticisms of one another's lifestyle, ideas, or activities.
- Household responsibilities.
- Lack of attention or affection toward one another.
- Disagreements about spending money.
- One or both have been hard to get along with.
- Disagreements about how to spend your leisure time.
- Disagreements about how to rear or discipline the children.
- One feels the two of you do not do enough things together.

SOURCE: Adopted from Sillars, Pike, Jones, and Redmon (1983).

stake is not the issue under discussion but the structure of the relationship.

In the studies reported in this section, the couples themselves defined the major issues that caused conflict between them. Couples separately completed questionnaires concerning the level of conflict and the salience of the disagreement over issues related to marital functioning. In Table 5.2, a set of such issues is presented. In the first study, two issues specific to the couple were discussed whereas in the second study, the couples discussed all issues but only the messages exchanged during the salient disagreements were categorized.

The multifunctionality of conflict avoidance. Conflict-resolution strategies can be broadly classified as prosocial or antisocial (Roloff, 1976). When faced with a conflict, an individual can choose to avoid (antisocial), to cooperate (prosocial), or to compete (antisocial). Within the dominant vision of intimacy in which relationships are devoted to both psychological closeness and change or "growth" (Bochner, 1983), avoidance is construed as an antisocial strategy because it precludes directly dealing with conflict and its ramifications. The implicit assumptions of these models is that the individual who avoids conflict is more constricted, less capable of solving problems, and more likely to be unhappy in the relationship.

Experiments testing modes of conflict resolution in marital dyads do not necessarily lend credence to these assumptions. Goodrich and his associates (1968) found that couples maintained marital harmony falsely by feigning agreement with one another. Other researchers were subsequently surprised to learn that couples who skillfully avoided conflict with one another by using hedging, denial, and disqualification with one

TABLE 5.3
Proportion of Conflict Management Acts
in Each Couple Type

	Traditional	Independent	Separate
Avoidance	.376	.520	.417
Cooperation	.426	.392	.441
Competition	.196	.088	.141

SOURCE: From Fitzpatrick, Fallis, and Vance, 1982. Reprinted by permission.

another had marriages that were no less compatible or comfortable than other marriages (Raush et al., 1974).

Avoiding the discussion of conflict issues does not, then, appear always to have a negative consequences for a marriage. Couples should postpone or avoid the discussion of serious conflicts until they have the time or energy to handle them (Bach & Wyden, 1968). Not only such short-term avoidance but also long-term avoidance may be functional in certain couples. When an issue is essentially unresolvable, functional approaches to communication suggest that the issue be avoided and the discussion channeled into more agreeable topics. In sum, the nature of the issue under discussion, the timing of the conversation, and specific communication tactics suggest that conflict avoidance can be either a prosocial or an antisocial strategy.

The first study compared couple types on their use of avoidance, cooperation, and competition. This study also addressed the multifunctionality of conflict avoidance in marital dialogues. Messages were coded into avoidance or nonavoidance categories and subsequently categorized as either prosocial or antisocial in character. We visited couples in their homes. While the couple discussed the conflict issues they had selected (Fitzpatrick, Fallis, & Vance, 1982), the researcher left the room. Few Mixed types emerged in this sample. Only the communication of the Pure types—12 Traditionals, 5 Independents, and 10 Separate couples—was analyzed. The three Pure couple types were significantly different (chi-square (4) = 11.78; p < .025) in their proportion of communication acts coded into one of these categories. There were no differences among the couple types in how frequently they used cooperation or competition. There were differences, however, in how often they used avoidance strategies.

The Traditionals used fewer avoidance acts than the other couples, whereas the Independents used more avoidance messages. This result is surprising because it is the Separates who report a greater willingness to avoid conflicts and disagreements than the other couples. Indeed, we predicted the Independents would be less likely than the other couples to avoid marital conflict. To understand what occurred in these dialogues, we constructed a 2 × 2 table with avoidance/nonavoidance as one dimension and prosocial and antisocial judgments as the other dimension. Coders made an extra pass through the data and coded the avoidance messages as either prosocial or antisocial. There were 291 avoidance acts and 53% were coded as prosocial and the remaining as antisocial acts. Goodman and Kruskal's (1965) lambda measure estimates 79% error in guessing prosocial or antisocial when the communication act is avoidance. Avoidance functions both prosocially and antisocially. Avoiding the discussion of a serious marital conflict is neither unambiguously positive nor negative. A smaller average number of avoidance acts by Separates ($\overline{X}$ = 4.00) were negative in contrast to the negative avoidance used by Independents ($\overline{X}$ = 9.00) or Traditionals ($\overline{X}$ = 7.11).

An examination of the nonverbal behavior of the Separates sheds some light on these findings. Separates psychologically withdraw from conflict by speaking to their spouses less often, for shorter periods, and with fewer interruptions than do other couples. This inaction is an extreme form of avoidance: It suggests that Separate concerns for both personal and partner outcomes are low (Pruitt & Rubin, 1986). The negative avoidance strategies displayed by Independents supports the Independent commitment to open communication between spouses. The Independent use of avoidance is an assertive one in that these couples use the antisocial or hostile forms of conflict avoidance.

Vocal tones during marital conflict. In a different study, Sillars and his colleagues (1983) coded vocal tones of couples as they discussed their conflicts. There were no differences among the couples on positive affect expressed during conflict but significant differences did arise for neutral and negative affect. Independents were less likely to use neutral vocal tones and significantly more likely to use negative tones of voice (e.g., cold, angry, accusing tones) when discussing tense issues with a spouse. At the nonverbal level, Independent couples in these situations clearly are engaging in conflict. The Independent relationship is one committed to the open expression of negative feelings and conflicts. Such a commitment spills over even when these couples verbally attempt to avoid conflict. Fitzpatrick (1984) argues that it is important to link marital interaction processes to other family processes than marital outcomes. Can children be expected to respond differently to adult marital conflict conducted in neutral versus negative voice tones?

Young children (1 to 2½ years old), who typically may not be able to follow adult verbal dialogue over conflict issues, experience distress on hearing angry vocal tones in interaction between adults. Typically, children respond to adult anger with some form of distress (Cummings et al., 1981; Cummings et al., 1985). Repeated exposure to interparent anger increased the likelihood of a negative emotional reaction on the part of a child and attempts to become actively involved in the conflict. Given the negative tones of the Independents, their marital conflicts may have negative emotional effects on their children.

Separates were significantly less likely to use a negative tone and more likely to use a neutral tone during conflict discussions. This neutrality suggests that it was not stressful or difficult for these couples to avoid confronting one another during conflict. Furthermore, the young children of Separates may be unlikely to experience negative affect as a consequence of parental discord. These children may only realize that there are tensions in the marriages of their parents when they are old enough to understand the dialogue. Traditionals decrease their neutral affect during conflict but do not have a clear positive or negative affect pattern. Although there are a number of ways to link the typology to larger family processes, the study of the communication of emotion during marital conflict and its potential impact on children is an important first step.

Sex differences in communication during conflict. Do husbands and wives differ in their use of evasive, cooperative, or confrontational tactics during conflict? Burgraff and Sillars (1986) analyzed conflict-resolution strategies of couples in the various types (approximately 76 couples) in order to see if sex differences could account for different tactics in marital conflict. These researchers were interested in the degree to which husbands and wives differed in levels of confrontation and evasiveness. As we can see in Table 5.4, there are no husband and wife differences in these communication behaviors in either the study conducted in the homes of couples or the study in which couples were invited into a laboratory. It is couple type and not the sex of the speaker that accounts for differential use of these tactics.

Table 5.4 displays the data for the two samples reported in the study. It is important to keep these data sets distinguishable because the methods used to collect the conversations between couples varied, and the relative proportions of various confrontational, evasive, and cooperative strategies differed between the contexts. The analysis of conditional proportions of conflict acts by couple types indicated that conflict avoidance was more likely when couples completed the discussion task at home (.51) than in the laboratory (.16) whereas informational acts were far more frequent (.43) in the laboratory than in the home (.18). The differences in

TABLE 5.4
Conditional Proportions of Conflict Acts by Couple Type

	Avoid	Confront	Analyze	Conciliate
Study 1				
Home Context				
Wives	.49	.25	.19	.07
Husbands	.53	.23	.17	.07
Couple Type				
Traditional	.73+++	.09---	.10	.08+++
Independent	---	----	----	----
Separate	.40---	.33+++	.20	.07-
Mixed	.51	.22	.21	.06
Total	.51	.24	.18	.07
Study 2				
Lab Context				
Wives	.14	.29	.45	.12
Husbands	.18	.30	.41	.10
Couple Type				
Traditional	---	----	----	----
Separate	.19	.56+++	.15---	.11
Independent	.18	.30	.44+++	.08--
Mixed	.15	.27---	.46+++	.12
Total	.16	.30	.43	.11

SOURCE: Burgraff and Sillars (1986).
NOTE: + or − = $p < .10$; ++ or −− = $p < .05$; +++ or −−− = $p < .01$.

the frequency of use of these message categories may be related to the different research contexts (home versus the laboratory), or to the fact that the second sample was more urban and less traditional than couples in the first sample.

Traditionals use significantly more avoidance, less confrontation, and more conciliation in managing conflict than expected by chance. Independents use significantly more information and less conciliation than expected by chance. In both data sets, Separates use significantly more confrontation than expected by chance. In the first data set, the Separates use less avoidance and conciliation and, in the second data set, Separates use less information seeking than expected by chance. Mixed types use less confrontation and more information strategies to manage their conflicts.

As hypothesized, Traditionals tend to cooperate and not to confront one another. Contrary to expectation, Traditionals utilize significantly more conflict avoidance (.73, p < .01) than expected by chance. In the Fitzpatrick et al. (1982) study, the proportion of avoidance messages used by Traditionals was .38: Traditionals report they are low on assertiveness and at the midpoint on a scale of openness to conflict (Fitzpatrick, 1984). In the dual concern model, Traditionals move from unassertive and uncooperative to assertive and cooperative. Their communication behavior during conflict reflects that Traditional concerns are either high for the outcomes of both parties or low for the outcomes for both parties. Depending on the issue discussed, the researcher may see either a great deal of avoidance or a great deal of cooperation between the Traditional couple.

Compared to couples in other types, Separates are low on interdependence, report a greater likelihood to avoid conflict, yet also state that they are assertive. Using the dual concern model, we hypothesized that Separates are unassertive and uncooperative, hence would use avoidance strategies. Conversationally, however, Separates are uncooperative yet assertive with their spouses. These couples are concerned with their own outcomes. The Separate style of conflict engagement is a subtly hostile one that depends on confrontation and depresses analytical and conciliatory moves. Separate couples tend to initiate confrontational acts (.55, p < .10) when there was no immediate antecedent act by the spouse. Separates couples do not reciprocate confrontational acts. Separates appear to be unable to coordinate either conflict engagement or conflict avoidance. The expression of hostility to engage the spouse in conflict is not responded to by the Separate partner. This "hit and run" style of communication over salient conflict issues shows up again in Separate compliance-gaining attempts reported in the next chapter.

True to form, Independent couples were less likely to be supportive, make concessions, or accept responsibility for the conflict. Independents were more likely to use analytical tactics. Independents, although not using the hostile confrontative category, do tend to engage in conflict with their spouses. Independents follow avoidance acts with confrontational acts (.38, p < .01) and not with conciliatory statements (.02, p < .05). Independents do not initiate confrontation unless provoked by the spouse (.12, p < .01). Independents react negatively to avoidance statements by the spouse.

Mixed couple types are noted for their use of analytical tactics and their inhibition of confrontation. The style of conflict engagement is a nonhostile one. Mixed couples followed informational acts with confrontation (.20, p < .05) but did not follow avoidance with confrontation (.13, p < .05). Informational acts yielded different outcomes for the Mixed types than such acts yielded for the Independents.

Summary

What general conclusions can we draw from these experiments about the conflict-management styles of couples in the various marital types? Traditionals are cooperative and conciliatory toward one another and may tend to avoid conflict to a greater degree than they realize. Independents do not respond well to a spouse's attempt to avoid discussing serious difficulties and confront them when they attempt to withdraw. Separates show hostility toward the spouse but appear to withdraw immediately from the discussion if the spouse contests their statements.

Marriage can be conceived of as a continuous confrontation between participants with conflicting—though not always opposing—interests. The focus of attention for our efforts then becomes the ways in which marital dyads negotiate the issues that arise from their joint participation in the institution of marriage and the family (Sprey, 1979). As communication researchers, we are interested in how these conflicting interests are managed through talk. Traditionals appear to manage and deal with interpersonal conflict by avoiding it. This approach to managing interpersonal conflict should not come as a surprise. A major conflict sociologist posits that "the most important effect of intense bonds is not to heighten conflict but to provide incentives to avoid and conciliate it" (Turner, 1970, p. 136). It is useful to compare the results presented in this section to a major study in the field. The conflict-avoidance strategies isolated in these studies bear close conceptual resemblance to the three types of avoidance moves discerned by Raush and his colleagues (1974) in their pioneering study.

Traditionals are more likely to collude with one another in avoiding interpersonal conflict. A husband's externalizations and denials will be supported by parallel externalizations and denials by a wife. A collusive joint pattern of avoidance seems particularly likely to foreclose the possibility of a shift to a metacommunicative level. Such avoidance suggests a static quality to the exchange between partners. From the standpoint of information theory, avoidance conveys little to the recipient (Raush et al., 1974). Changes over time in the marital relationship can not evolve from what goes on between the partners. Changes might derive from the press of external events—social and economic events, the birth and growth of children, and so forth. The relationship between the Traditionals is not the primary medium for learning. Is the conflict avoidance of these couples pathological?

If pathological means a condition that inhibits growth and the development of a relationship, then the Traditional style is pathological. Avoidance of conflict limits the possibility of learning about the spouse and of modifying one's relations with the other. Raush and his colleagues (1974), however, saw a number of young couples who exhibited a communication style similar to that of Traditionals. These couples were no less stable, comfortable, or compatible than were other couples in the sample. Constricted patterns of communication may not preclude relationships that are subjectively satisfying to the participants.

With these considerations in mind, the Traditional style is not pathological. Conflict avoidance is pragmatically benign according to Raush and his associates when the participants have accepted clearly differentiated roles, and when it is in the context of a bond of mutual affection. What the Traditionals mean by their reports of expressivity differ from their actual behaviors. For Traditional couples, it may simply be a mistake to assume that the open discussion of negative feelings and salient conflict issues is a critical part of their marriage. The metaphor that relationships are communicatively negotiated may be a weak one for Traditionals.

For the Separate couple, a sense of autonomy, privacy, and emotional distance predominates. These couples confront one another but immediately withdraw from the confrontation. Their lack of interdependence appears to be related to their inability to coordinate either the active sustained engagement in conflict and the open expression of feelings or the active negotiation of a pattern of joint avoidance. The Separates appear to be unable to negotiate their relationship communicatively.

Only the Independents match the dominant vision of intimacy in the culture in that their relationship is devoted to psychological closeness and "growth." Given their emphasis on sharing and the confrontation of conflict, such open communication is a symbol for Independents of the vitality of their marriage.

PROBLEM SOLVING DURING MARITAL CONFLICT

Use of the Sillars (1986) conflict coding scheme delineates some important behavioral differences among the couple types during inter-

TABLE 5.5
Content Codes of the Couples Interaction Scoring System (CISS)

Code	Example Statement
AG: Agreement	Ok.
DG: Disagreement	You're wrong.
CT: Communication Talk	We're getting off the topic.
MR: Mind Reading	You always get mad when this happens.
PS: Problem Solving and Information Exchange	I expected you to take care of this when we got married.
SO: Summarizing Other	You're saying I talk too much.
SS: Summarizing Self	All I'm saying is I don't want to do all the work around here.
PF: Expressing Feelings about a Problem	I am very upset about your difficulties with my family.

SOURCE: Adopted from Gottman (1979).

action. Pamela Kalbfleisch and I considered it important to examine couple type differences with a completely different coding paradigm. The major alternative in the marital literature to the conflict-engagement and conflict-avoidance paradigm is a consideration of problem-solving sequences and patterns in marital communication. Using the Couple's Communication Coding Scheme (CISS), we replicated and extended a classic study of conflict management in marital dyads (Gottman, Markman, & Notarius, 1977) by coding data from a sample of 51 couples (13 Traditionals, 10 Separates, 6 Independents, 5 Separate/Traditionals, and 17 Mixed couple types), using the same procedures and tasks as discussed in the Witteman and Fitzpatrick (1986) study. We tested the first-order lag sequential analysis sequences identified by Gottman (1979), although we used the Allison-Liker modification of the statistical analysis. These results offer strong support for the importance of the conflict-resolution sequences originally proposed by Gottman (1979) and found by Schaap, Buunke, and Kerkstra (1987).

Validation involves one spouse's expressions of feeling about a problem, followed by agreement by the other spouse. For example, one spouse says, "If you keep working so hard and ignoring me, it's really

TABLE 5.6
Problem-Solving in Marriage: CISS by Couple Types

	TRAD	INDEP	SEP	S/T	MIXED
Validation Sequences					
HPF * WAG * HPF				.09 .23	
WPF * HAG * WPF		.12 .14	.11 .11	.17 .21	.11 .12
HPF * WPS	.27				
WPF * HPS				.16 (−)	
Contract Sequences					
HPS * WAG				.12	
WPS * HAG				.14	
HPS * WPS	.42	.42	.37		.35
WPS * HPS	.40	.44	.40		.40
Metacommunication					
HCT * WCT					.05
HCT * WPS	.18 (−)	.14 (−)			.13 (−)
HPS * WCT	.06	.06		.06	
WCT * HPS	.18 (−)	.12 (−)			
Cross Complaining					
HPF * WPF		.13	.19	.19	
WPF * HPF					
HPS * WPF			.08 (−)	.08 (−)	
Disagreement					
WDIS * HDIS			.10		.11
HDIS * WPS	.16 (−)	.16 (−)			.11 (−)
WDIS * HPS	.14 (−)	.13 (−)	.14 (−)	.07 (−)	
Feeling Probe					
HMR * WMR	.03 (−)		.04 (−)		
WMR * HMR			.03 (−)		
HMR * WAG	.11	.09	.09		.11
WMR * HAG			.12	.18	.12
HMR * WDG	.09	.15			
HSO * WAG					.30
WSO * HAG					.42

NOTE: Only the conditional probabilities associated with statistically significant Z-scores are reported in this table. All scores are significant at the .05.

going to hurt our marriage," and the other spouse replies, "You're probably right." *Contract sequences* are problem solving and information exchanges, followed by agreement. For example, one spouse says, "Let's take out a loan to go to Venice," and the other one says, "Sounds good to me." *Cross-complaining* is an expression of feelings about a problem, followed by expression of feelings by the other spouse. For example, one spouse says, "I'm really nervous right now," and the other spouse says,

"Well, we've gone to these kinds of parties before, and I'm always miserable at them." *Probing for feelings* involves mind reading by one spouse, followed by agreement by the other. For example, a spouse says, "You always get mad in these situations," and the other spouse rejoins, "I guess you're right."

All couples employ contract sequences, except the Separate/Traditionals who do not expressly problem solve with one another. Rather, these couples tend to agree with their spouse when he or she offers a solution to a problem in the marriage. Traditionals employ a validation sequence where the wife offers a solution to the difficulty when her husband expresses his feelings about the problem. Metacommunication and disagreement by a husband or a wife in the Traditional marriage decreases problem-solving attempts by either spouse. This wife agrees with her husband when he attempts to read her mind.

Independents differ primarily from Traditionals in that these couples cross-complain and the Independent wife disagrees when her husband attempts to read her mind. The validation sequences for all couples except the Traditionals involve a "yes, dear" pattern on the part of the husband. When wives in these marriage discuss their feelings about problems, the husband agrees, and the wife continues her discussion in the same vein. Separates exhibit disagreement and cross-complaining sequences, and both parties agree with their spouses when they mind read.

Validation in the Separate/Traditional involves a parallelism in that both parties are likely to agree with the spouse's discussion of feelings and thus continue the discussion. In addition, when the wife discusses her feelings about a problem, her husband is less likely to engage in problem solving. Contract sequences in this marriage differ in that problem-solving attempts by one partner are followed by spousal agreement rather than more problem solving. These spouses cross-complain and the husband tends to agree when his wife reads his mind. Other Mixed couple types use the "yes, dear" validation sequence of the Independent, Separate, and Separate/Traditional couples, tend to match disagreement with disagreement, metacommunication with metacommunication, and often agree when the spouse reads their mind or summarizes what they have said.

Summary

The power of the coding scheme used in this research is demonstrated by the fact that not only can it discriminate among extremely happy and extremely distressed couples but is can also uncover subtle differences among couples who are above the midpoint, on the average, on a marital satisfaction scale.

An examination of the classic marital satisfaction measures (e.g., Locke & Wallace, 1959; Spanier, 1976) that discriminate couples into distressed and nondistressed groups reveals a conventionality bias (see Chapter 1). Although the Traditionals are more happily married than the Separates (see Chapter 3), individuals in these couple types share conventional orientations toward male and female roles. Couples recruited for marital interaction experiments on a distressed/nondistressed continuum may fall predominantly into categories of marriages that are traditional in their value orientations toward gender roles and male-female relationships. Such traditionalism may better explain empirical findings such as the happy wife edits her own negative behavior in the interest of cooling down an escalating conflict interaction (Gottman, 1979, pp. 119-120). Such couples may be skewing both therapy and theory on marital interaction in a traditional sex-role direction. This study indicates that couples with a commitment to traditional sex-role ideology (i.e., Traditionals, Separates, and Separate/Traditionals) also differ in their problem-solving strategies. The sampling of couples using a wider variety of indices than marital distress may help to correct this situation.

Validation and contract sequences may be viewed as prosocial marital conflict techniques, and couples in the various types rely on different tactics within these strategies in resolving their problems. Cross-complaining, disagreement, and feeling probes may be viewed as antisocial or confrontational techniques and couples also differ in the degree to which they systematically use these patterns. In the next chapter, we turn to a discussion of a subclass of such confrontational messages or compliance gaining. All couples, regardless of their relationship type, at times argue for their own concerns over those of their spouse. By analyzing these messages in greater detail, we hope to present a clearer picture of how couples in the various types confront one another over issues.

CONCLUSION

Three general observations can be drawn from this research on interaction in various types of marriages. First, this research offers empirical support and conceptual expansion to the various gender models of marital interaction. One model (Scanzoni & Fox, 1980) hypothesizes that couples in more traditional sex-role relationships will have less open conflict and negotiation because the roles, rules, and norms are more clearly established in the relationship. These couples fit the prototype of the Traditional couple. Traditional couples do not engage in power struggles with one another because, to some degree, the power matrix in the relationship is already established by the conventions and normative prescriptions of appropriate husband and wife behavior. Conflict is inevitable in long-term relationships, but Traditionals tend to conciliate and avoid the discussion of conflict issues. The arguments these couples do have may be focused more on content issues than on relational or structural issues. Perhaps Traditional couples need to be reminded that important issues are not handled solely by defining them as "trivial." Traditionals may tend to sweep their problems under the rug rather than dealing with them. These couples may profit from enrichment and training programs designed to build on reasonably good communication skills.

Couples in marriages in which the partners have little commitment to traditional sex roles will be more likely to engage in manifest conflict, negotiation, and bargaining with the marital partner (Scanzoni & Fox, 1980). The roles, rules, and norms of this marriage need to be defined and renegotiated with changes in the relationships or the environment. These couples clearly fit the Independent prototype. Attempts on the part of Independent couples to establish new role patterns and less sex-stereotypic interaction routines bring a certain level of conflict, stress, and tension to the relationship. The therapeutic implication of these findings is that Independents may need to be taught how to keep their conflicts and tensions within manageable bounds. Couples who deviate from well-established patterns experience more stress. Such couples may need help in handling these tensions within their own value orientations and comfortable levels of marital interdependence. Behavioral therapy (e.g., Jacobson & Margolin, 1979) that deals explicitly with power, influence, and decision-making issues may be helpful.

The marital typology expands the gender model of marital power to include Separate and Mixed type couples. With their traditional sex-role expectations combined with their lack of interdependence, Separates are emotionally divorced. The closeness of the Traditional relationship, as well as the certainty about traditional values, are missing in the Separate marriage. Separates do not openly discuss their conflicts and retreat immediately from the discussion of negative issues when the spouse begins to deal with any stressful topic. The Separates need to be taught techniques for dealing with marital issues and problems. In one study, the Separates were found to be the least accurate in predicting how their spouse saw himself or herself (see Chapter 3). Separates may overattribute the causes of their spouses' behavior to sex-role stereotypes (e.g., "Their feelings are just so easily hurt. That's just the way women are."). Thus some attributional therapy may be needed for this type of couple.

From a different perspective, Doherty and Colangelo (1984) argue that marital and family therapies may be categorized as those primarily dealing with inclusion issues, those with control issues, and those with affection issues. These authors further suggest that therapy must always proceed by dealing with inclusion, affection, and control, in that order. According to this perspective, therapy for Separates must start by dealing with inclusion issues such as the degree of commitment each spouse has to the marriage. Structural family therapy (Minuchin, 1974) may be necessary for Separates because its major emphasis is on membership, boundaries, commitment, and individual and couple identity.

Mixed couple types also have different interaction styles suggesting different strengths on which the therapist can build. In the Traditional/Independent marriage, for example, the husband may help keep conflict in the marriage within manageable bounds by strategically avoiding discussing issues that cannot be resolved; his wife may place fewer role burdens on him than would a more traditional wife. The type of therapy for these couples may depend more on the particular combination of marital identities within each marriage. In general, however, couples in these mixed relationships tend to have control problems and may profit from therapies dealing with power or control issues; these therapies include strategic therapy (Haley, 1980) or the interactional methods (Watzlawick, Weakland, & Fisch, 1974).

The second major implication of this research for the study of marital conflict, negotiation, and problem solving is that couples in various types of marriages use different verbal strategies of confronting, retreating from, and resolving conflict. The research has demonstrated the importance of examining in more detail the various global strategies that couples can use in conflict. The time has come to move from making general statements about positivity and negativity in verbal and nonverbal communication channels to exploring the specific tactics that couples in a variety of different types of marriages use to handle their problems.

The third major implication of this research for the study of marital conflict processes in general is that this research underscores the importance of considering the three levels of analysis in any systematic study of marriage. The typology points to the resources that spouses bring to interaction, predicts the messages chosen to deal with conflicts, and suggests the outcomes each couple type can expect to achieve with these message strategies. The relations between interdependence and ideological orientations, open conflict and marital outcomes are complex ones; yet there seems to be little justification for assuming that high levels of conflict are necessarily associated with imbalances of power or with dissatisfaction in marriage.

6

Getting Your Own Way
Strategies for Gaining Compliance

In marriage, as in all social and personal relationships, many instances occur in which spouses need to persuade or encourage one another to do something that the other may be reluctant to do. Spouses may have a variety of persuasive techniques for dealing with one another. These can range from calmly discussing the advantages and disadvantages of a given course of action, to pleading with the spouse for compliance because the issue is important to the partners' relationship, to power plays or threats demanding compliance or else.

Broadly speaking, the study of persuasion in interpersonal communication pursues answers to three basic questions. First, what individual characteristics of the speaker or the target tend to make them more persuasive or persuasible? Second, what messages strategies are more likely to be used and which are more effective in persuading the spouse? Third, does the relationship between the communicators affect persuasiveness? The focus of the research discussed in this chapter is on the last two of these major questions. In other words, rather than consider individual difference factors, we explore the various messages strategies employed, the outcomes of these strategies, and the nature and type of marriage that exists between the spouses.

There are three important reasons to study persuasion in marital interaction. First, the practice of rational persuasive discourse has always been seen as the antidote to the use of force or violence in civilized relations. The modern family, however, is a place in which hatred and violence are felt, expressed, and learned as consistently as love and rationality. Persuasion and demands for compliance span a continuum running from rationality to violence. Considering how far individual spouses will go in a laboratory interaction in pursuing their own ends and outcomes may give us insights into some of the darker aspects of family life. How far apart on an ethical threshold are power plays and threats from physical abuse and force?

Second, the in-depth study of compliance-gaining messages expands our knowledge of confrontation and the forms it takes in language. In the previous chapter, we learned about certain language forms, called confrontational or distributive, which tended to provoke more conflict. Confrontational strategies are used when the speaker is pursuing his or her own goals. Persuasion research reminds us, however, that there are positive or prosocial ways to pursue one's own goals. The most frequently cited list of persuasive techniques is that of Marwell and Schmitt (1967), who generated sixteen strategies that individuals can use to gain compliance. Some of these strategies were based on rewarding the target for complying whereas others were based on punishing the target for noncompliance.

Third, family life involves a legitimate monopoly of coercion. Socialization may be best viewed as a dynamic persuasive process with each member, at times, attempting to control the attitudes (Of course you're a Democrat), the behaviors (Stop smoking), and the feelings (Love me) of the others. Gaining the compliance of one's spouse for a variety of courses of action is a frequent occurrence in daily family life. When the negotiations go smoothly and the strategies are effective in both the short and long-term, partners probably do not realize persuasion has occurred. When resistance is met, however, a greater range and diversity of strategies may be employed to persuade the spouse.

In the previous chapter on marital conflict, I captured the unfolding of the balance of concerns in a marriage as couples discussed salient areas of disagreement. Under those conditions, Separates, Independents, and Mixed type couples used confrontational techniques more frequently than the Traditionals. Couple types also varied both in their frequency of use of avoidance, and in their responsiveness to their spouse's attempt to avoid the discussion of a serious problem. The research reported in this chapter experimentally induced a high level of concern for one's own outcomes: Each spouse pursued his or her own position over that of the partner. How do couples in the various types confront one another, when avoidance is removed as a communication possibility? Communication tactics used in these situations are called compliance-gaining moves.

In this chapter, my colleagues and I examine the actual messages that couples exchange when attempting to gain compliance. Based on a careful observation of the videotapes, the transcripts, and the extant literature on persuasion in general and compliance gaining in particular, we developed a coding scheme for compliance-gaining message behaviors. We present the results of two validation studies completed on the coding scheme as well as the results of the study examining how couples in the various types of marriages attempt to persuade the spouse

COMPLIANCE-GAINING MESSAGES

A number of analyses of compliance-gaining techniques have been undertaken in order to develop clusters of persuasive techniques that individuals see themselves using in relationships (e.g., Fitzpatrick & Winke, 1979; Marwell & Schmitt, 1967; Miller, Boster, Roloff, & Seibold, 1977). These studies rely on the perceptions that individuals hold concerning their communication behavior. This study examines how couples actually attempt to gain compliance from one another. Since all messages do not serve a compliance-gaining function, a sieve coding scheme was developed. This scheme is based on an analysis of the literature summarizing respondent perceptions of their compliance-gaining strategies as well as an analysis of the actual conversational ploys used by couples.

There are a myriad of ways for couples to be assertive with one another and these verbal strategies are captured in the Verbal Interaction Compliance-Gaining Scheme (VICS). A strategy is a conceptual route by which an actor makes his or her intentions manifest to the partner. Compliance-gaining strategies contain either implicitly or explicitly the response intended for the partner to make and an inducement that provides a reason or motivation for doing what the speaker wants (Schenck-Hamlin, Georgacarakos, & Wiseman, 1982). Compliance-gaining messages may be categorized according to one of three broad classes of reasons or motivations for complying (Witteman & Fitzpatrick, 1986). First, messages can induce compliance because of the expectancies or consequences associated with compliance or noncompliance. *Activity* and *Power* messages fall into this class. Activity messages stress the positive or negative outcomes an individual can expect by engaging in specific behaviors whereas Power messages emphasize consequences of compliance or noncompliance.

Second, messages can induce compliance because of the speaker's

TABLE 6.1
Verbal Interaction Compliance-Gaining Scheme (VICS)

References to Expectancies/Consequences

I. *Activity*: Force to comply comes from the nature of the specific activity, the importance of the activity, or from the outcome of the activity.
    A.   Positivity/Importance of Own Activity or Compromise.
    B.   Negativity/Unimportance of Own Activity or Compromise.
    C.   Positivity/Importance of Other's Activity or Compromise.
    D.   Negativity/Unimportance of Other's Activity or Compromise.

II. *Power*: Focus is on the exertion of control in the relationship. Control may be manifested in attempts to constrain behavior (both verbal and physical) and internal states or processes of either participant.
    A.   Exclamations/Cursing.
    B.   Constraining Self or Other.

Invocations of Identification/Relationship

III. *Us*: Force to comply comes from the relationship between the interactants.
    A.   Identity. Relationship's more stable characteristics.
    B.   Internal. Needs of the relationship.
    C.   Feelings between Spouses—Positive.
    D.   Feelings between Spouses—Negative.
    E.   Pet Names or Terms of Address.

IV. *Direct*: Nonevaluative statement or questions expressing past, current, or future activity, or activities (excluding behavioral regularities of Me, You, or Us).
    A.   Statement of Situation.
    B.   Direct Request for Compliance.

V. *Search*: Information search in question form. Questions are evaluatively neutral.
    A.   Relational/Self/Other Information.
    B.   External Information.

Appeals to Values/Obligations

VI. *Me*: Force to comply comes from within the actor.
    A.   Positive Self-Casting. The focus is on the actor as a "good" person.
    B.   Negative Self-Casting. The focus is on the actor as a "bad" person.
    C.   Identity. The focus is on the actor's stable characteristics.
    D.   Internal. The focus is on the actor's transient characteristics.

VII. *You*: Force to comply comes from within the other.
    A.   Positive Altercasting. The focus is on the target as a "good" person.
    B.   Negative Altercasting. The focus is on the target as a "bad" person.
    C.   Identity. The focus is on the target's stable characteristics.
    D.   Internal. The focus is on the target's transient characteristics.

VIII. *External*: Force to comply comes from a specific (enabling or disabling) agent or agents outside the participants or their relationship.
    A.   Time.
    B.   Cultural/Moral/Social Norms.
    C.   Third Parties.

SOURCE: Witteman and Fitzpatrick, 1984. Reprinted by permission.

conception of the relationship and the requirements entailed by belonging to it. *Us, Direct,* and *Search* fall into this class. Us messages specifically reference the relationship between the communicators or their feelings for one another. Direct messages reference the specific situation and actually ask for compliance, implying the relationship between communicators as the reason. Search messages are nonevaluative questions that ask for the opinions and so forth of the other person.

Third, messages can induce compliance because of the values or obligations held by the spouses. *Me, You,* and *External* messages concern how the speaker sees and values the self, the partner, and external factors affecting the persuasive act. Because the couples used compromises frequently throughout their conversations, we added compromises, or the alternatives that speakers propose in an attempt to reach a solution, to the scheme.

Table 6.2 shows the relationship between VICS and two major self-assessment schemes in the literature. The first scheme is the preformulated strategy list of Marwell and Schmitt (1967). The second comparison is to the work of Schenck-Hamlin and his associates who allowed respondents to construct their own lists of persuasive strategies.

There are a few differences between our observationally based categories and self-report compliance approaches. First, there is a lack of focus in the other systems on the speaker. Whereas many self-report categories focus on the other (i.e., the target of compliance), corresponding to our *You* category, there are few categories that parallel our *Me* category. Appeals such as "I need this" or "I always do it this way" are not represented in their categories. Second, very little attention is paid by these other schemes to the motivating force of appealing to the relationship between the parties as a reason for compliance. For married couples, the relationship is a resource that may motivate the compliance from a mate. Third, although our *External* category does appear in other schemes in the forms of moral appeals and third-party approvals or condemnations, our category encompasses a much wider array of external agents. This category may be expected to discriminate individuals who are heavily influenced by external factors. Fourth, none of the compliance schemes includes an information search category. In gaining compliance, information about the other's affective and cognitive states can be used by the actor in developing other messages. As such, *Search* can be conceived of as a "prestrategy message." The VICS includes examples from the direct-rational, exchange, manipulative, threat, and expertise categories (Cody, McLaughlin, & Jordan, 1980).

TABLE 6.2
Compliance-Gaining Behaviors, Preformulated Strategies, and Constructed Techniques for "Getting One's Own Way with the Spouse"

VICS BEHAVIORS	M & S PREFORMULATED	SH W & G CONSTRUCTED
Activity		
pos (2)	positive expertise	allurement
neg (s)	negative expertise	warning
pos (o)	positive expertise	allurement
neg (o)	negative expertise	warning
Power		
cursing	aversive stimulation	aversive stimulation
constraining (s)	promise	promise
constraining (o)	threat	threat
Us		
identity		
	altruism	altruism
internal		
feelings +	esteem + & liking	esteem & ingratiation
feelings −	esteem −	
Direct Request		
situation		
ask		direct request
Me		
self-casting +	self-feeling +	
self-casting −	self-feeling −	
identity		
internal		
You		
pos altercasting	positive altercasting pregiving	
neg altercasting	negative altercasting	guilt
identity	debt	
internal		
External		
time		
norms	moral appeals	
third parties		

NOTE: VICS is the communication coding scheme devised by my colleagues and I; the M & S refers to Marwell & Schmitt (1967); the SH, W & G refers to the work of Schenk-Hamlin and Associates (1982).

Categories included in other schemes that do not appear in ours appear to take two forms. The first set involves behaviors that would be difficult to pick up from observations of interactions. This group includes Hinting, Deceit, Indirect Strategies, Suggesting, and Withdrawal. Since all of these are indirect attempts to gain compliance, they are not apparent in interaction. Indeed, the strong point of the self-assessment procedures may lie in picking up such indirect persuasion techniques. All persuasion is not accomplished in one interaction nor with words alone. The second group consists of attempts at explanation, reasoning, and persuasion. These categories are often so broadly defined that they hold little promise for verbal message analysis. Explanation, reasoning, and persuasion can be better examined when the force behind the reason is explicated, as in the VICS.

The psychological thought unit (analogous to the sentence) is the unit of analysis, yet because all psychological thought units do not serve a persuasive function, this is a sieve coding scheme. The reliability for the psychological units was .95 (Guetzkow, 1950) and each unit (N = 2,170) was categorized into one of five main categories. That is, a psychological thought unit could represent an attempt to gain compliance, a statement refuting that attempt, a statement discounting the refutation, a simple agreement, or it could be none of the above. About 65% of the psychological thought units were coded as compliance-gaining behaviors. Cohen's kappas (1960) for these five categories were the following: Comply (.74), Refute (.69), Discount (.65), Agree (.80), and Other (.73).

Each of the Compliance units was subsequently coded into one of the eight categories, or a final category called Compromise. The overall Cohen's kappa at this level of the scheme was .79, and the figures ranged from a high of .91 for Search to a low of .62 for the Us category.

Validation of the Coding Scheme

Since the coding scheme was developed for use in this experiment, we felt that some validation was necessary. We validated this coding scheme in two ways. First, we demonstrated that the selection of compliance-gaining messages was differentially related to the outcome of a persuasive transaction and the marital satisfaction and happiness of the communicators. Curiously, most of the compliance-gaining literature focuses on message selection and not the relationship between a given message and outcomes. That is, although labeled "compliance gaining," no one has, as yet, examined the degree to which these strategies actually lead to compliance. Second, we translated the persuasive strategies defined in

TABLE 6.3
Proportions of Messages Used at Level Two
of VICS by Outcome Type

	W Wins		H Wins		M Res		No Res	
	H	W	H	W	H	W	H	W
Expectancy								
Activity	22 (+)	19 (+)	16 (−)	32 (+)	34 (+)	26 (+)	28 (−)	23 (−)
Power	20	12 (−)	24 (+)	29	17 (−)	17 (−)	39 (+)	42 (+)
Relationship								
Us	11 (−)	16	57 (+)	37 (+)	11 (−)	16 (−)	21 (−)	32 (+)
Direct	24 (+)	16 (−)	12 (−)	34 (+)	30 (+)	24 (+)	35	27 (−)
Search	22 (+)	15 (−)	20 (−)	33 (+)	26 (+)	23	32 (−)	30
Value								
Me	20	22 (+)	23 (+)	23 (−)	22 (−)	25 (+)	36 (+)	31 (+)
You	20	19 (+)	12 (−)	30	20 (−)	16 (−)	47 (+)	35 (+)
External	17 (−)	21 (+)	20	39 (+)	20 (−)	14 (−)	43 (+)	27 (−)
Compromise	21 (+)	19 (+)	24 (+)	24 (−)	29 (+)	31 (+)	27 (−)	26 (−)

NOTE: The proportions sum to one across the rows of the table for husband or wife. Wife wins, husband wins, mutual resolution, no resolution are the outcome types. A plus or minus signifies that the Freeman-Tukey deviates associated with the frequency in each cell is $p < .001$. The sign in parentheses indicates whether the observed value is more or less, respectively, than that expected by chance.

VICS into questions that could be used on a survey instrument. Married people were subsequently asked how likely they were to use these strategies in attempting to gain compliance from their spouses. Thus we can compare the likelihood of use data to actual behavioral frequencies observed in ongoing marital interaction.

VICS validation 1. The first validation of this coding scheme explored which of the strategies "worked." How do these contentious strategies affect marital outcomes? Two coders classified the outcome of each interaction: husband wins, wife wins, mutual resolution, or no resolution (Dillard & Fitzpatrick, 1985). Log-linear models with the four outcome types, the speaker (husband or wife), and the nine communication categories were calculated, as were post hoc Freeman-Tukey deviates. As we can see in Table 6.3, the use of these compliance-gaining messages does lead to the persuasive outcome desired by the speaker.

Wives gain compliance by emphasizing what can be expected from the activity desired, by referencing the shared values and obligations of the partners, and by offering compromises. Husbands gain compliance through the use of power plays and threats, by focusing on the nature of the relationship between the parties, or by focusing on themselves. If both spouses focus on the nature of the activity, use direct requests, and offer compromises, a mutually satisfactory resolution is achieved.

These persuasive messages do serve a compliance-gaining function, albeit the strategies are differentially effective for husbands and wives. Moreover, certain strategies decreases the spouses' chances of winning (see Table 6.3). Finally, the use of messages in the values or obligations class by either a husband or a wife increases the likelihood of no resolution to the disagreement.

The use of these messages was also correlated to the happiness and satisfaction of the husbands and wives. Even though we included marital satisfaction and marital happiness as "outcomes" in this study, we do not mean to imply that we are sure of the causal relationships between communication behavior and marital satisfaction. We pose the following as a research question: Is the frequent use of specific compliance-gaining message strategies correlated to marital happiness or distress? Simple correlation coefficients were calculated. Adjustments were made for individual differences in verbal output and an arcsin transformation was performed on each of the proportions to stabilize the variances (Winer, 1971).

Table 6.4 reports only the statistically significant findings. For husbands, the use of any messages in the values or obligations class is correlated to his marital distress. For husbands, appealing to values or obligations as a reason for requesting compliance correlates with his dissatisfaction although not necessarily to the distress of his wife. There are systematic relationships between the use of these persuasive messages and the outcomes of marital conversations. These findings show that some persuasive messages are more effective in the short run. A whole class of these messages (i.e., those in the values and obligations class) appear to be related to a husband's marital distress. Husbands and wives may only reference values when the other ties that bind are less strong. It is important to keep in mind that the wife "wins" when she uses these tactics although in marital as in martial life, they can be many Pyrrhic victories.

VICS validation 2. The second validation of the coding scheme involved asking a sample of married people how likely they would be to use the message strategies in attempting to gain compliance from their spouse. Many compliance-gaining studies rely on assessments of how likely individuals feel they are to use a certain persuasive tactic in a given situation. The directions for future research specified in this research paper genre frequently call for studying actual verbal behavior. In this study, we first explored what messages couples used to gain compliance

TABLE 6.4
Correlations Between Spouse's Use of VICS
and Relational State

		Relational State			
VICS	Speaker	HSAT	HHAP	WSAT	WHAP
Expectancy					
Activity	H			−.43*	
Values					
Me	H		−.25*		−.30*
You	W	.26*	−.24*		
External	H	−.46*	−.56*	.23*	
	W	−.29*	−.24*		

NOTE: There are no significant correlations between the measures of marital satisfaction and happiness and the compliance-gaining messages that invoke the "relationship" as the force to comply.
*p < .05. N = 51.

and then developed a self-report questionnaire concerning the likelihood of use of the tactics.

Four separate questions were written for each of the thirty-one subcategories of the VICS. These questions were based on actual couple dialogue coded into each category but written to be used in a survey instrument. For example, one question was, "How likely are to you to 'Tell your spouse he/she should do this because society expects it of him/her'?" This question measures the likelihood that an individual will appeal to external matters in the cultural values or morals class. A random sample telephone survey was conducted with 67 married individuals, approximately equal numbers of males and females (70% acceptance rate). One of the four versions of the survey instrument was chosen and respondents were asked how likely they would be to use the various messages types when attempting to convince their spouse to follow a certain course of action. Thirty-one one-way analyses of variance were conducted (p < .001) to ensure that the four questions for each category were similar in the minds of the respondents. There were no significant differences on likelihood of use, indicating that the four versions of the questions were exemplars of the same tactic. Table 6.5 presents the mean likelihood of use of each tactic and the actual frequency of use of the behaviors in the compliance-gaining situation.

In general, married individuals, drawn from the same population as the experimental subjects, are very good at predicting which tactics are likely to be used in compliance-gaining marital dialogues. Indeed, these respondents predicted behavioral data correctly about 70% of the time.

TABLE 6.5
Likelihood of Use and Actual Use of
Compliance-Gaining Messages

	Mean	Frequency (in percentages)
Expectancies		
I. *Activity*		
a. Positivity of own	3.84	6 i
b. Negativity of own	3.34	1 i
c. Positivity of other	3.49	1 i
d. Negativity of other	2.24	3 c
II *Power*		
a. Exclamation/cursing	1.75	1 c
b. Constraining self	2.09	7 c
c. Constraining other	1.83	1 c
Relationship		
III. *Us*		
a. Identity	2.99	2 c
b. Internal	2.34	1 c
c. Positive feelings	2.89	0 c
d. Negative feelings	1.53	0 c
e. Pet names	2.81	1 c
IV. *Direct*		
a. Statement of situation	3.88	19 c
b. Direct request	3.60	6 i
V. *Search*		
a. Internal information	4.27	10 c
b. External information	4.03	1 i
Values		
VI. *Me*		
a. Positive-self	2.69	1 c
b. Negative-self	2.45	0 c
c. Identity	3.78	2 i
d. Internal	3.58	19 c
VII. *You*		
a. Positive-other	3.35	1 i
b. Negative-other	1.99	3 c
c. Identity	3.12	1 i
d. Internal	3.45	4 i
VIII. *External*		
a. Time	2.70	2 c
b. Cultural norms	2.40	0 c
c. Third parties	2.58	3 c

NOTE: The mean likelihood of use is on a scale of (1) very unlikely to (5) very likely. The "c" assumes a mean likelihood of use under 3.00 and less than 10% of the overall compliance-gaining messages are the correct estimates of the behavior. The "i" represents incorrect estimates.

Married individuals say that they are not likely to use extreme negative tactics (any power tactic or focus on negative aspects of the other's idea or person), and behaviorally couples *do not tend* to use these tactics. Married people also say they are not likely to use the relationship as a compelling reason for compliance, and they actually do not use any of the messages in the Us category to any great degree. Finally, married people argue that they are not likely to use External messages and the behavioral data agrees with this perception. The married sample errs in predicting the likelihood of use of either the internal characteristics of themselves or any of the You messages that focus on characteristics or traits of the spouse. The survey data argue that these messages are very likely to be used yet they are used rarely in the behavioral data. In thinking about how to get one's own way, one may use attributions about the spouse although such attributional categories do not appear when actually engaged in message exchanges. Finally, the sample errs in predicting that they would focus on the characteristics of the activity as a primary means of getting their own way. The sample tends to see themselves as rational in focusing on the positive consequences of an activity yet very little of this occurs in actual compliance situations.

These data indicate that social desirability arguments against the use of checklists and self-reports of compliance-gaining techniques may need to be modified. Falbo and Peplau (1980) demonstrated that power strategies can be described on three continua: positive-negative, rational-irrational, and direct-indirect. These three continua help to organize our results comparing self-reports and behavioral persuasive strategies. People correctly report the use of negative strategies. When people report that they do not use power strategies and negative tactics, that is because they actually use these techniques very rarely. Social desirability may enter the equation only when considering the dimension of rationality-irrationality. Here, as in the activity category, people see themselves as referencing the "pros and cons" of an issue more than they tend to in conversation. People also see themselves taking the other's needs and desires into account more than they do behaviorally. Finally, the use of indirect strategies can be probed far better through questionnaires than in examining actual laboratory interaction. In discussing how they persuade the spouse, husbands and wives admit to some limited negative message strategy, and overemphasize their own rationality. Couples also pursue more in-directness than can be captured in dialogue.

Summary

In this section, we have presented and validated a scheme designed to measure how couples attempt to persuade one another to pursue a given course of action. The coding scheme is based on the concept that each persuasive messages specifies reasons for request-compliance. Broadly speaking, the persuader can reference the consequences of an action, the relationship between the communicator, or the values or obligations that each shares. The coding scheme, called VICS, was validated by examining how the use of these strategies led to specific interaction outcomes, correlated to the state of the marriage of the communicators, and judged as likely or unlikely persuasion strategies to be used on one's spouse. The latter was accomplished by translating the verbal messages into self-report assessments of compliance and asking married couples how likely they would be to use each strategy.

INDUCING SPOUSAL COMPLIANCE

How does the type of marriage affect the choice of persuasive strategies that husbands and wives employ in getting their own way? To answer this question, 51 couples participated in this study. The average length of the marriages was 7.8 years (range, < 1 year to 33 years). On the average, husbands were 31.7 years old (range, 22 to 57 years), and wives were 30.4 years old (range, 21 to 55). In this sample, there were 13 Traditionals, 10 Separates, 6 Independents, 5 Separate/Traditionals, and 17 Mixed types. The distribution of the frequencies in this sample of the three Pure types, the Mixed types, and the Separate/Traditionals does not differ significantly from that of the major random sample of couples (Fitzpatrick & Indvik, 1982).

Couples were asked to carry out two role plays, each of which took 15 minutes. The role-play situations represent areas of conflict that occur in most marriages at some time. One role play concerned the sharing of time; the other involved forming new friendships. Before the experiment, interviewers helped couples make the role plays conform as much as possible to the overall structure of their relationship and interaction style. Roles for husbands and wives were assigned on the basis of rather extensive probes (Gottman, 1979, pp. 138-140). After the coaching session, couples were brought into a simulated living room and instructed to try to gain compliance from their spouse for the course of action they had chosen. Compliance-gaining conversations were videotaped and transcribed. The manipulation checks indicated that all spouses saw themselves during these interactions as being natural and comfortable, and their behaviors as being similar to real-life situations. Because there were no significant differences in the perceptions of the respondents between the two discussion tasks, these two discussions were combined

TABLE 6.6
Frequency of Use and Correlation Between Husband
and Wife Compliance-Gaining Behaviors

	Frequency	Correlation
Referencing Expectancies		
Activity	14.75	.39*
Power	11.52	.07
Invocation of the Relationship		
Us	5.42	.28*
Direct	33.07	−.14
Search	15.39	.26*
Appeals to Values		
Me	26.02	.27*
You	10.96	.34*
External	10.52	.16
Compromise	12.78	.27*

* = $p < .05$.

for analyses. There were no significant differences in the number of psychological thought units coded for husbands and wives. The frequency of use of the various strategies differed. By far, the most popular method of attempting to gain compliance was to make a Direct Request apparently unadorned by a rationale whereas the least popular compliance-gaining message is Us. In invoking the relationship, couples do so indirectly rather than explicitly. The correlations between husband and wife compliance strategies suggest that spouses cue one another as to which strategies to use. Significant correlations hold for all but external, direct, and power strategies. The bluntness of the power and direct strategies may preclude a spouse from answering in kind whereas external reasons could only apply to the speaker's situation.

Couples in the various types are expected to differ in their persuasive techniques because each marital type relies on different forces for reasoning with the spouse when attempting to gain compliance. Predictions about the use of various persuasive strategies in marital types can be made at two different levels of the coding scheme hierarchy. Recall that at the first level of the scheme, a speaker's behavior was coded as compliance, refutation, discounting the refutation of the spouse, or simple agreement. A high use of discounts and refutations would suggest an argumentative style on the part of the communicator. Such a style is significantly different than the style where a partner uses many compliance strategies but does not necessarily refute or debate the partner. From their

TABLE 6.7
Proportions of Messages Used at Level One
of VICS by Couple Type

			Couple Type		
Message	Traditional	Separate	Independent	Separate/ Traditional	Mixed
Comply	.18 (+)*	.20 (+)*	.19 (−)*	.22	.21
Refute	.16 (−)*	.22 (+)*	.29 (+)*	.13 (−)*	.20
Discount	.13 (−)*	.24 (+)*	.35 (+)*	.12 (−)*	.17 (−)*
Agree	.18	.17 (−)*	.16 (−)*	.27 (+)*	.23 (+)*
Other	.16 (−)*	.17 (−)*	.22 (+)*	.26 (+)*	.19 (−)*

NOTE: The proportions sum to one across the rows of the table. These indicate differences among the couple types in their usage of messages. An asterisk signifies that the Freeman-Tukey deviates associated with the frequency in each cell is $p < .001$. Positive or negative signs in parentheses indicate whether the observed value is more or less, respectively, than that expected by chance.

communication style during conflict, we can predict that the Independents will engage one another during these dialogues and refute and debate the merits of what the spouse says in order to gain compliance.

The average frequency counts for each communication category were analyzed using log-linear analysis (Bishop, Feinberg, & Holland, 1975). Because we expected couples in different types of marriages to use different compliance-gaining strategies, we focused on models involving couple types. All of these models contain a sex-by-couple-type interaction because this interaction is automatically fixed by the sampling plan (see Swafford, 1980). A number of criteria was used to select the best fitting model. The first was based on the probability level of the model. The appropriate probability level ranges from anything over .05 as implied by Brown (1983) and Kennedy (1983) to between .10 to .35 (Knoke & Burke, 1980). We used the latter and more conservative standard to obtain a moderately robust yet parsimonious model to explain the data. If no model falls within this range, the model with a level of probability above and closest to .35 was selected. This again ensured parsimony. In addition, only the model that added a significant component chi-square was accepted. Once the best fitting model was selected, the respective Freeman-Tukey deviates for the best fitting model were examined. The deviates for the model were tested for significance at the $p < .001$ significance level (Bishop et al., 1975). Table 6.7 reveals the proportion of the messages used at level one of the coding scheme for the types.

It is clear from this table that the general persuasive styles of these couples are remarkably different. Independents tend to refute one

TABLE 6.8
Proportions of Messages Used at Level Two
of VICS by Couple Type

| | | | Couple Type | | |
Message	Traditional	Separate	Independent	Separate/ Traditional	Mixed
Expectancies					
Activity	.26 (+)*	.19 (−)*	.16 (−)*	.16 (−)*	.22 (+)*
Power	.15 (−)*	.25 (+)*	.24 (+)*	.11 (−)*	.26 (+)*
Relationship					
Us	.17	.16 (−)*	.14 (−)*	.33 (+)*	.21
Direct	.20 (+)*	.19 (−)*	.18 (−)*	.21 (−)*	.23 (+)*
Search	.20 (+)*	.17 (−)*	.24 (+)*	.18 (−)*	.22 (+)*
Values					
Me	.14 (−)*	.20	.19 (−)*	.29 (+)*	.18 (−)*
You	.14 (−)*	.22 (+)*	.20 (+)*	.29 (+)*	.15 (−)*
External	.17 (−)*	.26 (+)*	.17 (−)*	.22	.18 (−)*

NOTE: The proportions sum to one across the rows of the table. These indicate differences among the couple types in their usage of the compliance-gaining messages. An asterisk signifies that the Freeman-Tukey deviates associated with the frequency in each cell is $p < .001$. Positive or negative signs in parentheses indicate whether the observed value is more or less, respectively, than that expected by chance.

another in situations involving a conflict of interest, whereas Traditionals use relatively few refutations and discounts. The Separates were the most assertive and contentious: They used a high proportion of compliance moves, refuted one another's attempts and discounted one another's arguments, and were not very agreeable. The Mixed types in general were not likely to frame messages asking for compliance. Notably, the Mixed types and the Separate/Traditionals tended to use a good deal of agreement and tended not to discount the arguments of the spouse. Like the Traditionals, the Separate/Traditionals tended not to refute what the spouse said.

When these couples do frame persuasive messages, what form do these messages take? Independents use all three bases or classes of reasons when seeking spousal compliance, albeit a restricted range of messages within each category. Independents demand compliance from their spouses in that they rely on "you" strategies and power plays when attempting to persuade their spouses. Independents are likely to offer compromises and to question the spouse about their needs and wants. Independents use fewer compliance-gaining techniques overall, yet do engage in defending themselves and refuting what the spouse says. The techniques the Independents do use rely on a variety of bases.

Traditionals talk about their expectancies in trying to gain compliance. Given the shared, conventional value system of these couples and their levels of interdependence, Traditionals can discuss the positive and negative outcomes of a given course of action. This shared value orientation does not result in the Traditionals using any message in the values/obligations categories. Traditionals are significantly less likely than expected by chance to summon their values or any obligations in the relationship as a means to gain the compliance of a spouse. In attempting to get their own way, the Traditionals use the relationship and the identification that each has with the other as motivating forces to achieve compliance.

Separates avoid using identification or relationally based messages when seeking compliance from a spouse and tend to focus on the negative consequences of noncompliance. Only the Separates cite external reasons for spousal compliance. When Separates do engage in contentious behavior with the spouse, they use blatant attempts to constrain the behavior, and sometimes even the internal states, such as thoughts or feelings, of their spouses. Separates are not without intensity in their interactions but have a guerrilla-like communication style that demands acquiescence from the spouse without verbally staying to fight the whole battle.

Separate/Traditionals stress values and obligations and the relationship as means to gain compliance from a spouse. These couples ask the spouse to comply for them, for the spouse, and for the relationship. The Separate/Traditionals were the only couple type to inhibit their attempts to compromise when attempting to gain compliance from a spouse. Separate/Traditionals do not prematurely yield to their spouses when they are attempting to get their own way.

The other Mixed types rely on references to the consequences of noncompliance; they also rely on power plays, direct requests, and compromises as strategies to gain spousal compliance.

Summary

The three broad classes of influence that individuals can use to request compliance from a spouse with their associated different verbal strategies and tactics clearly differentiate the couples in the various types of marriages. This study is important because it shows the contentious nature of the communication in the Separate marriage. The Separates report that they avoid conflict in their marriages and also say that they are assertive toward their partners. Indeed, there are few coordinated exchanges of open conflict maneuvers between these partners. A range and diversity of assertiveness and then retreat appears to be the key to their communication style with one another. These couple use power plays, appear to avoid the rational discussion of issues, and hammer away at obligations and external causes for their own position holding sway. Power plays help the husband to win whereas appeals to values or obligations help the wife to win, although the latter is correlated to the husband's unhappiness in the marriage. A great deal of frustration may be building up in these marriages and these couples may be prone to violence or abuse.

CONCLUSION

The persuasion styles adopted by couples in each of these various types again supports the clear differences in interactions of couples in these types of marriages. One's ideological orientation to marriage, levels of interdependence, and openness to expressivity affect the reasons a spouse gives for requesting compliance, the outcomes such messages achieve, and the likelihood that certain tactics will be used in marital persuasion.

Two general directions need to be pursued in studying persuasion in marriage. First, a specific theoretical link needs to be made between these verbal persuasive strategies and violence in families. Straus (1978), for example, on his Conflict Tactics Scale, employs a Guttman scaling technique. Calm discussion anchors one end of the continuum and then very quickly moves into physical acts of force or violence. There is room on this continuum for a variety of techniques of rational persuasion. One approach to this topic is to examine the sequential structure of persuasion to see how far individuals move along this rational to violent continuum. A great deal probably depends on how much resistance a spouse meets from his or her partner to the persuasive attempt (Cody & McLaughlin, 1985). Second, the positivity-negativity, direct-indirect, and rational-irrational nature of the various tactics should be explored.

There is a legitimate monopoly of coercion in family life, with each member attempting to control the attitudes, behaviors, and feelings of the others. This control is rarely activated without a high degree of affect. The study of persuasion between intimates can illuminate important aspects of family socialization.

III

THE COMMUNICATION
OF EMOTIONS

7

Revealing Yourself
Self-Disclosure in Marriage

In the latter part of the twentieth century, the sharing of personal feelings and information about the self has become for some members of our culture the hallmark of a close relationship. The gradual exchange of intimate information about one's inner self is considered the major process through which relationships develop between people (Katriel & Philipsen, 1981). Many, if not most, theories of relational growth equate the development of a relationship with the exchange of increasingly more intimate information. Although theoretical work (e.g., Altman & Taylor, 1973) stresses the centrality of self-disclosure in the development of relationships, very little empirical work has examined the role that self-disclosure plays in established relationships.

There is a growing sense, however, that the role that self-disclosure plays in close relationships may not be as clear-cut as originally thought. Cultural critics such as Sennett (1978) contend that the emphasis on self-disclosure and expressivity is actually harmful to the satisfaction and stability of relationships. He indicts what he calls "the ideology of intimacy: [that] social relationships of all kinds are real, believable, and authentic the closer they approach the inner psychological concerns of each person . . . this ideology of intimacy defines the humanitarian spirit of a society without gods: Warmth is our god" (Sennett, 1978, p. 259). Paralleling this logic, some scholars of close relationships have refused to accept the premise that the closer the relationship, the greater the amount of shared verbal intimacy. Instead, close relationships are defined in terms of the interdependence between partners (Kelley et al., 1983). This interdependence takes many forms and the expression of the self in conversation is only one of them.

Nevertheless, self-disclosure is probably the most frequently studied communication variable in the area of personal relationships. This chapter examines self-disclosure in reference to other forms of inter-personal communication in the casual interaction of couples in various marital types. Two studies are reported, which consider the proportion of time spent in conversation disclosing to the spouse in comparison to other message types. This chapter also considers the public versus private nature of disclosure by examining how much one discloses to others in comparison to disclosure to one's spouse.

SELF-DISCLOSURE IN MARRIAGE

Self-disclosure has been approached as a personality trait and as a process variable (Pearce & Sharp, 1973). As a personality trait, disclosure has been linked to gender, to family and ethnic patterns, to race, and other cultural variables. As a process variable, self-disclosure has been studied as a facilitator of the development of interpersonal relationships. There are two major theories about how self-disclosure generates change in relationships. Social penetration theory (Altman & Taylor, 1973) specifies that relationships progress linearly and are marked by the exchange of personal information that grows in breadth of topics covered and depth of information shared. Many researchers agree that disclosure helps in the initial development of relationships by promoting mutual liking and reducing uncertainty about the partner's social status and personality characteristics (Berger & Bradac, 1982). A lack of self-disclosure may signal the end of a relationship as well. Self-disclosure appears to decrease as relationships move through various stages of deterioration (Baxter, 1985). In established relationships, such as marriage, however, the role of self-disclosure in the maintenance of the relationship is less clear.

Ongoing relationships may be maintained by illusions about the other, exaggerations of similarity, expectations of goodness, and less than full disclosure. In a classic longitudinal study of married couples, Raush and his colleagues (1974) expressed surprise at the use of what they considered communication pathology. Some of the happily married couples in their experiment avoided unpleasant topics, lied about their feelings, and disqualified their own or their spouse's statements. These data clearly indicate that optimal communication from one point of view (openness, honesty, self-disclosure) is not what is perceived as a good or functional relational style by all couples. The research suggests that the communication exchanges that maintain functional marriages are not necessarily characterized by high mutual self-disclosure.

Newer theoretical models (e.g., Bochner, 1983) question the role of self-disclosure in *maintaining* intimate relationships. These models argue that the notion of a unidirectional trend toward increasing openness between spouses should not be overstated. No relationship is able to sustain total openness and intimacy over long periods of time. Dialectical theories (e.g., Bochner, 1983; Bolton, 1961) posit that relationships follow a process characterized by continual cycling between superficial and deeper contact and a repeated ebb and flow of exchange. From the beginning, there is a tension between the need to self-disclose and the need to protect the partner from the consequences of such disclosure. Conversation in established relationships needs to serve a number of functions other than revealing the self to the other. For example, a growing expectation in an established relationship is that each person can trust the other to protect the vulnerability revealed early in relationships through the process of self-disclosure. To protect the vulnerability of a partner, however, it is sometimes necessary to conceal thoughts or feelings one has about the spouse that one now knows may hurt or anger the other. Revelation is always balanced against concealment in an ongoing relationship.

Conversation in ongoing relationships serves five basic functions that may require competing message choices in any given marital exchange. These five, interrelated and potentially contradictory, functions are (1) to foster favorable impressions, (2) to organize the relationship, (3) to construct and validate a joint worldview, (4) to express feelings and thoughts, and (5) to protect vulnerabilities (Bochner, 1983). These basic functions of communication can affect the direct expressions of feelings and thoughts in a close relationship. The need to validate the spouse can easily come into conflict with the need to be open and honest about one's thoughts or feelings. Additionally, self-disclosure to the marital partner takes place against a social background of self-disclosure to others in the network.

Within the various marital types, couples are expected to place different emphasis on the various functions of communication in maintaining a marriage. Consequently, the degree and kind of self-disclosure in the various types of marriages is expected to differ. With their concern for the other and for keeping a balance in the relationship, Traditionals are expected to moderate their levels of self-disclosure. The function of intimate communication in this marriage is more to protect the vulnerabilities of the spouse than to express personal feelings. Independents, on the other hand, are expected to express openly their personal feelings to one another as a sign of their intimate bond and their commitment to an ideology of expressivity. Separates are expected to have the least open communication style as the function of marital talk for these couples is the organization of the relationship rather than any open expression of personal emotions or feelings.

The Self and Other
Topics of Marital Talk

How important is the disclosure of one's feelings and thoughts to a marital partner? One way to contextualize self-disclosure is to examine the ongoing casual conversation of couples and compare the proportion of time spent self-disclosing to other forms of interpersonal communication. All other things being equal, the amount of time spent in a given conversational activity is a measure of its salience. There are a number of different ways to approach the coding of the communication between husbands and wives. Because we were particularly interested in coding spontaneous occurrence of self-disclosure in conversations between intimates, we chose to use the coding scheme developed by Stiles (1978a). Although this scheme is not limited to self-disclosure, it does offer a reliable way to code self-disclosure in ongoing interaction. Thus interaction of 50 couples who had been asked to "have a pleasant conversation" was coded with the Taxonomy of Verbal Response Modes (Stiles, 1978a). This taxonomy, also known as VRM, is a method of classifying and summarizing the interpersonal intent and grammatical form of the messages sent by participants in ongoing interpersonal exchanges. The VRM uses the psychological thought unit, or what Stiles (1978a) calls an utterance, as the basic unit of analysis. The VRM defines eight basic interpersonal communication messages based on the communication that has been previously coded into thought units: disclosure, edification, question, acknowledgment, advisement, confirmation, interpretation, and reflection. These eight messages are defined by the intersection of three dichotomous principles of classification: source of experience (whether the utterance concerns the speaker's or the other's experience), frame of reference (whether the utterance uses the speaker's viewpoint or a viewpoint shared with the other), and focus (whether the speaker presumes to know what the other's experience or frame of reference is or should be). Table 7.1 lists the VRM and examples of dialogue.

TABLE 7.1
Taxonomy of Verbal Response Modes

	Speaker Frame of Reference	Other Frame of Reference
Focus on Speaker		
Speaker's Experience	Disclosure	Edification
	"I'm worried about my health."	"Her husband is out of work."
Other's Experience	Question	Acknowledgment
	"Did you remember to pick up the tickets?"	"Yeah." "Mm-hmm."
Focus on Other		
Speaker's Experience	Advisement	Confirmation
	"You ought to stop smoking."	"We both feel the same way on that issue."
Other's Experience	Interpretation	Reflection
	"You have been working too hard."	"You want me to stop smoking."

SOURCE: Fitzpatrick, Vance, and Witteman (1984). Reprinted by permission.

This study involved 50 couples—13 Traditional, 9 Separate, 6 Independent, 5 Separate/Traditional, and the rest Mixed couples. Each couple was paid $20 for participating. Researchers made every effort to make the room where the experimental procedures and interviews were conducted as comfortable and nonthreatening as possible. Couples were asked to engage in a "pleasant conversation." Each couple was given a "fun deck" that contained possible topics of conversation designed to induce casual interaction (see Gottman, 1979). Couples were not restricted to these topics but were told that they should feel free to use the deck if they ran out of things to talk about during the 10-minute conversation. At the end of that period, couples completed a variety of self-report measures concerning the interaction. Within two weeks of the experiment, couples were visited in their homes by an interviewer who administered the Relational Dimensions Instrument and other self-report measures. A complete description of the sample, procedures, and methods of this experiment can be found in Vance (1981).

Although we had collected 10 minutes of interaction, we began by analyzing the middle 4 minutes of interaction. This segment was chosen to decrease any effect due to lack of comfort during the first and last few minutes in this section of the experiment. The 4-minute segment started with the first exchange of a speaking turn after the third minute. The conversation segments were transcribed by a professional court reporter. The transcripts were unitized according to the Stiles (1978a) rules. Each coder received a copy of the training manual, plus 14 weeks of instruction that included work with dialogue from selected plays as well as actual marital dialogues. Coder training reflected our primary interests—the intent dimensions of the Stiles system. We emphasized that the intent categories were to be discriminated on three principles of classification: source of experience, frame of reference, and focus. The intent of an utterance or psychological thought is scored by answering three questions: Is the topic of the utterance information held by the speaker or by the other? Does the utterance take the speaker's point of view or a point of view shared by the other? Does the speaker presume knowledge only of his or her own experience and frame of reference, or does the speaker also presume knowledge of the other's experience or frame of reference?

The 50 transcripts were distributed randomly among the three coders. Duplicate transcripts of nine couples were randomly selected and distributed to allow the computation of intercoder reliability. The mean intercoder reliability, based on Cohen's kappa (Cohen, 1960) for the intent categories, was 0.79. The mean intercoder reliability for the form (i.e., parts of speech, grammar) categories was 0.90. There are no gender differences: Husbands and wives are responsible for the same number of utterances. A test of the observed versus expected utterances among the couple types, however, was significant (chi-square = 13.35, df = 4; p > .01). Although there are no husband-wife differences, Separates used significantly fewer thought units during casual interactions than other couples.

Paralleling previous research (Fitzpatrick et al., 1982), which found that Separate couples spoke less frequently to one another during conflict, Separate couples used fewer thought units during casual interactions than did the other couple types. There were no differences for husbands across the couple types in how much they enjoyed the casual conversation (F = 0.823; df = 4, 49), nor for how much they felt their wives enjoyed the conversations (F = 1.17; df = 4, 49), nor for the wives in evaluating their own enjoyment (F = 0.219; df = 4, 49), nor their evaluations of their husbands' enjoyment (F = 0.226; df = 4, 49). Separates' reservation in these conversations reflects an avoidance of the spouse

TABLE 7.2

Proportions of Couple's Casual Talk in the Eight
Interpersonal Communication Categories

	Couple Type				
	Trad	Indep	Sep	Sep/Trad	Mixed
Message Type					
Disclosure	0.204	0.229	0.197	0.153	0.217
Edification	0.182	0.155	0.127	0.355	0.182
Question	0.191	0.221	0.235	0.162	0.191
Acknowledge	0.157	0.257	0.186	0.229	0.171
Advisement	0.200	0.267	0.133	0.200	0.200
Confirmation	0.235	0.235	0.206	0.176	0.147
Interpretation	0.500	0.250	0.000	0.250	0.000
Reflection	0.000	0.125	0.250	0.250	0.375
Total (481)					

NOTE: Proportions compare message usage across couple type. Results of the log-linear analysis were the same when the last two categories were collapsed in order that the few observations in those cells did not bias the statistical test. See Fitzpatrick, Vance, and Witteman (1984).

rather than any inherent displeasure with the task per se.

Most messages exchanged by the couples fell into the disclosure and edification categories. Approximately 56% of the utterances used in this interaction involved a speaker reporting his or her thoughts, feelings, desires, opinions, perceptions, and intentions (self-disclosure) or expressing what the speaker believes to be objective information, the accuracy of which could be judged by an objective observer (edification).

Table 7.3 shows the likelihood ratio chi-square values (G2), degrees of freedom, and the associated probabilities for a number of log-linear models that include an increasingly complex series.[1]

All four models that include the interaction between sex (S) and couple type (T) represent reasonably good fits to the data. The addition in model C of the (TC) interaction term (couple types by communication), however, makes a significant contribution to the fit of the model. Indeed, including all the interaction terms (model D) does not appear to yield a much better fit than model C. Not only is the interaction between couple types and the eight communication behaviors the best fit to the model, it is of greatest theoretical interest.

The Traditional couples, while engaging in a moderate amount of self-disclosure and edification during these interactions, were likely to interpret the spouse, although they also confirmed the comments of their spouse. Traditionals balance the functions of openness, protection, and regulation in their marital communication. These couples are as likely to

TABLE 7.3
Log-Linear Tests of Couple Type, Sex,
and Eight Communication Categories

Test of Fit Model	\	Added Effect	\	\	\	\
	df	G2	p	df	G2	p
ST x C (A)	54	28.13	> 0.05	7		
ST x SC (B)	47	25.35	> 0.05	7	2.78	> 0.01
ST x TC (C)	29	7.13	> 0.05	18	18.22	< 0.01
ST x S TC (D)	22	5.06	> 0.05	7	2.07	> 0.01

NOTE: S = Sex (Male or Female); T = Couple Type (Traditional, Independent, Separate, Separate/Traditional, Mixed); C = Communication Categories (8 Stiles categories). See Fitzpatrick, Vance, and Witteman (1984).

focus on their thoughts and opinions as their emotions and feelings in marital talk. Independents, on the other hand, use the highest proportion of disclosure, acknowledgment, advisement, and confirmation messages when asked to have a pleasant conversation with their spouses. These forms of communication closely approximate the style of interpersonal communication suggested in the humanistic schools of thought (e.g., Jourard, 1971; Rogers, 1961). Independents are expressive in their marital communication and open with the spouse in discussing their feelings.

The Separates engage in a higher proportion of questioning of the spouse and are not likely to express their feelings, state their opinions to the spouse, or to give the spouse advice. This muted style of casual interaction suggests that the function of marital dialogue for these couples is to regulate the relationship rather than to exchange feelings and points of view.

Separate/Traditionals are the least likely of these couples to disclose their feelings during these conversations but the most likely to state their opinions on factual matters to their mates. The raw frequencies indicated that the separate husbands in this marriage used very little self-disclosure and were predominantly responsible for the high proportion of edification statements. Their traditional wives were responsible for the self-disclosure that occurred in these conversations. This conversational pattern implies the creation of a joint worldview based on a strong commitment to gender roles. The Boston Couples study (Rubin, Hill, Peplau, & Dunke-Schetter, 1980), reported gender differences in self-disclosure closely approximating the pattern in this marriage. Women tended to disclose material that was personal, feeling oriented, and involved negative emotions. Males, on the other hand, disclosed more readily when the information was factual and relatively neutral or positive in tone. Behaviorally, the same patterns holds in these data with the husbands using edification and the wives the more personal disclosures.[2]

The other Mixed couple types used a similar (and moderate) amount of disclosure, edification, and questioning during these conversations as did the Traditionals. Mixed couples differed from the Traditionals in that they employed a smaller proportion of confirmation statements. Mixed couples also appear to be balancing openness, protection, and the regulation of the relationship in their conversation, although their disagreement on a basic relationship worldview shows up in their use of fewer confirmation messages.

The three principles of classification—source of experience, frame of reference, and focus—also can be extended to characterize interactions (Stiles, 1978b). A participant's role can be scored for its attentiveness, acquiescence, and presumptuousness in conversation (Stiles, 1979, 1980; Stiles, Waszak, & Barton, 1979).

Speakers are *attentive* to their conversational partners to the degree to which the speakers are concerned with "the other" as a source of experience in conversation. The number of utterances of a speaker being coded as "other" source of experience is divided by the total number of utterances. The higher this proportion, the more attentive a speaker is to his or her conversational partner. Questioning the other, for example, is a way that speakers attempt to use the other as a source of experience. A Z-test for attentiveness reveals significant differences between Separates and Traditionals ($Z = -2.737$; $p < 0.01$) and between Separates and the Separate/Traditionals ($Z = -2.974$; $p < 0.01$). Also, the Separate/Traditionals are significantly different from the Independents ($Z = -2.066$; $p < 0.01$). The Separates are significantly more attentive to their spouses than are the Separate/Traditionals or Traditionals. The Separate/Traditionals are the least attentive to their mates in casual social interaction.

Speakers are *acquiescent* to the other to the degree that they use the other as a frame of reference in conversation. Confirming the other's statements or reflecting on what the other has said are examples of ways that speakers have of being nondirective to others in conversation. The higher the proportion of "other" frames of reference remarks, the more acquiescent a speaker is to his or her conversational partner. A Z-test for the proportions of the other's frame of reference used by speakers in conversations with their spouses indicates that the Separate/Traditionals take a point of view shared by the other spouse significantly more often than the Traditional (Z = -6.275; p < 0.001), the Separate (Z = -6.408; p < 0.001), the Independent (Z = -5.958; p < 0.001), or the Mixed couple types (Z = -6.818; p < 0.001). Separate/Traditionals spend a greater portion of their conversational time than the other couple types acquiescing to their spouses.

Speakers are *presumptuous* to the degree that they assume that they understand their partners. Advising the partner or interpreting what the other has said are ways that a speaker presumes to understand the other individual. Presumptuousness suggests a personal familiarity or intimacy with the other, but it is similar to Gottman's (1979) use of mind reading and Sillars' (1986) category of presumptive attribution. The higher the proportion of "other"-focused utterances, the more presumptuous the speaker. A Z-test for the differences in proportions of utterances presuming knowledge of the frame of reference of the other indicates that the Separate/Traditionals are significantly different from the Independent (Z = 2.967; p < 0.01), the Traditional (Z = 4.139; p < 0.001), the Separate (Z = 2.976; p < 0.01), and the Mixed couple types (Z = 3.08; p < 0.01). The Separate/Traditionals are less likely to make presumptive attributions about their spouses.

Summary

Even in 4 minutes of interaction, couples in the marital typology can be discriminated from one another. Separates were the most attentive of the couple types. When Separates are attempting to have a pleasant conversation with their spouses, they tend to ask one another a number of questions and tend not to state their own opinions or to give one another advice. The attentiveness of the Separates suggests a kind of watchfulness in their casual interaction style with one another. Separates have little spontaneity in their casual interaction with one another and tend to limit the amount of communication they have with one another.

We expected the Traditionals to carry into their casual interaction the acquiescent style they adopt in conflict. Although willing to acquiesce during disagreements over trivial issues, Traditionals are not necessarily acquiescent to their spouses in other interaction contexts. Rather, the Separate/Traditional couples clearly emerged as the most acquiescent.

Separate/Traditionals were also the least presumptuous of the couples. When asked to have a pleasant conversation with their spouses, Separate/Traditionals neither disclosed to their spouses nor asked them questions but spent a good proportion of their time stating their opinions on factual matters. From a role perspective, these couples have the most defined speaker-role behavior of the couples. Separate/Traditionals are the least attentive to their spouses, the least presumptuous, and yet the most acquiescent. Although this couple type is made up of a separate husband and a traditional wife, their relationship and communication patterns are markedly different from the Separates and the Traditionals. Separates/Traditionals are not as watchful of what they say to their spouses as are the Separates, do not presume to understand the spouse as do the Traditionals, and are likely to acquiesce to their spouse, unlike the Traditionals.

The communication categories of self-disclosure and edification accounted for 56% of the messages exchange by these spouses during their casual interaction. Disclosing their own feelings or opinions and discussing both factual matters and other people with their spouses constitutes a casual conversation for marital partners. In their attempts to understand marital functioning, researchers have concentrated on how couples resolve conflicts. Equally important to understanding social relationships such as marriage is some appreciation of the different ways that various couples indicate their involvement with one another in casual conversations. In thinking about and evaluating their own marriages, couples undoubtedly compare the pleasantness of their daily exchanges against more disagreeable, conflict-ridden interactions. Relationships are built not only on the successful resolution of differences but also on the couple's ability to conduct pleasant, spontaneous conversations.

PUBLIC AND PRIVATE DISCLOSURE

The ideology of intimacy ties deep self-disclosure to the marital relationship and makes one's spouse the major and only confidante for one's innermost thoughts, feelings, and desires. Such an ideology represents a modern idea of marriage. As Hunt (1962, p. 199) says, "Among the many curious features of modern woman's life is one that would have thoroughly offended St. Paul, bewildered Tristan and amused Don Juan—namely, the fact that she is her husband's best friend and he is hers."

We have seen in the last section that there are significant differences among couple types in their interpersonal communication. Here, we examine self-referential talk by comparing it both to the dialogues that couples report, and those they actually have, with others. Communication styles both within and outside the marriage with spouses, strangers, friends, and acquaintances are considered.

Reports of Disclosure
to the Spouse and Others

The expressive or humanistic school of interpersonal communication, called the school of "expression, joy, and metaphor" by its critics (Hart & Burks, 1972) espouses openness and self-disclosure as the major form of communication between people. In opposition to this school of thought are the instrumentalists who argue that the expressivists preach dysfunctional practices such as stylized language, insensitivity to roles and social situations, and a lack of concern for information propriety (but, see Sillars, 1974). The instrumentalists argue that interpersonal communication should function in a rhetorically sensitive way, which means that communication must show a concern for the self, the partner, and the situation (Hart, Carlson, & Eadie, 1980).

Couple types are expected to differ in the degree of their perceived openness and instrumentality both to one another and to people outside the marriage. A couple may, for example, be very open with one another yet reserved in discussing their feelings or opinions with others in general.

Expressive marital communication was measured by the perceived amount of disclosure in the marriage and the open expression of feelings between partners. Instrumental marital communication was measured by the willingness of one partner to inhibit the expression of thoughts or feelings that he or she experienced when communicating with the spouse (Fitzpatrick, 1976; Swenson & Gilner, 1973). The general approach to instrumental and expressive communication was measured by the Rhetsen scale (Hart et al., 1980). The expressive component of this scale measures the degree to which respondents agree that under all circumstances individuals should "tell it like it is." The instrumental component of this measure asks whether the respondent is willing to restrain what he or she says in conversations with others in order to avoid hurting them. Data were available only for the Pure couple types in this study. In total, 16 Independent, 17 Separate, and 10 Traditional couples completed these questionnaires.

A multivariate analysis of variance was computed with couple type as the independent variable and the six communication measures as the dependent variables. The overall F-test for the equality of the mean vectors, using the Wilks's lambda criterion, was significant [$F(12, 70) = 4.63$, $p < 0.0001$]. Table 7.4 lists the observed means and the differences among the Pure couple types on each communication measure.

The most expressive marital communication style is that of the Traditionals. Traditionals are more likely to express their feelings to their

TABLE 7.4
Mean Self-Report of Communication Style
by Pure Couple Type

	Couple Type		
Communication Style	Trad	Indep	Sep
Marital			
—Expression of positive feelings	2.17a	1.90b	1.86b
—Inhibition of expression of positive feelings	1.39b	1.39b	1.71a
—Self-disclosure	2.51a	2.33a	2.07b
—Spouse disclosure	2.51a	2.21b	2.01b
General			
—Expressivity	0.72b	1.02a	1.26a
—Instrumentality	1.92a	1.40b	1.99a

SOURCE: From M. A. Fitzpatrick (1984) in L. Berkowitz (Ed.) *A Typological Approach to Marital Interaction.* ©1984 by Academic Press. Reprinted by permission.

spouse and perceive a good deal of self-disclosure in their marriage. With individuals other than the spouse, however, the Traditionals are the least expressive of the couple types and tend to be very instrumental in their nonmarital communication. The expressivity in the marriage of the Traditionals concerns sharing anxieties and concerns rather than negative feelings about the spouse. Each is the major confidant for the other.

The Independents also are relatively expressive in communicating with their spouse, although they rate their spouses as disclosing to them less than the Traditionals. Independents see their spouses as unable or unwilling to burden them with their anxieties and worries. Independents retain their own expressivity with individuals other than their spouses. Less likely than the other couple types to be instrumental in their communication, Independents are more expressive with outsiders than are Traditionals.

The Separates have the least expressive marital communication style of the couple types. Inhibiting the expression of their feelings on a variety of issues. Separates disclose less to their spouses and see their spouses disclosing less to them than the other couple types see. Outside the relationship, the Separates are more expressive than the Traditionals but do try to restrain their communication with others.

The Pure couple types differ from one another in their perceptions of their marital communication behavior as well as in their evaluations of their own general communication style. In the next section, we examine the self-disclosive behaviors of married couples in conversations with one another and with opposite-sex others. The perception that one can discuss vulnerabilities with the spouse may not hold up in a behavioral test.

Disclosing to the Spouse and Others

The exchange of "objective information" about the self is more common in early stages of a relationship. In examining spouse versus stranger interaction, we predict that more objective information about the self would be exchanged with strangers than with the spouse, especially in the first few conversations. Once partners feel they understand one another, the exchange of such objective or factual information about the self probably decreases. Only Separate/Traditional couples spent any appreciable amount of time exchanging objective self-information with one another during their interactions.

Self-disclosure in ongoing relationships continues to involve the disclosure of feelings about the self but it now also can involve feelings about the partner and the relationship. Individuals in ongoing relationships may discuss their emotional reactions to one another and these reactions may become a major part of the relationship. Involved in a close personal relationship, self-disclosure includes disclosing about one's partner. Indeed, it may be argued that there is no "self-disclosure" because by the act of revealing oneself to others, one automatically is revealing a good deal about his or her marriage. Opening up to others then becomes a matter of how one spouse protects the vulnerabilities of the other in conversations with those outside the marriage. Independents are, however, committed to an ideology of openness and expressivity not only to the spouse but also to those outside the marriage. Consequently, we expect more intimate self-disclosure from those who subscribe to an ideology of intimacy than from more traditional individuals. For those who subscribe to a traditional ideology of relationships, however, some behaviors, such as self-disclosure, are reserved for the partner and entirely limited, or rationed, to others.

My colleagues and I set out to explore the relative level of self-disclosure in spouse versus stranger interactions through time. Mailings were sent to a local church asking couples to complete and return a questionnaire about marriage and to participate in a study (Fitzpatrick & Dindia, 1986a). One dollar was donated to the church for each returned questionnaire. All couples were recruited from the same church because we intended to study self-disclosure as naturalistically as possible. That is, we wanted the participants to have some social tie to one another in order to prevent "the stranger on the train phenomenon" or the extreme self-disclosure that occurs when individuals know they will never meet again. The church had 110 couples and 58 questionnaires were returned. From the 58 couples who completed the questionnaires, 20 married couples were recruited for three experimental sessions. At the end of the sessions, couples were paid $30.00.

The original questionnaires contained the Locke-Wallace (1959) scales and a series of demographic questions. There were no significant differences on the demographic variables between the participants in the experiment and the couples who completed the questionnaires. The husbands were 46, had completed two years of postsecondary school, had been married 17 years, and had two children. Their wives were 42 and the combined annual income was over $25,000. There were no significant differences between the level of marital satisfaction experienced by the questionnaire respondents and the experimental participants [$t(85)$ = 1.48; ns]. There were no male-female satisfaction differences in either the participant [$t(19)$ = .242] or the questionnaire sample [$t(57)$ = –1.64]. Five groups of four couples each came to the laboratory on three evenings over approximately a one-month period. Four laboratories had been set up as living rooms because each person was to have a private conversation with every other person in the group. Participation in each conversation, each evening, was randomized. Thus each participant talked to seven other people, three opposite-sex strangers, three same-sex strangers, and the spouse, once a week for three weeks. Each conversation lasted approximately 10 minutes. We collected 420 conversations. The design is a round-robin block design in which all possible pairs of subjects within a set interact with one another. With the forty subjects (20 couples), we have enough degrees of freedom to test the effects of interest.

Self-disclosure was coded using the Stiles coding scheme. The scheme allows the researcher to focus on self-referential information that is both objective (Edification) and subjective (Disclosure). Raters coded all the self-referential information for depth of intimacy. Intimacy was scored on a five-point scale. Table 7.5 gives a shortened version of the coding rules given the raters. Originally, five levels of intimacy were coded. Since such a small proportion of the conversation actually received the higher intimacy ratings, the two highest levels were combined.

The first chapter suggests that there are three major approaches to studying marital communication: Coorientational, interactional, and typological. Each of these approaches can be classified as *interpersonal*

TABLE 7.5
Coding Rules for Intimacy Level

How intimate was the disclosure?

The coder should use any number from 1 (low) to 5 (high) with the following scale descriptions as guidelines.

(1) Absence of personal involvement or intimacy; the speaker reveals auto-biographical or nonintimate information about himself/herself; e.g., I'm from Tomah. I know the Cantors.

(2) . . . .

(3) Equal attention to superficial and personal aspects of the topic; e.g., My parents got back together last week. They were separated for six months. It looks like they can work things out.

(4) . . . .

(5) Highly personal involvement or intimacy. The individual expresses personal information about him/herself in a way that the observer truly understands where the speaker stands in terms of his/her feelings and thoughts regarding the topic; e.g., It really makes me happy that my parents are getting back together. That separation really shook my sisters and I.

approaches because they argue that meaning in marital communication resides in the communication between people rather than in any underlying psychological process, individual difference, or personality characteristic. In a similar vein, both the linear and the dialectical models of self-disclosure and relationship development are also *interpersonal* in that the focus of investigation is on the interaction between people rather than any individual communicator characteristic.

The individual difference perspective is, however, alive and well in the study of marital communication. Researchers and theorists, notably psychoanalysts and trait theorists, still suggest that *intrapersonal* traits, characteristics, and abilities make a marriage stable and mutually satisfying or unstable and full of discontent (Kelly & Conley, 1987). Specifically in the area of self-disclosure, the search for individual difference characteristics, which relate to the successful and unsuccessful use of self-disclosure, is a growth industry.

Interpersonal and intrapersonal models of marital communication are not mutually exclusive, despite the rhetoric on both sides (Berkowitz, 1985; Doherty & Rider, 1979). The interpersonal perspective may be construed as a description of how the intrapersonal one operates. High levels of self-disclosure by one communicator *because of* a disposition to

TABLE 7.6
Relative Variance Partitioning in the
Spouse-Stranger Design

	Actor		Partner		Relationship	
	Male	Female	Male	Female	Male	Female
Disclosure						
Intimacy						
Low	.00	.00	.00	.00	.92	.92
Medium	.00	.00	.12	.01	.74	.88
High	.17	.00	.07	.07	.69	.78
Edification						
Intimacy						
Low	.20	.01	.05	.08	.59	.74
Medium	.18	.00	.05	.00	.78	.93
High	.39	.00	.00	.22	.61	.78

NOTE: This is the percentage of variance accounted for across the entire spouse-stranger design for these variables, broken down by male and female communicators.

be open change the nature and the direction of the interaction between that communicator and others.

Until recently, we have not had the methodological tools to consider intrapersonal and interpersonal variables at the same time. The round-robin analysis of variance allows the simultaneous test of the intrapersonal and the interpersonal nature of self-disclosure in marital and stranger dyads. The intrapersonal perspective is tested by examining the actor and partner effects in the design. The actor effect examines how likely an individual is to self-disclose across conversational partners ("I am just an open person"). The partner effects test the degree to which an individual tends to elicit self-disclosure from others ("People always open up to me"). The interpersonal perspective is tested by examining the relationship effects in this design. The relationship effects test the degree to which the self-disclosive behaviors are a function of the particular adjustments that conversational partners make to one another. Table 7.6 lists the variance accounted for by the relationship effects for self-disclosure.

Two patterns emerge when examining the data for relationship variance. First, most of the variance in self-disclosure can be accounted for the subtle adjustments that conversational partners make to one another. The relationship-level variance displayed in Table 7.6 makes this clear. The high level of variance accounted for by the relationships between the communicators suggests that those theorists who study self-disclosure as a relationship or interpersonal phenomenon and consider the degree of reciprocity and so forth between interactants are on the right track.

Second, the role of actor and partner effects appears to grow in strength as the intimacy of the material exchanged increases. Relatively less variance is accounted for by relationship factors as the messages become more intimate. Actor and partner factors (i.e., intrapersonal factors) explain more of the variation in the exchange of highly intimate self-references than in the exchange of low-intimacy information. This suggests that the interpersonal perspective explains more of the variance in less intimate self-references. Members of a culture are able to negotiate an appropriate and dyad-specific level of low-intimacy self-disclosure in initial conversations, beyond their individual traits and or dispositions. It is in the disclosure of highly intimate information that the personality traits of a speaker or a listener can explain some of the variation in behavior. Intriguingly, this result supports models that suggest as relationships progress, communication becomes more idiosyncratic and tied to the individual characteristics of the communicators. Thus the individual difference perspective cannot be ignored when examining close relationships and the exchange of intimacies. The individual difference perspective shoule be given more attention in the study of communication in close relationships.

In combination, these two patterns warrant an examination of the factors that contribute to actor and partner variance in self-disclosure as well as a consideration of the reciprocity or compensation of self-disclosure across dyads. How do actor, partner, and relationship effects discriminate among the disclosures of husbands and wives?

The round-robin design does not allow a direct statistical comparison between couples in the various types as to their levels of self-disclosure to spouses and strangers. Rather it examines the differences between spouses and strangers, the strength of individual speaker and listener differences in directing message choices, and the role that various relational dimensions (i.e., ideology, interdependence, and so forth) play in accounting for message behavior. The components presented below may be said to tap what makes marriage a special relationship in terms of self-referential communication in comparison to the relationship established with others. These components may be said to represent the "intrapersonal" aspects of a model of self-disclosure.

Level. The difference between the average proportion of various intensities of disclosure to a spouse can be compared to disclosure to a

TABLE 7.7
Spouse Versus Stranger Differences in Self-Referential Talk

| | Female Behavior | | Male Behavior | |
	To Husbands	To Men	To Wives	To Women
Disclosure				
Low	.38	.40	.39	.42
Medium	.45	.39*	.40	.39
High	.41	.24*	.38	.24*
Edification				
Low	.52	.59	.51	.63*
Medium	.19	.13	.13	.13
High	.04	.02	.06	.04

NOTE: Asterisk indicates that there is a significant difference at the .05 or better between wives' (husbands') behavior directed toward husbands (wives) versus behavior directed toward opposite sex strangers.

stranger. Table 7.7 presents the difference between the average wife's response to her husband compared to the average female response to men in general and the average husband's response to his wife compared to average male response to women in general. Spouses disclose more to one another than to opposite-sex strangers. The exception to this rule is that males tend to reveal significantly more objective information about themselves at low levels of intimacy to female conversational partners than to their wives. In disclosing to women, males favored factual and nonemotional information. Women appear to engage in higher levels of self-disclosure, particularly in exchanging intimate information with their husbands, than do men.

Actor effect. We can examine the relationship between an individual's tendencies to self-disclose to opposite-sex others and the tendency to disclose to the spouse. This effect comes close to a behavioral test of the self-report data presented above. There is no systematic relationship for self-referential talk between how these women communicate with other men and how they communicate with their husbands. The more (less) a husband disclosed highly intimate information to his wife during these conversation, the more (less) he disclosed highly intimate facts about himself to the other women with whom he spoke. It appears that these husbands had particular characteristics that led them to be open to women, or not to be open with women, whereas the disclosure of the wives to their husbands was not systematically related to how they dealt with other men.

Partner effect. If the spouse tends to elicit self-disclosure from a mate, does that mean he or she is more (or less) likely to elicit disclosure in any form from opposite-sex others? Partner effects operate differently for husbands and wives. For highly intimate information, there is a strong positive relationship between a wife's elicitation ability with her husband and with other men. The more (less) intimate information a wife can elicit from her husband, the more (less) she can elicit from other men. Some women appear to be extremely good at drawing men out and this skill operates both with the husband and with other men. It appears clear, however, that if the woman is not very good at drawing men out in general, she will not be a particularly good receiver of her husband's self-disclosures.

Men appear to specialize in that the more intimate information a man receives from his wife, the less personal information he receives from other women. Husbands can be extremely good sounding boards for their wives yet not for other women.

Typological effect. Unfortunately, we cannot divide this sample of couples into couples types and explore the relationships among actor, partner, and relationship effects in this design. We did, however, correlate ideology, sharing, conflict avoidance, and marital satisfaction with the total disclosure and edification scores in the marital dialogues. These correlations replicate the behavioral pattern seen in the first study in this chapter. Those who subscribe to the ideology of traditionalism and have high degrees of companionship in the marriage (Traditionals) are less likely to self-disclose to the spouse whereas those with a less conventional ideology (Independents) use more self-disclosure. Avoiding conflict is related to suppressing self-disclosure in marriage.

Reciprocity of self-disclosure. Most of the variance in self-disclosive communication in these dyads can be accounted for by relationship factors. Self-disclosure is better predicted by the specific adjustments that individuals make to one another in conversations. Conceptually, these adjustments are discussed as reciprocal (or its opposite, compensatory) processes.

What is reciprocity? At least three "interpersonal" definitions of reciprocity exist. The first may be called *covariant reciprocity* in that changes in one partner's disclosure covary with changes in the other partner's disclosure (Hill & Stull, 1982). The rate of exchange of personal information by a husband may be correlated to the rate of exchange of personal information by the wife. Much of the extant literature measures this type of self-disclosure. In general, intersubjective perceptions of self-disclosure in families and personal relationships are positively related, objective observations of self-disclosures of dyadic partners are positively related, and a confederate's self-disclosure has a positive effect

TABLE 7.8
Correlation Between the Relational Dimensions and
Self-Referential Messages in Marital Dialogues

	Total Disclosure	Total Edification
Marital Satisfaction	−.18	−.32*
Ideology of Traditionalism	−.33*	.12
Ideology of Uncertainty	.34*	.19
Sharing	−.31*	−.06
Conflict Avoidance	−.39**	−.04

NOTE: These are Pearson product-moment correlations: *p < .10; **p < .05.

on a subject's actual disclosure (Dindia, 1982, 1985). The criticism leveled against this definition of reciprocity and its measurement is that it does not actually demonstrate a relationship between the self-disclosive behaviors of the communicators. Mary and John may have a high correlation in any given conversation for self-disclosive behaviors, but this correlation does not tell us, prima facie, that there is a systematic relationship between Mary's disclosures and John's disclosures. Methodologically, the correlation between the communication behaviors of this couple confounds base rates with levels of behavior.

The second interpersonal definition may be called *contiguous reciprocity* where one person's disclosure changes the probability of disclosure by the other. Gottman (1979) defines reciprocity as probability changes in behavior or an immediate lockstep trading of behaviors. In a similar vein, Cappella (1979) defines reciprocity as mutual positive influence. This definitions of reciprocity suggest a tit-for-tat exchange where the disclosure of a husband begets an immediate disclosure by the wife. Dindia (1982) has found that such a pattern of self-disclosure is not usually exhibited in conversation. I think this is because such a tit-for-tat reciprocity in self-disclosure is extremely inappropriate. This concept of self-disclosure predicts the following dialogue.

Husband: I think I'm getting a migraine. I had a terrible day at the office.
Wife: I'm the one who had the bad day. Your kids are driving me crazy. . . .

Dindia (1982) finds that self-disclosures usually lead to acknowledgments, requests for clarification, and so forth. Note how much more competent the following exchange is.

TABLE 7.9
**Reciprocity Versus Compensation in Self-Referential Talk
in Marital Dyads Across Three Conversations**

	DD1	DD2	DD3	DE1	DE2
Conversation One					
DD2	.44*				
DD3	−.57*	.04	.48*		
DE1	.04	−.10	−.34		
DE2	−.58*	−.29	.17	.08	
DE3	−.41	.50*	.26	−.44*	.66*
Conversation Two					
DD1	.50*				
DD2	.48*	.62*			
DD3	.46*	.57*			
DE1	−.55*	−.18	−.16		
DE2	−.41	−.09	−.23	.70*	
DE3	−.25	.16	.68*	−.08	
Conversation Three					
DD1	.47*				
DD2	−.57*				
DD3	−.59*	.77*			
DE1	.05	−.31	−.52*		
DE2	−.33	.38	.32		

NOTE: Asterisk marks correlation significant at the .05.

Husband:	I think I'm getting a migraine. I had a terrible day at the office.
Wife:	Oh, what happened? Are you having trouble getting that request to the vendors finished?

The third interpersonal concept of reciprocity may be called *delayed reciprocity* where disclosure is reciprocated, but not necessarily in such a tit-for-tat manner. Spouses may reciprocate disclosures over an extended period of time. Reciprocity delayed over time may be the essence of an interpersonal relationship yet it is one not easily studied in an experimental context.

Apart from the issues of timing of the response that undergird the three interpersonal forms of reciprocity, the disclosures exchanged may or may not be equal in value on some predetermined dimension of breadth, depth, and so forth. The reciprocity examined in this study is a form of covariant reciprocity in which the reciprocity correlation between spouses has been adjusted, statistically, for individual speaker and listener differences in self-disclosure. Furthermore, by rating the intimacy level of the information exchanged, we can examine the degree to which the reciprocal exchange of self-disclosive behaviors is equivalent (or not).

The high amount of variance accounted for suggests a good deal of behavioral adjustment took place in these conversations. In the first conversation for the spouses in this experiment, disclosures at the same level of intensity or only one level above or below tend to be reciprocated: Disclosures two units apart in personalness tend to be compensated. This suggests a rule for marital dialogue: Be only as personal in conversation as is your spouse and only gradually increase the personalness of your remarks, being careful to match that of your partner. This rule needs to be modified in the second and third conversations. In this conversation, spouses show a high degree of reciprocity of the self-disclosures of their partners. After extracting individual differences, and examining these dialogues through time, reciprocity of self-disclosure occurs in marital dialogues. This reciprocity is not the contiguous form discussed by Gottman and Cappella but rather the average matching that occurs across a conversation for spouses.

Summary

Folk wisdom suggests that men are less expressive than women and social scientists have written of what they see as the "tragedy of the inexpressive male" (Balswick & Peek, 1971). Men, the argument goes, are socialized not to show any weakness and become so skillful at hiding their feelings and thoughts that not even their closest associates know when they are depressed, anxious, or afraid. Women, on the other hand, are socialized to show their emotions and to discuss their feelings with their friends and romantic partners.

A good deal of recent evidence, however, indicates that in close relationships, the pattern of the silent male and the talkative female may not be a good description of the interaction. Reis, Senchak, and Solomon (1985) show that whereas men may inhibit their disclosure in conversations with other men and with women with whom they are not well acquainted, men do disclose at relatively high levels to their opposite-sex romantic partners. Thus close relationships with women are one context (perhaps the only context) in which males can be expressive. Expressivity for males may occur, when it occurs at all, only with the spouse.

The sex roles of the Traditionals are very conventional ones in that the male is expected to be task oriented, concerned with problem solving, and dominant while his wife is nurturant and concerned with the relationship

(Fitzpatrick & Indvik, 1982). The women in this marriage type see themselves as very feminine and the males see themselves as masculine. Communicatively, this would suggest that the Traditional husband would not discuss his feelings with his wife or with others. Contrary to expectations, the Traditional husband can share his positive feelings about his spouse as well as his own anxieties and worries with his wife. However, this is the limit of the expressivity of this male, and his wife is the traditional husband's only confidant. This wife appears to be able to draw the husband out and helps him to express his feelings.

The traditional ideology specifies that spouses should fulfill marriage roles defined as important by society. Traditionals approach marriage like "structuralists" (e.g., Parsons, 1951) in that they define their marital roles according to culturally based categories about appropriate behavior for husbands and wives. Recently, two new family roles have emerged in American culture: the therapeutic and the companionship roles. Both of these roles specify that it is the duty of spouses to listen to one another, to help with each other's worries and anxieties, and to be pleasant companions with similar leisure time interests (Nye, 1976). A commitment to these new roles specifies that a spouse, even a husband, must communicate with his wife. He is to be assisted in this endeavor by an understanding wife. Thus what appears at first to be an anomaly, the Traditional husband disclosing to his wife, is actually now part of the appropriate role behavior for males when married. This communication is limited, however, by the views of the Traditionals on conflict. Traditionals believe in exercising restraint in expressing negative feelings to the spouse.

In contrast, Independents believe in less conventional sex roles and these husbands and wives are more likely to see themselves as androgynous (having positive masculine and feminine traits) than the other couple types. Androgynous people are more flexible in adopting interpersonal behaviors not usually associated with their own sex. Both husbands and wives in these couples are able to express their feelings, including those feelings that society traditionally limits to the opposite sex. Thus the husband can express his vulnerability and the wife, her anger.

The ideology of the Independents values spontaneity and change in relationships. Couples who adhere to this viewpoint attempt to construct their own husband and wife roles according to their individualized preferences. These couples approach marriage like "interactionists" (e.g., Turner, 1970) in that they attempt to negotiate and create rules in the course of the marriage rather than to follow culturally prescribed roles.

All the values of the Independents stress disclosing to the spouse whether the disclosure is positive or negative.

The disengagement of the Separates from one another means that they rarely experience emotion in the relationship. When they do, their extreme preferences to avoid conflict and limit their expressiveness indicate that these couples engage in a minimum of affective self-disclosure. The Separates are extremely conventional in their sex-role orientations. The Separate husband sees himself as masculine sex-typed yet his wife sees herself as unable to engage in typical feminine behaviors. Unlike the Traditional relationship where the wife draws her husband out and helps him to express his emotions, this Separate wife lacks this interpersonal skill.

CONCLUSION

The typology answers some basic questions concerning communication in close relationships. First, the typology argues that individuals use communication in diverse ways based on implicit assumptions about what constitutes appropriate or desirable communication in maintaining a marital relationship. Second, these implicit assumptions determine the functional relationship between communication and satisfaction (Fitzpatrick, 1976). In the post-1960s culture, open and supportive communication was considered the essence of a good relationship. Research with the typology, however, clearly indicates that openness in disclosing oneself to the spouse is not an effective marital communication strategy for all couples.

Traditionals value self-disclosure in marriage and they behaviorally disclose to their spouses. The kind of openness in a Traditional marriage limits self-disclosure to positive feelings and topics about the partner and the relationship. This pattern of self-disclosure leads to a very satisfying and adjusted relationship between the partners. For Traditional couples, it is inaccurate to assume that open communication is a critical mediator of marital satisfaction. Many roles are defined by conventional belief in this type of marriage, hence there is less need to negotiate openly with the spouse. Furthermore, these couples may have less negative affect to exchange with the spouse than others have.

Independents also value self-disclosure and have been found to disclose substantially more to their spouses than do the other couples. The openness of the Independents is less restrained in that these couples are willing to disclose both positive and negative feelings to one another.

This kind of openness is related to tension and conflict in the relationship. The Independents, albeit very cohesive as a couple, exhibit dissatisfaction with the marriage, disagree with one another on a variety of topics, and have serious conflicts with the spouse. The expressivity of these couples is related to marital dysfunctioning. For the Independents, however, relationships are meaningful only to the extent that they are dedicated both to psychological closeness and to growth and change. Open communication and the confrontation of conflict are a sign of relational vitality for these couples although they pay a price in satisfaction for the intensity of the relationship.

The open style of communication is likely to violate the autonomy, privacy, and emotional distance of the Separates. Separates do not value openness and disclosure in marriage and also do not self-disclose to their spouses. The reserve of the Separates may be a communication strategy that promotes moderate satisfaction in marriage. The Separates, who agree with their spouse on a number of marital and family issues, are not very cohesive as a couple, or affectionate with one another. Neither the extreme openness of the Independents nor the extreme reserve of the Separates leads to the highest possible outcome for the marriage. Moderation in the degree and kind of self-disclosure seems to lead to more satisfaction in marriage.

The literature needs a more pluralistic view of what constitutes "good" communication in marriage and other close relationships. The potentially oppressive result for couples seeking help is that "good communication" may require conformity to someone else's idea of what constitutes a satisfying relationship. Within prescriptive communication programs, couples are urged to confront conflicts, self-disclose, and speak in terms that are descriptive, consistent, and direct. Indeed, couples regardless of their ideological orientation or levels of interdependence in marriage are urged to become Independents. The Independent relationship matches the dominant ideology of relationships promulgated in the literature of interpersonal communication and may even match the marital type of most researchers in close relationships. The Independent relationship is not the only marital type or even necessarily the most satisfying.

NOTES

1. The interaction term sex by couple type (ST) is included in all the models because that is fixed by the sampling plan. Its inclusion will keep the estimated, expected two-dimensional marginal totals for sex (S) and couple type (T) equal to the observed totals fixed

by design. No further interpretation of this interaction (ST) is warranted (Bishop et al., 1975, pp. 70-73).

It should be understood that this model constitutes a nested hierarchy, and the inclusion of a higher-order term implies the inclusion of all lower-order effects involving the same variables. In addition, in interpreting the test of fit of the model, it is important to remember that the chi-square is due to error generated by the restriction of the model. If the chi-square is not statistically significant, then the model is a reasonably good fit to the observed frequencies (Swafford, 1980).

2. Gender differences in interpersonal communication must be studied in the context of the attitudes and values that males and females hold on gender issues and sex roles. The continuation of the study of "sex differences" without anchoring these differences in cultural values, norms, and so forth will lead to more confusion than enlightenment.

8

Communicating
Without Words
Sending and Receiving Nonverbal Messages

Not all human communication is linguistic or verbal. A spouse is rarely confronted with a disembodied transcript of a marital conversation. Gestures, facial expressions, pacing or position, touch, posture, gaze, and paralinguistic cues (e.g., pitch, volume, tone of voice, rate of speech, pausing, interruptions) are all part of nonverbal communication. And, these facets of communication reveal important emotional dynamics of the marital relationship. Nonverbal channels are continually attended to and seem to communicate information that is primarily affective in quality and reflective of personal relationships with, and attitudes toward, others (Brown, 1986). Throughout this book, we have seen that couples in various types of marriages use language differently to communicate with their spouses. In this chapter, we are concerned with nonverbal communication in various types of marriages, especially with what nonverbal communication can tell us about the nature of the emotional relationship between spouses. We have completed only two studies on the nonverbal communication of emotion in couples. Consequently, this chapter ends on a more speculative and theoretical note than do the previous chapters. The first of the two studies is an interaction study that examines the spontaneous display of nonverbal cues indicating the actor's underlying feelings or attitudes toward the spouse (Patterson, 1985). This study measures the responsiveness of couples to one another by examining decreased distance, increased gaze and touch, more direct body orientation, and greater facial expressiveness in marital interaction. The second study employs a standard content paradigm that examines the symbolic display of emotion to the spouse through nonverbal communication.[1] One spouse communicates neutral or ambiguous sentences and uses the nonverbal channels to convey a number of different intentions and emotions to the other. The listener-spouse decides which message is communicated by interpreting the nonverbal cues. These two studies illuminate how couples respond to one another in interaction nonverbally and how accurate (inaccurate) each is in picking up the emotional meaning behind the words.

After reporting the two studies, I speculate about how the level of interdependence in the various couples may predict different emotional reactions to themselves, to one another, and in reference to their relationship. Future research is needed on the emotional connections among the spouses in the various marital types and on the nonverbal communication that expresses the state of that emotional connection.

NONVERBAL COMMUNICATION OF EMOTION

In considering how couples communicate their feelings, emotions, and attitudes toward one another through nonverbal communication, we are not assuming that the only function of nonverbal communication is the communication of emotion. Nonverbal communication may serve purposes other than the communication of emotion. The use of certain gestures, tones, and so forth may, for example, help the speaker to be better understood by the listener. Nor do we assume that nonverbal communication is inherently better able than language to communicate affect. The love sonnets of Shakespeare do a remarkably good job of communicating emotion to the reader (or the one being read to) yet the author's exclusively verbal contribution is the key factor. Our position is that language is a universal medium capable of expressing anything that can be thought or felt, whereas nonverbal communication is specialized to a restricted domain of meanings (Brown, 1986). In that restricted domain, the communication of affect is a primary function of nonverbal channels.

Nonverbal Responsiveness

What behaviors signal closeness (or lack of closeness) between husbands and wives in the various couple types? A functional approach to

TABLE 8.1
Average Nonverbal Responsiveness Cues for
Husbands and Wives Across Couple Types

	Husbands	Wives
Traditional	40.54	47.23
Independent	31.17	31.83
Separate	23.90	32.20
Separate/Traditional	24.50	43.67
Mixed	37.58	51.17

NOTE: These cues include postural orientation (body lean and touch), gaze, smiling, and laughter.

answering this question stresses the related and patterned nature of communication behavior in contrast to the channel approach that analyses behaviors in isolation. The functional perspective demands an examination of a variety of nonverbal cues in one interaction and an assessment of the exchange of cues between partners. In a functional model (Patterson, 1983) intimacy and closeness between people are signaled by close interpersonal distance (including touch, lean, and body orientation), postural openness and head nods, and gaze and facial expressiveness. Touching and mutual gaze are especially important. Increased intimacy is indicated by decreased distance, increased gaze and touch, more direct body orientation, more forward lean, greater facial expressiveness, and increased postural openness. The Separates, although above the midpoint on scales of marital satisfaction, are expected to demonstrate less openness and union with the spouse than do the other couples. Separates keep a distance in their relationship and this distance should be reflected in the nonverbal communication of the spouses. Since the Separates are less interdependent with one another, these couples are expected to demonstrate nonverbally less involvement with one another than couples in the other types.

In total, 13 Traditionals, 10 Separates, 6 Independents, 5 Separate Traditionals, and 17 Mixed types participated in this experiment. Touching the spouse, forward body lean toward the spouse, direct body orientation to the spouse, gazing at the spouse, smiling and laughter were positive intimacy cues. Fifteen minutes of interaction were analyzed. The onset, duration, and direction of the intimacy cues was measured.

The Separates displayed fewer intimacy cues in this fifteen-minute interaction segment than did the other couples. The emotional distance in the Separate marriage appears in their use of these nonverbal intimacy cues. Traditional and Mixed husbands displayed more positive cues than

TABLE 8.2
First-Order Lag Sequential Analysis
Results for Responsiveness

	TRAD		INDEP		SEP		SEP/TRAD		MIXED	
	Z	PHI	Z	PHI	Z	PHI	Z	PHI	Z	PHI
WH	3.28	.15	1.83	.13	3.67	.23	2.67	.20	5.39	.21
HW	4.92	.23	4.33	.30	2.15	.14	3.85	.29	4.12	.16

NOTE: Responsiveness involves the exchange of positive involvement cues. The phi coefficients are better estimates of the strength of the relationship than the z-score because these coefficients are not affected by sample size.

did the other husbands whereas traditional wives in both Traditional and Separate/Traditional and the Mixed couples displayed a high number of positive intimacy cues.

We were interested not only in average differences in these cues but also the level of responsiveness between partners to the nonverbal intimacy cues of the spouse. Responsiveness was defined as the reciprocation of positive affiliation cues. A functional view of interpersonal communication stresses the equivalence of different behaviors in serving the same function (see Street & Cappella, 1985). When a wife smiles at her husband, he may return that intimate and friendly gesture with a touch or a look, not necessarily with a smile (although he may, of course, return the smile with a smile).

The lag sequential analysis results indicated that wives in the Separate and Mixed couple types are more likely to be responsive to their husbands than are the wives in the other marriages and than their own husbands are to them. Gottman and Levenson (1987) argue that the process of marital disintegration begins with the husband's emotional retreat from the marriage. This retreat can be seen in the nonverbal behavior of husbands and wives: Husbands display less positive affect in response to their wives whereas wives become even more responsive to the positive affect of their husbands. This *husband-retreat, wife-entreat pattern* appears with the Separate and Mixed couples. These husbands are withdrawn from the marriage: Any positive sign of interest on their part is immediately reciprocated by their wives.

In contrast, husbands in the Traditional, Independent, and Separate/Traditional marriages are much more likely to respond to the positive cues of their wives. These males are more responsive than are males in the other marital types. The Separate/Traditional marriage, despite the husband's emotional distance, is one in which the husband is emotionally invested.

Separates are less involved in these marital conversations when nonverbal measures of intimacy and affiliation are taken. The emotional distance in the Separate marriage is indicated by less smiling, laughter, forward body lean, touching and gazing at the spouse in their dialogues. The husband in this marriage is not likely to respond to the positive intimacy moves by his wife. Traditionals in line with their discussions of themselves as close and emotionally united exhibit a high average number of positive intimacy cues. Traditional husbands are very responsive to their wives' positive affiliation cues. Both Independent husbands and wives exhibit on the average fewer positive intimacy cues but the husband in this marriage is very responsive to his wife's positive cues. In the Separate/Traditional marriage, the husband emits fewer overall positive intimacy and his wife emits a large average number. This husband is extremely responsive, nonverbally, to his wife. In the other Mixed types, the husband emits a moderately high number of positive cues and his wife emits more positive cues on the average than anyone. This wife is more responsive to her husband than he is to her. In the next section, we explore closeness and distance in these marriages by focusing on intentional emotional exchanges.

Accuracy in the Nonverbal Communication of Emotion

Couples in the various types of marriage are differentially responsive to the positive cues of their mates. To what degree are couples in the various types able to communicate both positive and negative emotions to one another accurately? A lack of responsiveness to one's spouse may come about because the mate has not perceived positive cues. To test for accuracy, we employed a standard content paradigm. Standard content tasks involve the use of neutral or ambiguous words to express a number of different intentions. Participants may ask a question such as "What are you doing?" to express anger, surprise, or interest. Noller (1984) has conducted a series of studies requesting happily and unhappily married couples, using a set of standard messages, to communicate a positive, negative, or neutral message to the spouse. The partner's task was to decide which of the three alternative intentions the partner was actually sending.

In a recent study, Guthrie and Noller (1988) discovered that happily and unhappily married spouses differed in communicating specific emotions. For example, all couples clearly communicated anger (anger could be perceived accurately regardless of the relationship happiness) yet

TABLE 8.3
Example of a Standard Content Message

SITUATION:
You walk into the room where your husband is:
  INTENTION
    Version 1:
      (a)   You are really angry, because he is doing something that you have asked him repeatedly not to do.
    Version 2:
      (b)   You are really pleased, because he is obviously trying to do you a favor.
    Version 3:
      (c)   You are not sure what he is up to, and you are a bit curious.
  STATEMENT
  You say:

  WHAT ARE YOU DOING?

---

the unhappily married had more trouble with depression. Consequently, Patricia Noller and I extended the standard content paradigm to include specific emotions. We measured the communication of pleasure, affection, depression, and anger in couples of various types.

In total, 18 Traditionals, 13 Independents, 8 Separates, and 26 Mixed type couples participated in this experiment. Ten situations with different phrasings for husbands and wives were constructed with three versions. Spouses were to communicate either a positive (affection or pleasure), negative (anger or depression), or neutral emotion. The task for each couple was to decide whether the spouse intended to communicate affection, pleasure, depression, anger, or neutrality. The spouse was presented with the same three situations as the communicator and had to decide whether the emotion communicated was positive, negative, or neutral. In addition, each speaker rated their own communication clarity on each item and each listener rated how confident he or she was of the rating made of each item. Turns were randomized, with one spouse starting as the speaker for all 30 situations.

Across the entire sample, husbands and wives were more accurate in communicating anger and depression than in communicating affection and pleasure. Couples also gave themselves the highest scores on both their ability to communicate anger and their ability to understand anger when communicated to them. Although all couples were as good at seeing depression as they were at perceiving anger, married couples were less

TABLE 8.4
Grand Means for Dependent Variables

	Accuracy	Speaker Clarity		Listener Confidence	
		Correct	Incorrect	Correct	Incorrect
Affection	3.45	4.85	4.11	4.93	4.38
Pleasure	3.38	4.95	4.42	5.08	4.40
Depression	4.06	4.76	4.29	5.10	4.27
Anger	4.15	5.22	4.72	5.28	4.40

NOTE: The accuracy measures can range from 0 to 5 for each emotion, whereas the confidence and clarity ratings can range from 1 to 6.

TABLE 8.5
Accuracy in Interpreting Nonverbal Emotional Cues
of the Spouse

	Affection	Pleasure	Depression	Anger	Neutrality
Traditional					
Husband	3.44	3.83	4.11	3.94	6.89
Wife	3.72	2.61	4.28	3.94	6.50
Independent					
Husband	4.08	4.23	4.39	4.46	10.00
Wife	3.31	3.15	4.08	4.15	7.54
Separate					
Husband	3.38	3.75	3.63	3.63	6.00
Wife	2.38	3.13	3.50	3.63	6.75
Mixed					
Husband	3.81	3.85	4.12	4.46	9.77
Wife	3.04	2.77	3.96	4.31	9.62
$F (4, 121)$	2.29	4.76	.22	.16	.37
$P <$	.06	.001	nsd	nsd	nsd

sure that they could clearly communicate or recognize the communication of depression.

Table 8.5 indicates that across all the emotional states, the Separate husbands were the least accurate of the husbands in any of the couple types in interpreting their wives. Their wives also were less accurate for all emotional expressions, except their husband's pleasure. The Independent husband more accurately perceived the communication of both affection and pleasure from his wife, although it is the Traditional wife who more accurately perceives the communication of affection or sexual interest on

TABLE 8.6

Average Correlations Between Speaker Clarity and
Listener Confidence Ratings for Each Couple Type

	Traditional	Independent	Separate	Mixed
Affection	.31	.40*	.35	.25
Pleasure	.20	.33	.02	.19
Depression	.27	.36*	.42	.31*
Anger	.25	.23	.50*	.26

NOTE: Asterisk indicates that the correlation is significant at the .05 level. The correlations reported are based on different sample sizes. Little importance can be attached to correlation coefficients calculated on small samples unless they are fairly large.

the part of her husband. Independent wives accurately perceive their husbands' expressions of pleasure.

For the Traditionals, there was no significant relationship between how the speaker rated his or her clarity in communicating and how confident the listener was in his or her evaluation of the emotion expressed. For Independents, significant relationships existed for clarity and confidence for affection or sexual interest and for depression. The better Independents rated their clarity in communicating affection or depression, the more confident the Independent receiver. Mixed types were also connected for their depression ratings whereas Separates had a high correlation between clarity and confidence only for anger.

Regardless of their wives' accuracy, Separate husbands rated themselves as significantly less clear in communicating their pleasure than did the other husbands.[2] Separate wives saw themselves communicating less clearly than did the other wives on the items their husbands judged correctly. Both partners in the Separate marriage saw themselves as unable to communicate their pleasure or happiness to one another. The wife in this marriage accurately perceived her husband's nonverbal communication of pleasure yet was no more confident in that judgment than other wives. Separates were also less accurate in perceiving the communication of sexual interest or affection on the part of their spouses. Separate wives were extremely inaccurate in understanding their husband's sexual interest, although the husband rates himself as good at communicating these emotions as other husbands.

Affection dealt with the communication of sexual attention or interest. In all of the marriages except for the Traditional one, husbands were significantly better than wives in accurately interpreting the communication of sexual interest and affection. The Traditional wife rated

TABLE 8.7
**Speaker Judgments of Clarity for Correct and Incorrect
Pleasure Items**

| | Pleasure | |
| | Speaker Clarity | |
	Correct	Incorrect
Traditional		
Husband	4.70	3.97
Wife	5.25	4.69
Independent		
Husband	4.93	3.66
Wife	5.40	4.59
Separate		
Husband	4.27	3.51
Wife	4.82	4.61
Mixed		
Husband	4.55	4.52
Wife	5.13	5.30
	$F (4, 110) = 3.18$	$F (4, 94) = 4.29$
	$p < .01$	$p < .003$

herself as communicating clearly on those items that her husband missed. Husbands were good at interpreting displays of pleasure, with the Independent husband the most accurate. And, wives rated themselves highly on their ability to communicate accurately their pleasure to their husbands with wives in the Mixed couple types giving themselves the highest ratings.

Summary

The Separates are the least accurate in decoding the emotional communications of their spouses because close emotional connections are not part of the Separate schema of marriage. The most inaccurate of the spouses are the Separates and these couples have difficulty in recognizing the positive emotions of pleasure and sexual interest. Independent couples, who include strong emotional states in their construction of marriage, recognize these emotions significantly more frequently than couples in the other types of marriages.

These results for nonverbal communication accuracy parallel the findings in Chapter 3 for coorientational accuracy: Separates are the least accurate of the couples in predicting the gender attributions of their spouses and in understanding the emotional communications of their spouses. The Separate wife does poorly in interpreting her husband's sexual interest. Although this husband feels he cannot clearly communicate his positive affect to his wife, in general, this couple does not appear to "know" that they do not communicate very well. They are equally as confident in their judgments of the nonverbal communication of emotions of their spouse as are other couples.

Separates think they are able to communicate their anger and hostility to one another and feel confident when they see this emotion but the confidence is misplaced. Anger is poorly communicated in this marriage. The conflict avoidance of the Separates may be related to the fact that when one spouse thinks they are clearly communicating their anger and hostility, the other misperceives that emotion and is very confident in that misperception. Separates misconstrue anger as some other emotion, usually neutrality. The schematic commitment to emotional distance and conflict avoidance affects the interpretation of anger and hostility in this marriage. The misperception occurs yet both are confident in their communication clarity and their communication accuracy.

The Independents are the most accurate in understanding the emotional messages of their spouses and significantly more accurate than other couples for affection and pleasure. The Independent wife credits herself with being extremely clear in communicating pleasure to her spouse and both are confident that they have good communication. This communication system demonstrates strong positive correlations between clarity and confidence for affection and depression. As Independents clearly communicate their sexual interest, the spouse is confident that he or she understands the message. The accuracy data for affection suggests that Independents do have clear, open sexual communication. For depression, the same pattern holds. Independents see themselves as clearly communicating depression and confidently understanding the depressive communication of their spouses. The accuracy data for these couples indicate that this confidence is well-placed. Independent couples have clear, open emotional communication systems and are confident in their ability to understand the nonverbal messages of their spouses. Their overall accuracy suggests that the Independent listeners should be confident in their judgments of the emotions expressed by their spouses.

Traditional couples are confident that they can read the nonverbal communications of their spouses and think they communicate very well nonverbally yet are not particularly accurate in deciding which emotion their spouse intended to communicate. Indeed, Traditional husbands do as poorly as Separate ones in seeing their wives' sexual interest although the wives think they have clearly communicated such an interest. The major form of accurate emotional communication in this marriage is that the Traditional wife is good in discerning her husband's sexual interest. Her husband does moderately well in discerning her pleasure whereas she does poorly in understanding his pleasant moods. The emotional communication system in this marriage suggests some clearly sex-differentiated understanding of nonverbal communication. The wife understands her husband's communication of sexual interest yet not his pleasure, whereas he understands her pleasant moods but not her sexual interest.

Mixed couple types demonstrate different patterns for husbands and wives. Husbands in this marriages do as well as the Traditional husbands in understanding their wives' affection and pleasure and do almost as well as the Independent husbands on the other emotions. The confidence that these husbands have in their judgments of their wives' emotional communication is better placed than is the confidence of the Traditional husbands. For Mixed couples, the extreme confidence of the wives in their ability to read the emotional communications of their husbands is misplaced.

These two studies have just scratched the surface of the emotional connections in couples in these various types of marriages. In the next section, we offer some theoretical speculations on the experience of emotion in marriage.

THE EXPERIENCE OF
EMOTION IN MARRIAGE

The emotional systems of couples in the various types of marriages appear to be remarkably different both in what couples spontaneously express in one another's presence and in their differential ability to manipulate signals of emotional displays in order that their spouses can correctly read those displays. Does the typology have any insights as to why these emotional systems differ? To suggest an answer to this complex question, we need to turn to models of the cognitive bases of affect (Fitzpatrick, 1987b).

Research on the cognitive bases of affect suggests that the interruption of complex goal sequences causes arousal and emotion. The amount of cognitive interruption guides the intensity and direction of one's affective reaction. Two people who are intimate have a greater chance of interrupting each other's plans and violating each other's expectations. Within the context of a marriage, an individual can experience a number of emotional states that can possibly be communicated to the spouse. An emotional state can be positive or negative. Further, this positive or negative affect can be (Sprecher, 1985) *Directed toward the Self* (happiness or depression), *Directed toward the Partner* (lust or anger), or *Directed toward the Relationship* (commitment or dissatisfaction).

These emotional states are experienced at different rates in the various couple types. The interdependence established by couples directly affects the experience of emotion in close relationships. The *experience* of an emotion is, however, a necessary but not a sufficient condition for the expression of that emotion to the spouse. The ideological orientation that an individual holds concerning marriage and family life affects the meaning that he or she assigns to an emotion-producing stimuli. Further, this ideological orientation and openness to conflict predict the *expression* of what is experienced.

This section differentiates between the experience of emotion and the expression of that emotion to the spouse and shows that different underlying psychological processes can be used to account for experience and expression. It is this differential that predicts both emotional responsivity to a spouse and the accuracy and inaccuracy of couples in these communication systems.

The Experience of Emotion

In an intriguing analysis, Berscheid (1983) has applied Mandler's (1984) theory of emotion to close relationships (see Chapter 1). A necessary condition for the experience of emotion is the presence of physiological arousal. Physiological arousal is said to occur when an individual is interrupted in the completion of an organized behavioral sequence. After the interruption occurs and alternate routes to complete the sequence are blocked, then emotion is experienced. The valence (positivity or negativity) of the experienced emotion depends on the context in which the interruption occurs. Positive affect results if the interruption is seen as benign or controllable, leads to the accomplishment of a goal sooner than expected, or removes something previously disruptive. Since interruptions are usually uncontrollable, however, most of them lead to negative affect.

When this model is applied to close relationships such as marriage by Berscheid (1983), the concept of interdependence is central to understanding what the individual may or may not experience as interrupting. Between spouses, there are a number of sequences of events in which each event in one person's causal chain is causally connected to an event for the other. That is, couples develop a series of organized behavioral sequences that necessitate the spouse as a partner in the action in order to achieve successful completion. The sequences that require the spouse for completion are called interchain sequences (e.g., lovemaking, marital conversations). The event in each person's chain is causally connected to an event in the spouse's chain and each needs the actions of the other to complete the sequence.

Individuals also have intrachain sequences or ongoing goal-directed activities that need to be completed once they have begun. Interchain causal connections are viewed as necessary, but not sufficient, conditions for emotion to occur. Autonomic arousal and emotion occurs when some interchain connection interfaces or interrupts the completion of an individual's intrachain sequence. Berscheid (1983) defines an individual's emotional investment in a relationship as the extent to which there are interchain causal connections to one's own intrachain sequences. Because connections of this sort lead to the experience of emotion in marriage, emotional investment refers to the potential amount of emotion that might be experienced. In certain types of relationships with very well-meshed sequences, however, one may tend to underestimate one's own emotional investment in a relationship because the experience of emotion does not occur very frequently.

The use of the term interdependence in Berscheid's (1983) model is very similar to its use in the typology as a defining feature of marriage. The occurrence of organized behavioral sequences was measured indirectly in the typology by the level of sharing in the marriage as well as the couple's organization of time and space in the household. Using this model of emotion and the levels of interdependence achieved by couples, it is possible to generate predictions concerning the degree of meshing in organized behavioral sequences in the various couple types.

The more highly interdependent the couple, the greater the number of meshed intrachain sequences. In other words, husbands and wives simultaneously engage in highly organized intrachain sequences and the events in each person's chain facilitate the performance of the other's sequence. A great number of meshed intrachain sequences occur for the Traditionals. Meshing makes it possible for many interconnected and highly organized event sequences to be performed by Traditionals without the smallest interruptive hitch. The connections between the Traditionals are symmetrical in that each partner facilitates the completion of the organized behavioral sequences for the other person. The connections between these couples are also facilitative. Because of their meshed and mutually facilitative intrachain sequences, the Traditionals are significantly less likely than the other couple types to experience emotion in reference to either the partner or the relationship on a daily basis. Under the tranquil exterior of the Traditional marriage, however, lies a very committed partnership. The Traditionals have a high degree of emotional investment in the relationship although these couples do not experience emotion on a daily basis. The paradox of the Traditional form of interdependence is that the mutual facilitation of intrachain sequences by each spouse for the other goes unnoticed (and does not produce even positive emotion) until the facilitation ceases.

The Separates have a marriage in which there are very few meshed intrachain sequences. This means that there are few or no causal connections between the intrachain sequences simultaneously enacted by the individuals in this marriage. Separates are disengaged from one another. These couples neither facilitate nor inhibit the organized behavioral sequences of one another. Since they are like children at parallel play, the Separates are not expected to experience much emotion in reference to the partner or to the relationship. This lack of emotional experience with respect to the marriage is qualitatively different than that of the tranquil exterior of the Traditional relationship. There are few connections between the Separate spouses. Under the surface of the Separate marriage, neither spouse is emotionally invested in the marriage since the potential to experience emotion in interaction with one's spouse is small.

The Independents represent couples with a number of nonmeshed sequences. The causal connections between the intrachain sequences interfere with the enactment of behavioral sequences for one spouse or the other. The Independents experience a greater range and intensity of emotions on a daily basis than do the other couples. These couples have been shown to engage in conflict significantly more than other couples and they have also reported having more fun, good times, and laughter than the other couples (Fitzpatrick, 1984). These couples probably experience negative emotion in reference to the spouse and to the marriage because the experience of interruption is most often regarded as negative.

The emotional state of each participant in the pure couple types is symmetrical, in that the facilitation or interference in the completion of behavioral sequences is balanced equally between husbands and wives. Husbands and wives have the same level of interdependence in the marriage and hence are more similar in the emotional experiences that the marriage can generate. The mixed couple types show that asymmetries do exist. In the Separate/Traditional relationship, for example, the traditional wife facilitates the completion of a number of intrachain sequences for her husband although he does not facilitate the completion of a number of intrachain sequences for her. Emotionally, this separate needs his wife more than she needs him. Although neither one may experience emotion on a daily basis as a consequence of the relationship, the husband is more emotionally invested in the marriage than is the wife. This husband may hold the power in a number of the spheres of their life together but the wife has more power to precipitate emotion in her husband (by interrupting her facilitation of his intrachain sequences) than he does in his wife. The emotional paradox of this marriage is that if the marriage ends, the "separate" male may experience greater distress. He loses the facilitation provided by his wife, of which he is unaware until it ceases. His traditional wife may be surprised to find herself less distressed at the end of marriage since so few of her behavioral sequences were facilitated by her husband.

The Meaning Analysis

Although the level of interdependence in the marriage governs the degree to which emotion can be experienced in the marriage, the assignment of meaning to the interrupting stimuli is controlled by the second major typological dimension, that is, ideology. Once the interruption has caused arousal, two decisions are made. The first concerns the class to which an emotion belongs; that is, whether the interruption can be attributed to the self, the partner, or to the relationship. Emotion directed toward the self occurs when individuals decide that they interrupted one of their own organized behavioral sequences. The emotion is directed toward the partner when the meaning analysis places the onus on the partner for the interruption. Finally, emotion is directed toward the relationship when the individual decides that the marriage per se is interfering in the accomplishment of higher-order plans or goals. The second decision involves whether the interruption can be considered positive or negative.

The Traditionals are expected to experience few interruptions and those that they do experience when related to the partner or the marriage will be experienced as positive ones. Even when Traditionals are interrupted in an important organized behavioral sequence, the interruption will be perceived as benign because marriage or the relationship to the partner is a higher-order plan within the Traditional ideological framework. The meaning analysis engaged in by the Traditionals would show that an interruption by the spouse, although interfering with the completion of a lower-order plan, actually facilitates the completion of a higher-order plan (that is, the maintenance of the relationship between parties). Thus the interruption is likely to lead to positive feelings toward the relationship. In support of these predictions, we find that Traditionals report a good deal of satisfaction and commitment to the marriage (Fitzpatrick & Best, 1979).

Interruptions occur frequently for the Independents giving the marriage a strong emotional tone yet one that is largely negative. These interruptions are viewed negatively because a meaning analysis of the interruptive behavior of the spouse would not show that this behavior fits into any higher-order plan. The Independents believe that marriage should not constrain the achievement of an individual's goals or plans. Independents attribute the interruption to the relationship, and experience a good deal of negative affect and dissatisfaction toward the marriage (Fitzpatrick & Best, 1979). Furthermore, the overall number of interruptions is high because Independents have nonmeshed intrachained sequences. When these interruptions are ascribed to the partner, the Independent may be more willing to view them positively. Independents are hypothesized to have strong positive feelings toward the partner and strong negative feelings toward the relationship.

Interruptions occur rarely for the Separates because the points of contact are few. When these interruptions do occur, however, the Separates ascribe them to the relationship but may view them as positive or negative. The Separates are ambivalent about the importance of the marriage in their higher-order plans, sometimes giving it high importance, other times less importance. Thus sometimes the interruption by the spouse will be viewed as positive because it aids the attainment of higher-order goals; at other times, such an interruption will be viewed negatively as interfering with higher-order goals for individualism. Emotional ambivalence is usually resolved in one direction or another (Gergen & Jones, 1963). Negative information appears to be more heavily weighted in all types of social interaction (Kellermann, 1984). We predict that the Separates will remember the negative emotional reactions to the relationship and indicate more dissatisfaction and a lack of commitment to the marriage.

Using this model, clear predictions can be made about the experience of emotion directed toward the spouse and toward the marriage. To understand emotions directed toward the self as a consequence of some marital process, we need to turn to Higgins's (1987) self-discrepancy theory. Different types of discrepancies between self-state representations predict different kinds of emotional vulnerabilities. Discrepancies between the actual/own self-state (i.e., the self-concept) and the ideal self-states (i.e., representations of an individual's beliefs about his or her own or a significant other's hopes, wishes, or aspirations for the individual) are associated with dejection-related emotions such as sadness, disappointment, and so forth. In contrast, discrepancies between the actual/own self-state and the ought self-states (i.e., representations about the individuals beliefs about his or her own or a significant other's beliefs about the individual's duties, obligations, or responsibilities) are associated with agitation-related emotions such as fear, anxiety, and restlessness.

This theory can be applied to the typology in the interest of examining the emotional states directed toward the self as a consequence of a discrepancy between one's own definition of the desired state in a marriage versus the definition of what marriage should be. Discrepancy in ideal/own guide is expected to result in dissatisfaction and disappointment; discrepancy in ideal/other guide results in shame. Discrepancy in ought/own guide leads to guilt; discrepancy in other/ought guide leads to apprehension, panic, and insecurity. Since traditionals and separates base their marital interaction schemata on learned social roles and conventionalism, they would have more "shoulds" than ideals for marriage. Further, the separates may have more discrepancies in their guides leading them to experience more guilt, and/or apprehension and insecurity. Independents may use more ideal guides and hence when discrepancies arise, experience disappointment rather than guilt.

CONCLUSION

Emotionally, these couples have very different marital systems. Separates exhibit fewer positive cues in one another's presence. The Separates are the least accurate in understanding the emotions their spouses are trying to communicate although both spouses are confident in their judgments. The communication of anger is problematic in this marriage. Objectively, the level of accuracy for anger recognition by Separates is low. These spouses think they are clearly communicating hostility yet the other person does not pick up on this anger and does not know that they are wrong. Indeed, the Separate spouse as a listener is quite confident that he or she understands what the spouse meant.

Traditionals exhibit more positive cues in one another's presence and the husbands are responsive to their wives' positive nonverbal communication. The Traditionals are moderately accurate in predicting their spouses' emotional messages although they are overconfident in their judgments. Since there are no correlations between listener and speaker ratings for Traditionals, there seems to be no systematic emotional distortions in this communication system.

Independents display moderate amounts of positive emotional cues in one another's presence yet the husband is very responsive to his wife. Independents are very accurate in understanding their spouses' emotional communications. These couples are accurate in expressing sexual interest and personal pleasure and the more confident the speaker in showing sexual interest, the more confident and correct the receiver. The communication of positive and negative emotions appears to be accomplished clearly and confidently in the Independent marriage.

We have conducted two laboratory studies examining the communication of emotion between partners. To understand the emotional connections between spouses, however, more research is needed. In the interest of generating more theoretically based research on nonverbal communication among couples in the various types, this chapter proposed a theoretical model that can be applied to the experience and expression of emotion in these marriages. In this model, we differentiated between positive and negative emotions experienced in reference to the self, the spouse, and the marriage as an entity. We also argued that theoretical work needs to differentiate the experience of emotions from the communication of those states to one's spouse. Everything one feels cannot be, and usually is not, communicated to one's spouse.

In my laboratory, I intend to study the communication of emotion by coding the facial and vocal expressions of the couples in the accuracy study. By having observer-judges also guess the emotion that each spouse is attempting to convey, we can establish "good" versus "bad" communications and link these evaluations to specific processes. Furthermore, we can examine those couples who have developed "idiosyncratic" emotional communication systems that work well for them. Finally, males and females in various types of marriages may specialize in a given nonverbal communication channel to communicate their emotions to one another. Hall (1987) proposes a cue-specialization explanation for male and female differences in judgment accuracy. The face contains information on positivity-negativity, and women, who are more concerned with this dimension, attend more to the face. The voice contains information on dominance-submission and is attended to more by males who care whether the speaker feels in control.

In my laboratory, we also intend to complete a diary study to probe the daily emotional life of couples. The diary method would require having couples keep records of emotional experiences in order to uncover the changing nature of these marriages. Given a well-designed diary and careful supervision of its completion, a good deal could be learned about spouse's emotional reactions to one another as they occur, not after the fact. People can report a good deal about their inner life if the questions are reasonable and asked close in time to the events that precipitate the emotional experience. Listen to the eloquent response of a 23-year-old working-class housewife, mother of two and married six years, when asked to describe her feelings about her husband:

> God, I was so scared: I didn't know what to do. I felt sorry for him and I felt angry at him. It was like the two feelings were always there inside me, fighting with each other, until I got a terrible headache. (Rubin, 1976, p. 76)

NOTES

1. Some critics of the paradigm argue that it is artificial to have couples attempt to send angry or depressed messages to the spouse in a "cold, laboratory" situation where the spouse might not actually feel the emotion he or she is asked to communicate. This criticism misses two important points: one related to the nature of human communication and the other to the purpose of laboratory research. First, human communication exists on a continuum from totally spontaneous to purely symbolic (Buck, 1984). The communication of emotion is not exclusively at the spontaneous end of this continuum. Every culture has display rules that guide the communicator as to the appropriate degree and intensity with which they should display their feelings. The point of the standard content paradigm is not to uncover spontaneous feelings between married partners but rather to examine the accuracy of their symbolic emotional exchanges. Second, the efficacy of this paradigm is demonstrated by the number of marital interaction studies that have been able to demonstrate differential accuracy in various channels for the happily and the unhappily married (e.g., Noller, 1984).

2. Across all the emotions, for correct and incorrect decisions, the only differences on speaker clarity and listener confidence ratings emerged for the speaker clarity ratings on both the correct and incorrect pleasure items.

IV

THINKING ABOUT MARRIAGE

9

Psychological Realities
The Views of Marital
Insiders and Outsiders

In this chapter, I go beyond merely expanding or checking the validity of individual's self-reports about power, conflict, and expressivity: I demonstrate the psychological reality of this typology by proving that certain propositions about marriage cohere together. Such coherence in the minds of the members of this culture suggests the marital types are psychologically real categorizations of marriage. Both married and unmarried individuals use the relational dimensions to categorize marriage in meaningful ways. Such marital categorizations drive both the encoding and decoding of marital communication. This chapter presents the results of six investigations. The first three experiments study how the typology affects the encoding of marital messages. Within this set, we examine the syntactic and pragmatic code usage of various couples, the content themes of marital dialogues, and married individuals' processing of relationship-relevant content from television shows.

I also present three investigations on the decoding side. The first study examines what couples remember about their "first meeting," or "first encounters of the close kind" (Fitzpatrick & Hein, 1986). The second study considers whether outsiders (in this case, the children of married couples) use the relational dimensions to categorize their parents' marriages. The third study examines psychological reality by manipulating discussions of various relational forms and having participants rate couples on their communication. Taken together, these six studies offer strong support that the couple types, with their particular patterns of communication, are psychologically real and structure the way individuals think about marriage.

ENCODING MARITAL COMMUNICATION

Communication between people necessitates a shared code or a systematic arrangement of symbols (e.g., letters, words, gestures) that have arbitrary meanings known and used by the communicators. Codes can be verbal or nonverbal and can be analyzed at very different levels of abstraction. Encoding is the process of putting a message into a code, and decoding is the process of assigning meaning to a message according to the code. In this section, we demonstrate that the marital type controls the encoding of messages by couples at various levels of analysis.

Pragmatic and Syntactic Codes

The couple types represent different private cultures of relationships, with different values, time, space, and companionship orientations. Consequently, we expect differences in the codes that various couples use. Codes are symbol systems that represent the different ways speakers can structure their knowledge about reality. As such, codes can demonstrate how an individual produces (interprets) language in accordance with certain processing norms. Couples in various marital types utilize different lexical and syntactic structures in conversations with one another because these couples differ in their interdependence and ideological orientations.

Codes can be pragmatic or syntactic (Ellis & Hamilton, 1986). Traditional relationships are reflected in the use of a pragmatic code. In the pragmatic code, meaning resides in the situation and depends on the communicators' expectancies. In the Traditional relationship, the expectations of the self and the spouse are based on relatively clear role prescriptions and conventional patterns of behavior. Consequently, there is simply less need for talk. The interaction that does occur for Traditionals does more work; that is, because the interactants share more presuppositions, a word or a clause does the work of a complete sentence. Traditional discourse should display loose coordination with few explicit cohesion devices because these devices are simply unnecessary (Ellis & Hamilton, 1986). The Separate relationship also is marked with a good deal of agreement over basic issues related to family life and extremely clear role prescriptions. Like Traditionals, Separates are hypothesized to use a pragmatic code. A major difference between the two types of marriages, however, is that because of the emotional distance in Separates' marriage, these people tend to speak less to their spouses overall. Separates use the pragmatic code, but over an even greater range and variety of issues than do the Traditionals.

The syntactic code is used by Independents because linguistic elaboration and modification is the hallmark of the Independent marriage. Independents are involved in a greater variety of interaction than are other couple types; Independents spend more time negotiating the roles and rules of the relationship. Consequently, Independent discourse should include more linguistic cohesion devices, with greater use of direct semantic elaboration. For the Independents, language connects ideas and not relational presuppositions. Mixed couple types, because of their disagreements on many fundamental issues in the marriage, also are expected to use the syntactic code; they need to elaborate and modify symbolic reality in conversations with their spouses.

The concepts of syntactic and pragmatic codes are similar to the elaborated and restricted code concepts presented by Bernstein (1973). Therefore, the reader may be concerned that these linguistic differences occur because these couples come from different social classes. As we have seen, however, the couple types are equally distributed across social classes. Furthermore, Bernstein (1973) argues that codes are fixed as a consequence of one's social class. Individuals have the ability to switch codes; hence codes may be better analyzed as relying on the regulative nature of the situation, the relationship established between the partners, and their dispositions (Ellis & Hamilton, 1986). This concept of a code is more flexible and takes into account that codes represent the psychological and situational adaptations made by the interactants. A speaker may adapt one code in a personal or family situation and quite another in a professional or work context. Independents' syntactic code usage in their marital conversations, for example, does not necessarily extend to their interactions with coworkers.

In total, 30 married couples—6 Traditional couples, 6 Separate couples, 7 Independent couples, and 11 Mixed types—took part in this study. We made transcripts of the middle four minutes of the conversation of the 30 couples, who were waiting for another experiment to begin. We chose the short interaction (i.e., four minutes) because it was a stringent test of the encoding hypothesis. These couples' dialogue was coded with Ellis and Hamilton's (1986) scheme, which examines the natural language of the speakers by coding such indicators as personal pronoun use, verb

TABLE 9.1
Discriminant Function Analyses of Language Use

Function I–Couple References	
We	.56
Personal pronouns	−.29
Infinite verbs	.18
F = 47.80; df = 3, 57; p < .0000	
Function II–Linguistic Complexity	
Relative pronoun	.32
Disfluencies	.31
Finite transitive verb	.31
Disjunctive pronouns	.24
Subordinate clause	.17
Adjectives	.16
Possessives	.11
F = 17.31; df = 3, 57; p < .0000	
Function III–Linguistic Elaboration	
Finite verb	−.45
I	.31
Adverbs	−.23
Intransitive verb	.22
Gerund	.17
Participle	.07
F = 5.42; df = 3, 57; p < .0025	

SOURCE: Fitzpatrick, Bauman, and Lindaas (1987).

forms, uncommon adjectives, and so forth. The variables are organized around four themes: personal reference, structural complexity, verb complexity, and elaboration. Three coders spent eight weeks learning the coding system. They did not begin work until they had reached a 95% reliability level; their reliabilities were checked throughout the data collection period. The reliabilities never fell below .83 during the coding.

We converted the variables to proportions and calculated arcsin transformations. When the 16 variables were submitted to a discriminant function analysis, three functions emerged. The couple types differed significantly on each of the three functions, and 80% of the couples could be correctly classified based on this solution. As we can see in Table 9.1, function one is basically defined by the use of the words "we" and, in the opposite direction, the use of personal pronouns ("he," "she"). We have labeled this function *Couple References*. The group centroids indicate that the Traditionals are significantly different from the other couples on this measure. An examination of the means indicates that the Traditionals use significantly more "we" messages and significantly fewer personal

TABLE 9.2
The Group Centroids

	Function 1	Function 2	Function 3
Traditional	2.74	.09	.17
Separate	−.62	−1.66	−.25
Independent	−1.50	.25	1.04
Mixed	−.73	.85	−.46

NOTE: Each function clearly defines one of the three Pure couple types.

pronouns than do the other couples, whereas the Independents use significantly more personal pronouns and significantly fewer "we" references. This function may represent part of the pragmatic code in that the Traditionals couples high on this function are reasonably certain enough about their shared presuppositions that they frequently assert the right to say "we."

The second function is labeled *Linguistic Complexity* (Table 9.1) because it includes verbal complexity and such measures as disfluencies. The speech disfluencies coded here are those that indicate cognitive planning, such as pauses filled with "Ah" and so forth. The Separates are significantly different from the other types (Table 9.2) in this function. An examination of the variables' means indicates that the Separates are not linguistically complex in their marital interaction. Because this function represents part of the syntactic code, we see that the Separates are lower than all the other couple types on linguistic complexity in marital communication.

The final function is labeled *Linguistic Elaboration* (Table 9.1), and the group centroids (Table 9.2) indicate that the Independents are discriminated from the other types on this measure. The Independents use significantly more references to themselves in the form of the word "I" and tend to embroider their marital conversations with more complex verb forms.

In these data, we see the closeness and interdependence of the Traditional couples as represented by their consistent use of references to themselves as a couple and the relative absence of references to the spouse as an individual. Traditionals assert the right to say "we" in the relationship. Although the Traditional relationship is marked by the absence of linguistic elaboration and complexity, the Separates are even more strongly represented by the pragmatic code. Separates employ less linguistic complexity and more implicit roles and rules to communicate with the spouse. For the Separates, everything they say to the spouse (and in general they say as little as possible) does more work. The Independents do appear to have a more elaborated code than the other couples. Less is assumed in this discourse, and more attention is paid to linking topics. The Independent use of the syntactic code involves more precise symbolization. Such precision is necessary because the Independent marriage involves flexible roles, change, and novelty. Although the Independents had a large number of disfluencies, the Mixed couples had even more. At least for some indicators of the syntactic code, the Mixed types were similar to the Independents.

We have shown that in casual conversations lasting only a few minutes we can make conceptually reasonable discriminations in the encoding behaviors of married couples. At a natural language level of analysis, the private culture of the relationship is reflected in the linguistic choices of these couples. We turn, now, to a more abstract analysis of marital talk and encoding choices. Let us examine topics of marital conversation.

Content Themes in
Marital Conversations

Marriage creates for people the sort of order in which they can experience their world as making sense (Berger & Kellner, 1975). It is through conversations with one another that married partners construct a shared reality and subsequently define their identities. Through conversations, a "couple identity" is not only built but also is kept in a state of repair and is ongoingly refurbished. As Berger and Kellner (1975, p. 226) so eloquently phrase it:

> The nomic instrumentality of marriage is concretized over and over again, from bed to the breakfast table, as partners carry on the endless conversation that feeds on nearly all they individually or jointly experience.

The building of these joint couple identities is accomplished at the level of conversational topics and themes. Specific themes in marital talk may be linked to more general, pervasive, and fundamental perceptions of the relationship (Hess & Handel, 1959). We have seen that couples in various types of marriages have different views of marriage, and that these views explain the content of their talk with one another. Differences in the content of couples' communications emerge from their pervasive underlying beliefs about the nature of marriage. Perception of a mutual identity, cohesion, and interdependence is manifest in communal themes such as shared rights and obligations, togetherness, and cooperation. Individuals may focus their marital talk on their own individual traits and behaviors in order to express that they have distinct personalities and that personalistic factors account for events in the marriage (Sillars, Weisberg, Burgraff, & Wilson, 1987). In sum, the content of marital talk can be broadly categorized into three themes: Communal, Individual, or Impersonal. These three categories are loosely derived from attribution theory and represent the themes that couples see as important in understanding their marriage, and marriage in general.

Sillars and his group used the content-themes coding scheme to recode the conversations from two earlier projects (see Chapter 5, this volume). They coded usable transcripts from 69 couples. Couples were given 10 topics to discuss, each representing a common marital conflict (e.g., lack of time spent together, a lack of communication, and so forth). Couples were asked to discuss whether they perceived each of the topics as representing a problem in their relationship. Instructions stressed that couples could skip topics if they wished and that there was no time limit on the discussion. In order to avoid confusing content themes with speech act categories, all categories were defined to have positive, negative, and neutral categories. For example, separateness refers to positive comments about freedom in the marriage, as well as to complaints about too much or too little freedom. Content themes were identified with the semantic object given the most emphasis as a causal or controlling factor in the marriage. Table 9.3 defines the categories and their subthemes and presents the results for the various couple types.

Because Traditionals emphasize sharing and togetherness, they express communal themes in their dialogues. Traditional conversations include references to sharing activities, interests, and time; they also include expressive communication and sharing. These couples are likely to refer to romantic themes such as being in love and having mutual affection. Traditionals are less likely to mention individual traits, characteristics, habits, or skills of themselves or their spouses. Finally, an important impersonal theme for these couples is stoicism, or the calm acceptance of moderate standards of satisfaction with life and marriage and a perception that all marriages inherently have difficulties.

Separates are as conventional in their orientations as are Traditionals, yet their conventionalism takes different thematic forms in conversations. Separates de-emphasize togetherness and sharing interests and activities; they present marriage as a product of separate identities or roles. Separates talk about their individual activities, interests, and hobbies and also their distinctive personalities, traits, habits, and skills. The impersonal themes of these couples, in contrast to the Traditionals, are not stoical acceptance of moderate standards of happiness. When Separates

TABLE 9.3

Conditional Proportions of Content Themes in Couple Types

			T	S	I	M
		Communal Themes–Marriage is seen as the product of an active interdependence.				
	A.	Togetherness includes references to sharing of time,	+.18	−.11	−.08	.14
		activities, interests, etc.	−	.07	.09	.11
	B.	Cooperation conscious, active, working together	.08	.06	.08	.06
		to resolve problems	−	.04	.06	.05
	C.	Communication expressive communication and verbal	+.08	.06	−.01	.06
		sharing	−	.03	.07	.07
	D.	Romanticism being in love, having shared	+.03	.01	.02	−.01
		affection	−	.02	.01	.01
	E.	Interdependence mutual influence and joint	.01	.01	.00	−.00
		patterns of behavior.	−	.02	.01	.01

II. Individual Themes–Marriage is seen as the product of separate identities or roles.

			T	S	I	M
	A.	Separateness having separate time, activities,	.07	+.11	.06	.07
		interests	−	.09	.10	.09
	B.	Personality having distinct individual traits,	−.12	+.26	−.12	+.25
		habits, skills	−	+.39	.27	.26
	C.	Role having separate instrumental roles	.05	.04	.08	.06
		and performing adequately or not.	−	.04	.06	.06

III. Impersonal Themes–Marriage is seen as the product of factors that are largely or partly beyond the direct, personal control of the couple.

			T	S	I	M
	A.	Organic properties normative, developmental, intrinsic	.07	+.12	.11	.08
		facts that determine marriage	−	.12	−.07	.11
	B.	Stoicism problems inherent in marriage, accept	+.19	−.09	.19	.14
		moderate standards of satisfaction.	−	.08	.11	.08
	C.	Environmental influence couple's situation preempts	.12	.12	+.24	.13
		individual choice.	−	.10	.16	.15

SOURCE: Sillars, Weisberg, Burgraff, and Wilson (1987).
NOTE: + = significantly greater than expected; − = significantly less than expected; $p < .05$. T = Traditionals; S = Separates; I = Independents; M = Mixed.

discuss factors that influence marriage and that they perceive as beyond their control, these couples emphasize the normative or developmental issues that affect marital interaction.

Independents do not necessarily see marriage as a product of active interdependence; they tend to suppress the kinds of references to togetherness and communication that Traditionals use. Although themes of interdependence did not predominate for the Independents, these couples are significantly more likely than are other couples to pick up partners' topics. Independents picked upon themes introduced by the spouse more frequently (19%) than did Traditionals (8%), Separates (7%), or the Mixed types (8%). Independents are cohesive both in their use of topics and themes introduced by the spouse and in their reliance on a syntactic code. Independents continue the topics introduced by their spouses in conversation and use linguistic devices that help clarify the connections in the conversation between partners. These couples also do not see marriage as the product of separate identities or roles. The nature of the negotiated identity of Independent couples is neither the form of interdependence adapted by Traditionals nor is it the autonomy of the Separates. The Independents are working out a new worldview of relationships and negotiating the roles and rules of the relationships; the interdependence of the Independent marriage is not captured in this coding scheme. In sharp contrast to the other Pure couple types, the Independents use environmental explanations for aspects of marital interaction that are seen as beyond the couple's control. An important theme for Independents centers on those times when their individual choices are usurped.

Mixed types do not see marriage as the product of an active interdependence; they inhibit the discussion of romantic themes and any treatment of joint patterns of behavior and mutual influence. These couples, like the Separates, focus on personality themes in discussing marriage. Unlike the other couples, however, these Mixed couple types do not use impersonal themes to describe some aspect of marital interaction. This lack of an attributional structure that focuses on external factors in dealing with problem issues may cause problems for these couples. Undoubtedly, it is very functional at times in a marriage for a couple to be able to say, "It's not you, it's not me, it's not us, it just is. It's just the way things are." Being able to attribute problems or difficulties to some factor external to the partner or the relationship may help couples deal more effectively with one another. All the Pure couple types at times describe some impersonal force for a conflict or problem in their marriage.

Conversational themes identify the factors that couples decide are important in discussing the difficulties of marriage. The factors may be communal, individual, or impersonal. The results of this study present strong evidence that couples' ideologies about marriage and their views of interdependence lead to making suggestive causal statements about how marital interaction can best be explained. The next study examines encoding in a very different manner; it considers one common daily experience of married life as filtered through couples' marital definitions. In this study, we examined television viewing and its effect on setting agendas for marital talk.

Television Content and Marital Reality

Perhaps the only issue on which media-effects researchers, cultural-studies scholars, and ethnomethodologists agree is the pervasiveness of television in American life; the television set is turned on in the average home approximately 7.5 hours a day. The effects of such widespread exposure to television, however, are hotly debated. In this section, we take the position that exposure to aspects of television content related to marriage and the family affects marital interaction. Close relationships frequently are portrayed on television, and the interaction between partners often deals directly with relational issues. Over a 32-year period (1946-1978), 218 family serials appeared (Glennon & Butsch, 1982). Between 40 and 50 family serials are televised weekly during prime time and Saturday morning (Greenberg, 1982), and soap operas are an abundant source of relationship portrayals (Fine, 1981). Does television depict an array of relationships (i.e., various values and structures), or do viewers encounter a limited range of relationship characterizations?

One way to answer this question is to turn to content analyses of the media. Such analyses often address the nature of gender-role portrayals. Television persists in depicting men and women as opposites (Greenberg, 1982; Roberts, 1982). Ambition, dominance, and the ability to cope characterize males; females are portrayed as submissive, romantic, and emotional. In addition, 90% of TV conversations between family members are affiliative, rather than evasive or conflictual (Greenberg, 1982). In the realm of the family, we find considerable evidence that traditional values are the televised norm. That the television portrayal of the family typically mirrors a conventional ideology is in itself instructive for our purposes, but traditionalism is more strongly reinforced when characters deviate from traditionalism. Traditional complementary sex roles (e.g., the nurturant female and the controlling male) are associated with relational harmony on TV; conflict arises when partners share roles (Phelps, 1976). If TV women have successful careers outside the home, they frequently encounter relationship difficulties (Roberts, 1982). Negative sanctions appear to accompany situations where traditional wisdom is rejected.

Television portrays a rather singular view of close relationships. The predominant image of intimate associations strongly reinforces traditional sex roles and family values. In this conventional context, relational partners are extremely affiliative and apparently are not reticent to express intimate thoughts and feelings. Such a view closely resembles the Traditional prototype. What effect does the frequent presentation of the Traditional marital type have on married couples?

Predictions about the results of exposure to televised relationship information are not straightforward. Indirect evidence suggests that television viewing affects marital processes, especially in terms of TV's impact on attitudes and beliefs regarding sex roles, family values, and family structure. A number of studies have been concerned with the relationship between the amount of viewing and the acquisition of sex-role stereotypes (Hawkins & Pingree, 1982). Heavy television viewing appears to be associated with an increase in traditional sex-role attitudes.

Both adults and children are influenced by portrayals of family life on television. There are subgroups, however, for whom the effects are more pronounced. We know, for example, that viewing soap operas changes the perception of the number of happy marriages, divorces, extramarital affairs, and careers; the effect is particularly strong for people with low self-concept or low satisfaction with life (Buerkel-Rothfus & Mayes, 1981). Dissatisfied individuals are only one subgroup that may be affected by TV portrayals of close relationships. Television viewing affects social reality, but the relationship between television and its cultivation of certain social realities depends on certain viewer characteristics. An individual's marital definition is expected to affect how he or she processes information about relationships and marriage as shown on TV. Marital definition causes people to construe differently what they see.

Much of television content positively portrays traditional family relationships. An individual's marital type affects how responsive he or she is to relationship-oriented television content. Specifically, the types control whether the typical television content is responded to as relevant and consistent, as irrelevant, or as relevant and inconsistent (Hastie,

1981). Only those viewers who see the content as relevant yet inconsistent with their marital definitions are likely to attend to and discuss that content with their spouses.

Independents will see most of what they watch on television (that is, portrayals of traditional marriages) as irrelevant to their concept of marriage and hence will not attend particularly to such content. High television viewing for Independents should prompt little talk about their marriage. Traditionals also will be less likely to talk about personal issues as a consequence of what they see on television, but this outcome occurs for a different underlying reason. Television marriages are relevant to traditionals because these marriages represent "reality" for traditionals. A viewer is less likely to pay attention to information that is relevant but very consistent; thus traditionals are less likely to pay attention to these portrayals and are less likely to talk about family or personal issues, even after viewing a good deal of television.

Television content provides an avenue for discussion in a relationship in which the separate individual does not share, is not affiliative or expressive, and tends to avoid conflict. Family and intimate portrayals are particularly salient for individuals who see their relationship as lacking interdependence yet constrained by traditional ideological views. These couples see TV couples who are as traditional as they are, yet appear to remain close to one another.

In this study, each couple was visited at home, where they individually completed a questionnaire containing the Relational Dimensions Instrument (RDI) and other items. Participants answered questions about their television viewing and topics that they discussed with their spouse as a result of seeing something on television. We asked our subjects to report the number of hours per day that they typically watch television alone and with their spouses. Husbands and wives reported the frequency of discussions about (1) political/social issues, (2) subjects related to the family, (3) subjects related to the job, (4) subjects related to the marriage, (5) subjects related to the children, and (6) subjects related to physical/mental health. These spouses also estimated general frequencies of talk prompted by something seen on television.

The amount of television viewing in general is an important covariate in the social reality literature (with effects always stronger in the high-viewing groups). Therefore, we classified respondents into high- and low-viewing groups. Table 9.4 presents the results for the six discussion topics. Significant differences emerged only for the separates. High- and low-viewing separates differ in the amount they report discussing the

TABLE 9.4
Frequency of Talk for High Versus Low Viewing by Type

Topics	High	Low	t (df)		p (1-tail)
Political Issues					
Traditional	5.000	4.765	.70	(29)	NS
Independent	5.111	5.000	.23	(15)	NS
Separate	4.727	4.688	.09	(25)	NS
Family Subjects					
Traditional	4.429	4.177	.51	(29)	NS
Independent	4.556	3.875	.81	(15)	NS
Separate	5.273	3.813	2.92	(25)	.004*
Job Issues					
Traditional	3.643	3.353	.54	(29)	NS
Independent	4.000	4.500	−.63	(15)	NS
Separate	4.546	3.938	1.12	(25)	NS
Marital Issues					
Traditional	4.000	3.706	.53	(29)	NS
Independent	4.111	4.125	−.02	(15)	NS
Separate	4.727	3.250	2.64	(25)	.007*
Parental Issues					
Traditional	3.556	3.688	−.17	(23)	NS
Independent	3.714	3.250	.35	(13)	NS
Separates	4.444	3.308	1.30	(20)	NS
Health Issues					
Traditional	4.000	3.647	.67	(29)	.254
Independent	4.000	3.875	.17	(15)	.434
Separate	5.091	3.375	4.41	(25)	.000*

SOURCE: Fallis, Fitzpatrick, and Friestad (1985).

three relationship-relevant issues as a result of watching television. Viewing by separates encourages conversation about subjects related to the family, to the relationship with the spouse, and to personal physical/mental health. Not only does television appear to influence discussion for separates, as opposed to the traditionals and independents, but this effect is noted only for topics relevant to the relationship. Heavy-viewing separates increase the amount of personal talk with the spouse as a consequence of what they see on television. However, all couple types are equally likely to discuss political or social issues, their jobs, or their children. In an effort to clarify the relationship between viewing and marital conversation, total daily viewing hours and hours spent viewing with spouse each were correlated with the general frequency of discussion of something seen on television.

TABLE 9.5
Relational Definition by Topic for Hours Viewing
Alone and Hours Viewing with Spouse

	Pol	Fam	Job	Mar	Par	Heal	Total
All Alone							
Trad	.07	.18	.10	.06	.04	.09	.27
Indep	−.14	.06	−.19	.06	.20	.07	−.29
Sep	.15	.30*	.01	.41***	.39**	.57***	.20
With Spouse							
Trad	.18	.06	.04	.04	.03	.07	.21
Indep	−.14	−.13	−.19	−.19	−.17	−.01	−.25
Sep	.20	.14	.17	.36*	.11	.26	.59***

SOURCE: Fallis, Fitzpatrick, and Friestad (1985).
*p < .15; **p < .10; ***p < .05.

Table 9.5 shows a very strong relationship—but only for separates—between watching television as a couple and frequency of interaction (r = .59). No other correlations of viewing with frequency of discussion were statistically significant. Evidently, separates frequently talk about what they view together, whereas traditionals and independents are not so inclined. There are no significant differences across the relational definitions by frequency of television-viewing behaviors, proving that these insignificant correlations are not due to a restriction in the range of the variables. A one-way ANOVA for relational definition by television viewing alone was not significant (F = 1.69; df = 2, 72; ns), nor was the one-way ANOVA for relational definition by television viewing with spouse significant (F = 1.55; df = 2, 57; ns).

Summary

These three studies suggest that the couple types are psychologically real in that these types control the encoding of messages to the spouse at both the code and content level. Such types can even be used to predict the effect of a high dosage of traditional images on the topics discussed by partners. Television viewing has an effect on marital interaction when the television content is processed by a particular orientation to marriage. In the next section, we demonstrate the psychological reality of the typology from the decoding point of view.

DECODING MARITAL INTERACTION

In this section, we take up the issue of the assignment of meaning to the couple types, not only by married couples but also by people in general.

TABLE 9.6
Positivity of Memory for First Encounter with Spouse

	Husband	Wife
Traditional	4.14	5.07
Independent	2.59	5.45
Separate	2.62	3.50
Sep/Trad	2.18	5.43
Mixed	4.48	5.04

NOTE: These scores are adjusted by subtracting 3.1 from each trait value.

First, we consider what married couples remember about their first meeting. Second, we test whether college-age students can use the typological dimensions to evaluate their parents' marriages. Third, we directly examine how people link the dimensions of the typology to different marital interaction patterns.

First Encounters

When asked to recall their first encounter with one another, most married couples are able to recall, in some detail, the impressions that each had of the other. Indeed, many of the themes of marriage are represented in these accounts. How positive are the memories that husbands and wives have of their first encounter? We intensively interviewed 102 people about their first impressions of one another. We categorized the descriptions of their partner into personality traits and then went to Anderson's (1968) list and got average ratings of likability on the traits. Table 9.6 shows that wives have more positive memories of their first meeting than do husbands; wives also gave more (3.8) traits than did husbands (2.9). Husbands in the Traditional marriage and in various Mixed types have substantially more positive images of their first encounters than do other husbands. All wives but those involved in Separate marriages rate the husbands positively; Separate wives are less likely to remember positive characteristics of the spouse.

Rating One's Parents

Do the three definitive types of relationships exist in the minds of observers? How do college-age children perceive the marriages of their parents? Is one of these relationship types more "ideal" in the minds of the participants than another (Fitzpatrick, 1981)? We asked 510 college students to complete the Relational Dimensions Instrument under one of

TABLE 9.7
Relational Types by Desirability

	Ideal	Worst	My Parents
Traditional	46	13	27
Independent	38	14	43
Separate	16	73	29

NOTE: The number represents the percentages in each conditions choosing the various relational definitions.

two sets of instructions. The first set asked the participants to complete the RDI, role playing their parents. Males were to respond as their fathers would, and females were to answer as their mothers would, presenting an honest picture of the marriage. The second set tapped an evaluation of marriage in general; participants were asked to complete the RDI as if they had the best or the worst marriage they could imagine.

On the average, the students' parents had been married 25 years and 81% of the parental marriages were still intact; the children were reporting on relatively stable relationships. The RDIs completed by these respondents were submitted to factor analysis and linear typal analysis (see Chapter 2). The same three basic types—Traditional, Independent, and Separate—emerged from the analysis, with one exception. Children rate parents who are Separates as significantly more assertive than the Separates usually rate themselves. As we have seen in Chapter 5, Separates are indeed more confrontative than they would like to be with one another. Of the respondents, 43% defined their same-sex parent as independent, whereas 27% rated the parent as traditional, and 29% as separate.

Table 9.7 lists marital types by desirability. The ideal relationship is the Traditional one. Observers clearly differentiate marriage into three basic categories, can assign a parent to one of the three, and demonstrate clear stereotypes about the best and worst possible marriages.

Psycholinguistic Reality
and Relational Identities

Would providing listeners with information about a couple's marital adjustment or their marital type evoke stereotyped communication beliefs about the couple? Tables 9.8 and 9.9 display what should exist in the minds of listeners about communication in various types of marriages. Table 9.8 shows some differentiating characteristics of the happily and unhappily married. Table 9.9 displays some of the major differences for

TABLE 9.8
Communication Correlates of Marital Adjustment/
Nonadjustment as Predictions for the Present Investigation

		Couple Type	
Items		Adjusted	Nonadjusted
Marital adjustment	1[a]	+	−
Self-disclosed	2[a]	+	−
Talked frequently	2[a]	+	−
Stopped communication less often	2[a]	+	−
Accurate interpretations	3[a]	+	−
Generally positive	4[b]	+	−
Generally negative	4[b]	−	+
Cross-complaining sequences	4[b]	−	+
First reciprocated positivity, then stopped	4[b]	−	+
Interaction patterned	4[b]	−	−
Discussing a problem, wife uses a negative tone	5[b]	−	+

NOTE: a. refers to findings from self-report studies, while b. indicates behavioral observation studies. Numbers refer to the study in question, namely, 1, Spanier (1976); 2, Kahn (1970); 3, Bienvenu (1970); 4, Gottman (1979); 5, Noller (1980). + indicates this item is evoked by the couple type. − indicates that item is not clearly apparent.

the couple types. Relational identities (marital adjustment and type) have psychological reality and hence bias listeners' judgments of a couple. Furthermore, these stereotypes are in line with the profiles displayed in Tables 9.8 and 9.9.

Naive listeners have knowledge that links descriptive characteristics of marriage to certain frequencies and patterns of communication between spouses. For example, a cognitive representation would link a traditional value orientation and a high degree of companionship to sharing feelings with the spouse but not necessarily with anyone else. These stereotyped beliefs could bias listeners' linguistic judgments of an unfamiliar couple's talk. Hence items appearing in Table 9.9 also were included as dependent measures in the study to follow.

In our investigation, 244 undergraduates in an introductory communication class at a midwestern university were assigned randomly to a marital adjustment study or the typology experiments. All participants listened to the same 90-second conversation, showing a young married couple discussing the purchase of a used car. The speaking roles of husband and wife were equalized; they engaged in the same number of speaking turns and used the same number of words. In addition, the number of agreements and disagreements used by each spouse was not

TABLE 9.9
Predicted Communication Correlates
of the Marital Typology

		Couple Types		
Items		Trad	Indep	Sep
Showed affection	1[a]	++	+	+
Marital adjustment	2[a]	++	+	+
Agreed with each other	2[a]	++	−	+
Took partner into account	3[a]	++	+	−
Self-disclosed	3[a]	++	+	−
Husband (sounded) masculine	4[a]	+	+	++
Husband (sounded) feminine	4[a]	−	+	−
Wife (sounded) feminine	4[a]	+	+	−
Wife (sounded) masculine	4[a]	−	+	−
Talked frequently	5[b]	+	+	−
Cooperated in conflicts	5[b]	+	−	−
Negotiated verbally	6[b]	+	−	−
Flexible communication	7[b]	+	−	−
Vocal tones negative	8[b]	−	+	−
Each tried to control the conversation	9[b]	−	++	−−
Complementary in style	9[b]	−	−−	+

NOTE: a. refers to findings from self-report studies, while b. indicates behavioral observation studies. Numbers refer to the study in question, namely, 1, Fitzpatrick (1976); 2, Fitzpatrick and Best (1979); 3, Fitzpatrick (1977); 4, Fitzpatrick and Indvik (1982); 5, Fitzpatrick, Fallis, and Vance (1982); 6, Witteman and Fitzpatrick (1986); 7, Fitzpatrick (1983); 8, Sillars, Pike, Jones, and Redman (1983); 9, Williamson (1983). + indicates that this item is evoked by the couple type, and ++ indicates this is extremely so. − indicates this item is not clearly apparent, and −− suggests it is definitely not evoked.

significantly different. A pretest of the conversation showed that the conversation was not slanted toward any particular type of marriage. We were satisfied that this conversation was emotionally neutral. All participants in the main study listened to the tape in the knowledge that they would be required to answer questions about it afterward. Immediately after listening to the taped couple, and just before making a series of ratings along nine-point scales, listeners were provided with typewritten information about the couple (see Ball et al., 1982). In the marital adjustment study, participants received one of the following descriptions of the couple:

Description 1: John and Susan want to stay together very much and have few intense or serious conflicts. They have never discussed separation or divorce. They are very satisfied with their marriage and tend to kiss one another every day.

Description 2: John and Susan do not want to stay together very much; they have frequently discussed separation or divorce. They are very dissatisfied with their marriage and tend not to kiss one another every day.

In the typology study, participants received one of the following three paragraphs representing the basic marriage types:

The Traditional description—John and Susan have very strong traditional values on marriage and family life. They share almost all aspects of their lives with one another. They have very regular daily time schedules and do not feel the need for private space in their home away from one another.

The Independent description—John and Susan have very strong non-traditional values on marriage and family life. They share many, but not all, aspects of their lives with one another. They have irregular daily time schedules and feel the need for private space in their home away from one another.

The Separate description—John and Susan outwardly have very traditional values about marriage and family life but often doubt these values. They share few aspects of their lives with one another. They have very regular daily time schedules and feel the need for private space in their home away from one another.

All participants listened to exactly the same tape recording of a couple talking. The only difference between the five subgroups of listeners was in the information provided them concerning John and Susan. Few explicit details were provided about the couple's communication. Having read this brief information, all participants rated the communication behaviors of the couple they had just heard. Ratings were made on a 40-item questionnaire derived from Tables 9.8 and 9.9. It also included a large number of items relating to social evaluation (see Table 9.10 for a synopsis of most of these scales).

A correlation matrix for the 40 dependent measures for all participants was submitted to a Principal Components Analysis to determine the number of factors utilized by raters. Cattell's Scree test suggested that five factors appeared to define this data set, accounting for 51% of the variance. The relatively small amount of variance accounted for here may well have been due to the very heavy cognitive demands placed on our respondents; that is, assessing a more or less bland conversation by using 40 nine-point rating scales. Obviously, future work should use an evaluatively easier judgmental task. A subsequent factor analysis—using squared multiple correlations in the diagonals of the matrix, followed by a varimax rotation—yielded five interpretable factors that could serve as

TABLE 9.10
Factors and Item Loadings

(1) *Social evaluation* (eigenvalue = 6.79; 48.2% variance)
Would you like to have a marriage like theirs?   .79
Would you like them as close friends?   .76
Would you go to them for advice?   .73
Would you discuss issues as they do?   .69
Do you think they are really compatible?   .57
Do you respect this couple?   .56
Do they seem a typical married couple to you?   .52
It is clear that this couple does not talk much together.   −.50
Do you think their marriage will last?   .47

(2) *Negative communication style* (eigenvalue - 2.68; 19% variance)
This couple was generally negative toward one another.   .61
When she was discussing a problem with her husband, the wife
had a negative tone.   .58
Each tried to control the conversation.   .57
This couple engaged in "cross-complaining sequences."   .55
This couple was quick to reciprocate a negative remark of the spouse.   .53
This couple initially reciprocated positive remarks but later in the
conversation stopped doing so.   .46
The vocal emotional undertones of this couple were negative.   .45
This couple interrupted one another fairly frequently.   .37

(3) *Open communication style* (eigenvalue = 1.97; 14% variance)
This couple took into account each other's feelings.   .65
This couple shared their thoughts and feelings.   .63
Overall, this couple shows a high degree of marital adjustment.   .57
This couple showed their affection for one another.   .51
This couple verbally negotiated with one another.   .48

(4) *Cooperative communication style* (eigenvalue = 1.54; 10.9% variance)
This couple was generally positive toward one another.   .43
This couple agreed with one another on most matters.   .41
This couple used a neutral tone of voice.   .40
Overall, this couple used far more agreement than disagreement.   .38
The interaction between this couple was extremely "patterned"
in that one remark can easily be predicted from another.   .38
This couple gave in to one another.   .33

(5) *Sex-stereotyped voices* (eigenvalue = 1.12; 7.9% variance)
The husband in this marriage sounded masculine.   .56
The husband in this marriage sounded feminine.   −.57
The wife in this marriage sounded feminine.   .63
The wife in this marriage sounded masculine.   −.57

TABLE 9.11
Mean Ratings and F-Values for Listeners' Judgments
in the Marital Adjustment Ministudy

Dependent Measures	Mean Ratings		Fs	Ps
	Adjusted	Nonadjusted	(df = 1,108)	
Social evaluation	3.65	3.33	4.22	.04
Open communication	5.46	5.04	2.19	.14
Showed affection	3.18	2.18	6.38	.01
Marital adjustment	5.63	4.62	6.29	.01
Generally positive	6.12	4.93	8.70	.003
Generally negative	2.45	3.27	4.04	.04
Cooperated in conflict	7.16	6.40	4.84	.03
Made each other laugh	1.16	0.53	5.92	.01
Agreed with other	6.59	5.82	4.83	.03
Talked too frequently	4.98	3.85	4.41	.04
Went to for advice	2.98	2.03	4.90	.03
Really compatible	4.49	3.62	3.79	.05
Marriage will last	5.29	3.33	20.71	.0001

NOTE: The higher the mean rating, the more listeners perceived the dependent measures in question.

dependent measures, in addition to the individual item data, in further analyses.

The first factor was labeled "social evaluation" and was defined by such questions as: "Would you like this couple as close friends?" and "Would you go to them for advice?" The second factor was labeled "negative communication style" and included items that viewed the couple as using negative voice tones with one another, engaging in cross-complaining sequences, and other items. The third factor was labeled "open communication style" and included such items as sharing thoughts and feelings, showing affection, and taking one another into account. The fourth factor was labeled "cooperative communication style" and included items suggesting that the couple generally agreed with, and were positive about, each other. The fifth factor was labeled "sex-stereotyped voices" (see Smith, 1980) and included items asking for evaluations of the masculine or feminine nature of the voices of the husband and wife on tape.

Thus the first factor that emerged was an overall evaluation of the couple, whereas the other four factors dealt with the makeup of that identity. Respondents appeared to have little trouble in evaluating these couple identities or in seeing relationships among the component parts of these identities. In the adjustment, the communication behaviors linked

TABLE 9.12
Mean Ratings and F-Values for Listeners' Judgment
in the Typology Study

Dependent Measures	Couple Type			Fs	Ps
	Trad	Indep	Sep	(df = 2,131)	
Social evaluation	4.13	3.14	2.71	3.06	.05
Open communication	6.21	5.66	4.89	14.35	.00
Showed affection	3.68	3.45	2.09	9.95	.0001
Marital adjustment	6.45	5.50	5.09	6.60	.002
Generally positive	6.30	6.13	5.40	3.59	.03
Generally negative	2.06	2.05	2.81	3.06	.05
Cooperated in conflict	7.58	6.87	6.75	3.54	.03
Took partner into account	6.58	6.00	5.62	3.31	.04
Self-disclosed	6.34	5.95	4.28	11.45	.0001
Stopped positive reciprocation	3.19	3.45	4.19	3.36	.04
Flexible communication	3.64	4.66	2.85	5.36	.005
Patterned communication	6.53	5.58	7.00	5.10	.007
Respected this couple	5.11	4.53	4.00	2.92	.05

NOTE: The higher the mean rating, the more listeners perceived the dependent measure in question.

to the happy and the unhappy couples were significantly different. One-way ANOVAs were computed for each of the six factors, as well as for the individual items. As can be seen from Table 9.11, a significant difference emerged on the social evaluation factor (i.e., factor 1). Respondents were more favorably disposed toward the adjusted couple. Table 9.11 also pinpoints the individual items of social evaluation that were also significantly disposed in this direction. Although the overall mean values for open communication (factor 3) in Table 9.11 were not significantly different statistically, an examination of the means on the individual items indicates that listeners viewed the maritally adjusted as having a more "open" and "cooperative" communication style.

In the typology study, an overall MANOVA on these data differentiated ratings for the three couple types ($p < .01$); similar ANOVAs provided somewhat more extensive differences than the foregoing. As Table 9.12 indicates, both the factors of "social evaluation" and "open communication" were significantly different for the couple types. An examination of the individual items specifies this trend. Here, the Traditionals were perceived to have shown more affection, to have been more adjusted, to have been generally more positive and hence less negative, to have cooperated in conflict, to have self-disclosed more, and to have been less likely to stop positive-reciprocity cycles in their communication than the Independents; the Independents, in turn, were more "open" and "cooperative" than were the Separates. In addition, respondents evaluated the Traditionals significantly more favorably than the Independents, who in turn were judged more positively than the Separates.

In general, the differences across both studies, although not numerous, are nonetheless striking and in line with our predictions. Interestingly, items that we had not predicted would differentiate adjusted and nonadjusted marriages did emerge in Table 9.11 (e.g., "made each other laugh"). Similarly, items not formally predicted to differentiate between the three couple types also appeared in the perceptual profile of Table 9.12 (e.g., "stopped positive reciprocation"). Nevertheless, there is a good degree of similarity between the two. An exception emerged with the measures of flexibility and patterning of communication styles in Table 9.12. In line with previous observational research on the couple types, the Separates were viewed as the most rigid in their communication with the spouse. The predicted differences for the Traditionals and the Independents, however, did not occur. Indeed, our respondents viewed the Traditionals as more rigid and patterned in their communication than the respondents viewed the Independents. In the couple realm, this may be akin to the phenomenon of "psychological convergence but linguistic divergence" (see Thakerar, Giles, & Chesire, 1982). The patterns that emerge in the stereotype of the various relationships do not reflect what occurs linguistically when researchers analyze the interaction of actual couples. Although psychologically our respondents linked the conservative ideological orientation in marriage and family life of the Traditionals to a rigid communication style, linguistically such rigidity does not occur in Traditional dialogues with a spouse. Similarly, the Independents are not as flexible as our respondents believed. Respondents did converge, however, on questions concerning the frequency of certain communicative behaviors (e.g., self-disclosure, being generally positive). Only on questions concerning interaction patterns did reactions shift away from our predictions.

Perhaps our respondents, and even couples themselves, do not notice and store interaction patterns; perhaps they respond instead to the frequency of occurrence of specific communicative behaviors. When respondents—and again couples themselves—evaluate dyadic encounters, they may remember only first-order acts (he said/she said) and not the complex strings of interaction favored by observational researchers. The relationships among self-reports, behavioral frequencies, and interaction patterns in the minds of people who are evaluating couple identities may differ from actual relationships among these factors in couple communication. Such questions will be of obvious import for future work in this realm. We believe that if the taped conversation had been less "bland," with the couple showing a little more interpersonal conflict and tension, retrospective speech halo effects may well have permeated other judgmental dimensions as well (e.g., the negative communication factor). We also think that, had the contextual information regarding couple types been introduced prospectively rather than retrospectively, similar findings would have emerged (see Snyder, 1981). Indeed, previous research on this phenomenon at the individual level (Ball et al., 1982; Thakerar & Giles 1981) supports such a contention. In this research, listeners could listen to the stimulus tape a second time and modify their ratings. In both studies, respondents rerated in a manner identical to their original—biased—linguistic judgments.

Summary

These three studies suggest that the couple types are psychologically real in that the couples types control the decoding of messages about marriage. The couple types are systematically related to the memories spouses have of their first meeting. The typology also organizes how children view the marriages of their parents and how people in general evaluate couples' communication. Future work should probe the social environments that weaken and strengthen the decoding effects found in these studies. Moreover, would superimposing the linguistic and communication behaviors in Table 9.9 onto an emotionally neutral conversation between spouses induce raters to see them along the lines of the typology (see Bradac, 1983)? I think it would.

CONCLUSION

From both an encoding and a decoding perspective, we have demonstrated that the marital typology is psychologically real. The typology relates to what spouses talk about with one another and to how evaluations are made about marriage and memories of first encounters. Future research on the psychological reality of the couples types could take a number of different directions. The encoding studies reported in this chapter are from the point of view of the couples themselves and two of the decoding studies deal with individuals outside the relationship. The points of view from these two communication perspectives could be broadened.[1] Encoding studies could be conducted with people outside the marital relationship. For example, do children interact differently with parents or adults who are in one of the couple types? A decoding study from the insider point of view would request married couples to evaluate marriages in terms of the communication behaviors.

A major question still unresolved is the following: Do couples themselves recognize the categorizations of their own marriages? To explore this question, the labels "traditional," "independent," and "separate" should not be used with research participants, as these names have a number of connotations attached to them that differ from the empirical results. Scientific language often differs from ordinary language use. For example, a recent description of the family life of a public figure reads like this:

> The North household was a *traditional* one. Ollie was the breadwinner, and his wife, Betsy, was a homemaker and fulltime mother to their four children. . . . (*The Washingtonian,* July 1987, p.142)

The journalist's use of the phrase "traditional" gives us no idea of the psychological nature of the marriage or of the communication patterns and outcomes experienced by this couple. In this typology, a traditional marriage has a highly specific and detailed set of meanings that differ from the use of the term by naive language users and other theorists. Given the widespread use of these terms, however, the terms themselves need to be avoided in asking about a couple's marriage. Instead, couples should be given descriptions of the basic characteristics of the types and asked to identify their marriage.

NOTE

1. This general point was suggested to me by Bryan Crow in a personal conversation in May 1987. Thank you, Bryan.

Epilogue
New Directions
for Marital Research

The fundamental goals of a science of relationships are to describe, predict, and explain. How well has this typology accomplished these fundamental goals? On balance, the marital typology does very well in describing the private culture of marriage by categorizing couples with conceptually important dimensions of relationships. Couples' reports about their interdependence, their ideological views on the nature of personal relationships, and their levels of conflict and expressivity describe the variety of marital systems in some detail. The marital typology also has done extremely well in predicting not only the self-reports but also the communication behaviors and interaction sequences of married couples in various types. Although strong in description and prediction, the typology has been less useful in explaining the nature of marriage. Indeed, many scholars oppose typological or taxonomical formulations *because* these formulations are not theoretical explanations (e.g., Berger, 1985).

Admittedly, the typology in its current state offers little scientific explanation. The naming of constructs implies little about the relationships among those constructs. It has never been my viewpoint, however, that the typology, per se, is an explanatory mechanism suggesting either causes or reasons for communication in marriage. To state that Independents confront disagreements in their relationship is descriptive and predictive, yet it does not answer the question "why" or offer any explanation or understanding for the statement. In other words, why do Independent couples, defined by a combination of nonconventional ideological approaches to marriage and high levels of sharing and interdependence, confront disagreements and negative interactions rather than avoid them?

Despite the apparent pessimism of the previous paragraph, this typology's power to describe and predict marital patterns suggests the building blocks of a theory of marital communication are embedded within the typology. My purpose in this epilogue is to offer an explanation of marriage based on this typology. In attempting to build theory from the typology, I could proceed in two general directions at this point. In other words, there are two ways in which the typology can serve as a heuristic device in the study of communication in intimate relationships. First, the relational dimensions that categorize couples could be used to generate theoretical predictions about specific communication behaviors and outcomes. Rather than grouping individuals and couples, individuals could be allowed to vary along the relational dimensions, and specific main effect and interaction predictions could be made about interaction sequences. The specifics of marital types can be used to specify multivariate hypotheses (Hage, 1972, pp. 47-50). To understand the potential causal role of these dimensions, my colleagues and I could follow couples through time to plot the effect of sharing, ideology, and expressivity on relational change; causal modeling techniques could be employed.

The second way to begin to explain marriage is to use the typology as a starting point and to suggest, from other theoretical perspectives, explanations for the sequences and patterns uncovered in this work. Such a move is similar to conceptual developments in the biological sciences. In biology, early taxonomic methods used morphological characteristics to type species. Each type became associated with a large bundle of empirically connected traits. The morphological basis gradually began to be replaced with a phylogenetic basis, more deeply embedded in the theory of evolution. This theory did not emerge from the typing of the species, yet the theory did explain the systematic regularities derived from empirical observations. The various species are now defined in phylogenetic and genetic terms. The original morphological characteristics still provide criteria for assigning organisms to species. Without the original description and taxonomy of the species, however, the phylogenetic basis might not have emerged (Sneath & Sokal, 1973).

In my current research, I have chosen the second path in an attempt to explore what underlies the dimensions of relationships. Theory development is important not only within the structure of this typology but also in reference to many other descriptions of family life. This chapter moves toward the development of a marital communication theory that offers conceptual explanations for the empirical regularities observed in this program of research.

A THEORETICAL EXTENSION

The theoretical explanation is a social cognitive one. As an initial move toward a social cognitive theory of marital communication, I presented evidence that the types of marriages uncovered in this program of research are "psychologically real"—that is, individuals have and use knowledge representations about marriage that link the descriptive characteristics of a marriage to the major communication characteristics exhibited by various types of couples.

Based on this research, I argue that individuals have "marital schemata," knowledge structures that represent the external world of marriage and provide guidelines about how to interpret incoming data. Marital schemata specify the nature and organization of information relevant to the partner and the marriage (Neisser, 1967). The Relational Dimensions Instrument (RDI), on which the categorization of couples is based, does not contain all the major dimensions of marital interaction; the RDI also fails to isolate the content of an individual's marital schemata. But, the RDI does allow the researcher to tap into subgroups of individuals who hold similar marital schemata. The schemata affect the encoding, retrieval, and processing of marital messages.

There are four advantages to treating the basic marital orientations uncovered in previous research as marital schemata. First, this view allows the researcher to make a number of specific theoretically derived predictions about message processing. Schemata can be said to direct attentional focus; they make classes of messages from a spouse—for example, messages that deviate from prior expectations—salient (Hastie, 1981; Taylor & Fiske, 1978). Second, this theoretical stance leads to predictions about what spouses remember about interactions with one another. Because the dimensions of the typology contain more information than the level of marital satisfaction of a couple, the marital schema yields more information concerning inputs to marital interaction, not only outcomes. Such a perspective helps explain why different interaction patterns lead to specific levels of marital satisfaction.

Third, proof of the existence and operation of marital schemata advances our understanding of social cognitive processes in general because this work could show how schemata operate in domains where emotion runs high. In Chapter 8, we argue that emotion may occur because of the discrepancy between the marital schema and a spouse's behavior.

Fourth, adopting a social cognitive perspective offers a way to understand how couples assign meaning to their own messages. Many programs of research (Fitzpatrick, 1984; Gottman, 1979; Markman, 1984; Weiss, 1985) have coded the ongoing interaction of spouses and demonstrated the patterned nature of that interaction. Researchers rarely study how the couples evaluate these messages. One exception can be found in the talk table studies (Markman, 1984), which demonstrate that distressed couples have different schemata and pay attention to different aspects of the communication. These schemata are not necessarily those held by the observers.

The marital typology research reported in this chapter implies that the three relational definitions are marital schemata. Individuals appear to have stable views of relationships; these views correspond to the marital types. Furthermore, the views contain clear specifications of the kinds of messages exchanged in various couple types. These views of various marital forms affect the amount and kind of marital communication. This evidence for the existence of marital schemata is obviously indirect. The arguments for gender schemata (Bem, 1984) and for role schemata (Kinder, Peters, Abelson, & Fiske, 1980) suggest that individuals may encode and process messages from the spouse and about the marriage in terms of the traditional, independent, and separate schemata.

Little research has been conducted on the social cognitive processes underlying marital communication. Communication is the very essence of social cognition (Forgas, 1981). According to Markus and Zajonc (1985, p. 231), "social cognitions are both the sources and the products of a social process in which communication is the main vehicle." The study of communication in marriage represents a potentially rich intersection of the cognitive and the social. The construction of dialogues is the way social cognition manifests itself. Conversation is inherently social because it involves the transmission of messages between at least two people and it is cognitive in that communication requires cognitive activity.

The social cognitive perspective has pragmatic and therapeutic implications as well as theoretical ones. For example, interventions from a behavioral marital therapy perspective (e.g., Jacobson & Margolin, 1979) designed to increase positive and decrease negative behaviors, must be individualized to fit into a couple's interpretations of their own interactions. Married individuals may see more negative or positive events than outsiders or a spouse may become perceptually set over time to react in a certain way to the spouse.

CONCLUSION

My studies of communication in marriage have used a broad range of methods: perceptual tests and questionnaires, direct observations of verbal and nonverbal communication both in laboratories and in homes, and comparisons of spouse and stranger interactions. I have used coding schemes, both abstract and concrete in the level of inference they require, and multiple-sampling methods and a variety of experimental techniques. The main objective of this research has been to demonstrate that couples can be categorized and such categorizations predict communication behaviors and outcomes. Although communication is central to the relationship between husbands and wives, the meaning of "good communication" differs systematically among couples according to their attitudes and values, their degrees of interdependence, and their levels of expressivity.

It is my hope that other scholars will take up some of the themes and ideas about marital communication presented in this book. According to Reiss (1981), models of family processes are intriguing to other scholars only after the scholar has made a number of decisions. First, the scholar must find something familiar and plausible in the typology. Given the similarity of this perspective to many other views on marriage, the typological model should not be foreign nor should its assertions be improbable to the reader. Second, a scholar, recognizing the robustness of the underlying structure, must see ways in which the model can be improved. The fundamental structure of the typology is strong enough to support revisions and reworkings. Third, the scholar must have a sense that additional work on the typology will expand what we know about marital and family processes. I believe that the marital typology has this heuristic potential. The reader is the final judge of the potential of this marital typology.

Appendix I
The Relational Dimensions Instrument

COMMUNICATION BETWEEN MATES

This questionnaire is concerned with how husbands and wives communicate with one another and how they organize their family life. The answers will provide information about couples in ongoing relationships and will have direct practical application in counseling and marital enrichment programs. Your responses will be used for the purposes of research only. All responses will be kept confidential and anonymous, so please do not sign your name.

INSTRUCTIONS

Although the questionnaire is rather lengthy, much of it requires only short answers and can be completed rather quickly. There are no right or wrong answers to these questions, so try to answer them as honestly as possible. Give each question a moment's thought and then answer it. Please answer the questions without help from your partner. Your partner should not see your answers nor try to help you with them. Please feel free to add comments if none of the responses describe how you feel or fit your situation. Thank you participating in this project.

On the following pages, you will find a number of statements. Each statement is followed by a scale. This scale requires you to make a judgment of how frequently a particular activity or behavior occurs OR how frequently a given statement can be considered true for you or your relationship. Please CIRCLE the number that best shows how you feel about the statement.

(1) We try to make our guests feel free to enter any room of our house.
(2) We talk about the future of our relationship.
(3) We share responsibility for deciding when, for how long, and at what speed chores around the house should be completed.

(4) We go out together to public places in the community such as zoos, sporting events, public parks, amusement parks, museums, libraries, and so on.

(5) We visit with our friends in their houses or apartments.

(6) My spouse/mate has taken vacations without me (even if only for a day or two).

(7) We try to resolve our disagreements immediately.

(8) We embrace in public places.

(9) We tell each other how much we love or care about each other.

(10) My spouse/mate tells me (i.e., tries to influence) what magazines or books to read and/or what television shows to watch.

(11) We decide together how to arrange the furniture and set up various rooms in our home.

(12) We go to bed at different times.

(13) My spouse/mate encourages me to use my talents, even if it means some inconvenience to him/her.

(14) Most of our friends know each other.

(15) We talk more about tasks and accomplishments than about feelings and affection.

(16) We feel a need to resolve the disagreements or oppositions that arise between us.

(17) I open my spouse's/mate's personal mail without asking permission.

(18) I feel free to interrupt my spouse/mate when he/she is concentrating on something if he/she is in my presence.

(19) I tell (i.e., try to influence) my spouse/mate which magazines or books to read and/or what television shows to watch.

(20) My spouse/mate reassures and comforts me when I am feeling low.

(21) My spouse/mate forces me to do things that I do not want to do.

(22) My spouse/mate expresses his/her feelings and reactions to me.

(23) I get the feeling that my spouse/mate can read my mind.

(24) We eat our meals (i.e., the ones at home) at the same time every day.

(25) We seek new friends and outside experiences.

(26) We are likely to argue in front of friends or in public places.

(27) I have my own private workspace (study, workshop, utility room, etc.).

(28) We cook and eat our meals separately, even when we are both at home.

(29) I feel free to invite guests home without informing my spouse/mate.

(30) I have taken separate vacations from my spouse/mate even if only for a day or two.

(31) We express anger with each other.

(32) I feel free to ask my spouse/mate to communicate his/her true feelings to me.

(33) In our house, we keep a fairly regular daily time schedule.

(34) We share many of our personal belongings with each other.

(35) If I can avoid arguing about some problems, they will disappear.

(36) My spouse has his/her own private workspace (workshop, utility room, study, and so on).

(37) My spouse/mate tries to persuade me to do something that I do not want to do.

(38) We talk about the present.

(39) We serve the main meal at the same time every day.

(40) My mate complains if I open his/her personal mail without permission.

(41) It bothers me if a guest goes into our refrigerator or fixes himself/herself some coffee in our home.

(42) If I am working or concentrating on something, I ignore the presence of my spouse/mate.

(43) When I am angry with my spouse/mate, I'll say nothing rather than something that I will be sorry for later.

(44) We openly express our disagreements with each other.

(45) Events in our house/apartment occur without any regularity.

(46) Our time schedule varies quite a bit from day to day.

---

(1) Always; (2) Usually; (3) Often; (4) Occasionally; (5) Often Not; (6) Usually Not; (7) Never.

The next set of questions is followed by scales which ask for a judgment of how strongly you agree or disagree with particular statements concerning a variety of issues. Please CIRCLE the number that best shows how you feel about the statement.

(47) Life is filled with so many contradictions that I am not certain how to interpret what it all means.

(48) Our life together seems more exciting than that of most couples I know.

(49) We cooperate well in resolving our conflicts.

(50) It is more important to share good feelings with each other than it is to share bad feelings.

(51) I think that we joke around and have more fun than most couples.

(52) Infidelity (unfaithfulness) in marriage is inexcusable.

(53) Relationships should not interfere with each person's pursuit to discover his/her own potential.

(54) Often the only way to gain perspective on a situation is to see its absurdity.

(55) Our wedding ceremony was (will be) very important to us.

(56) Pictures, mementos, and other objects that have a special meaning for a couple should be displayed in their home so that others can see them.

(57) A good motto for our relationship is "Care deeply but remain composed."

(58) It is important for a couple (or a family) to attend church (synagogue) and, when possible, to attend together.

(59) Sex is very important in our relationship.

(60) I think it is important for one to have some private space which is all his/her own and separate from one's mate.

(61) Children should be taught the traditions and customs which are their heritage.

(62) Once family plans are made, they should not be changed without a very good reason.

(63) Family secrets should not be shared with friends, no matter how close they are.

(64) Our society, as we see it, needs to regain faith in the law and in our institutions.

(65) The meaning of life and our purpose in it is very clear to us.

(66) The ideal relationship is one which is marked by novelty, humor, and spontaneity.

(67) In marriage/close relationships there should be no constraints or restrictions on individual freedom.

(68) There seem to be many minor crises in our lives.

(69) A woman should take her husband's last name when she marries.

(70) We can go for long periods of time without spending much time together as a couple.

(71) We communicate to one another with a greater range and intensity of feelings than most couples I know.

(72) It is better to hide one's true feelings in order to avoid hurting your spouse/mate.

(73) With my spouse/mate, I tell it like it is no matter what the consequences.

(74) Partners should be frank and spontaneous in conversations with one another even if it leads to disagreements.

(75) In a marriage/close relationship, privacy is more important than togetherness.

(76) In a relationship, each individual should be permitted to establish the daily rhythm and time schedule that suits him/her best.

(77) In our relationship, we feel that it is better to engage in conflicts than to avoid them.

---

(1) Strongly Agree; (2) Agree; (3) Moderately Agree; (4) Undecided; (5) Moderately Disagree; (6) Disagree; (7) Strongly Disagree.

Appendix II
Computing Couple Types

The search for relatively homogeneous groups of people or objects is facilitated by cluster analysis. In the initial stages of this research, I used a linear typal analysis program developed by Overall and Klett (1972). The program, however, is not easily available and has not been written for use on a microcomputer. In the past few years, we have calculated couple types using the SPSSPC+ "Quick Cluster" program (the reader using other versions of SPSS needs to check program commands carefully). Quick cluster requires that the researcher know the number of clusters and the mean values for the cluster centers before data analysis. In our case, we are looking for three clusters and we have eight different means values (i.e., RDI scores) for each of the three marital definitions. The eight different mean values for each of the three marital definitions are taken from the 1,600 person sample reported in Fitzpatrick (1984). The use of such a large database to estimate mean values adds to the stability of the findings for those researchers working with smaller samples.

These values are listed in order from sharing to conflict in the runstream below. The runstream lists the items in the RDI that need to be reflected. The item numbers correspond to the numbers on the RDI in the first appendix. The cluster centers are the following: mean values for traditionals on all eight rational dimensions, the mean values for independents on all eight dimensions, and, finally, the mean values for separates on all eight dimensions.

Each spouse completes the RDI separately. The output from this runstream yields a printout of the individual's marital definition. The researcher compares husband and wife definitions to compute couple types.

THE RUNSTREAM

Check the computer manual for exact instructions (Norusis, 1986, pp. B-91-B-101). I have included some annotation on the runstream.

The first few lines of the following runstream set up the file, define couple numbers, sort cases, and define missing data.

```
set printers =  on/length = 59/more = off.
data list file = 'rdidat.dat'
/cnum 1-3 sex 4 rl to r46 5-50
/r47 to r77 1-31.
recode rl to r77 1-31.
recode rl to r77 (0 =  4) (9 = 4).
sort cases by cnum sex.
value labels sex 0 "male" 1 "female."
```

The data are redefined in order that a high score indicates agreement with the relational dimension.

```
recode rl to r77 (7 = 1) (6 = 2) (5 = 3) (4 = 4) (3 = 5) (2 = 6) (1 = 7)
```

Eleven variables are recoded.

```
recode r12 (7 = 1 ) (6 = 2) (5 = 3) (4 = 4) (3 = 5) (2 = 6) (1 = 7).
recode r15 (7 = 1 ) (6 = 2) (5 = 3) (4 = 4) (3 = 5) (2 = 6) (1 = 7).
recode r31 (7 = 1 ) (6 = 2) (5 = 3) (4 = 4) (3 = 5) (2 = 6) (1 = 7).
recode r40 (7 = 1 ) (6 = 2) (5 = 3) (4 = 4) (3 = 5) (2 = 6) (1 = 7).
recode r41 (7 = 1 ) (6 = 2) (5 = 3) (4 = 4) (3 = 5) (2 = 6) (1 = 7).
recode r44 (7 = 1 ) (6 = 2) (5 = 3) (4 = 4) (3 = 5) (2 = 6) (1 = 7).
recode r45 (7 = 1) (6 = 2) (5 = 3) (4 = 4) (3 = 5) (2 = 6) (1 = 7).
recode r46 (7 = 1 ) (6 = 2) (5 = 3) (4 = 4) (3 = 5) (2 = 6) (1 = 7).
recode r73 (7 = 1 ) (6 = 2) (5 = 3) (4 = 4) (3 = 5) (2 = 6) (1 = 7).
recode r74 (7 = 1 ) (6 = 2) (5 = 3) (4 = 4) (3 = 5) (2 = 6) (1 = 7).
recode r77 (7 = 1 ) (6 = 2) (5 = 3) (4 = 4) (3 = 5) (2 = 6) (1 = 7).
```

The eight RDI factors are computed.

```
compute s = r2 +r3 + r4 + r5 + r7 + r8 + r9 + r11 + r12 + r13 + r15 + r16 + r20 + r22 +
   r23 + r25.
compute sharing = (s + r32 + r38 +r48 + r49 + r51 + r59 + r71)/23.
compute tradit = (r14 + r52 + r55 + r56 + r57 + r58 + r61 + r62 + r63 + r64 + r65 +
   r69)/12.
compute uncert = (r47 + r53 + r54 + r66 + r67 + r68 + r75 + r76)/8.
compute tempreg = (r24 + r33 + r39 + r45 + r46)/5.
compute autonom = (r6 + r27 + r30 + r36 + r60 + r70)/6.
compute assert = (r10 + r19 + r21 + r26 + r28 + r37)/6.
compute space = (r1 + r17 + r18 + r29 + r34 + r40 + r41 + r42)/8.
compute conflict = (r31 + r35 + r43 + r44 + r50 + r72 + r73 + r74 + r77)/9.
```

Some descriptive statistics are requested.

descriptives sharing to conflict
/ options = 3
/ statistics = 13

The quick cluster commands are included. In this set up, marital definition 1 is traditional, marital definition 2 is independent, and marital definition 3 is separate. This is arbitrary. If you change the order of the cluster means, be sure you know how to make your marital definitions.

quick cluster sharing to conflict
/ criteria = clusters (3)
/ initial= (5.01 4.97 3.52 4.71 3.20 2.80 4.44 3.94
        4.73 3.93 4.35 3.23 4.39 3.54 4.41 3.60
        4.07 4.88 4.19 4.41 4.40 3.27 3.88 4.54)

Calculate an analysis of variances comparing the three marital definitions on these eight dimensions. And, save your cluster definitions for the whole sample in order to type couples.

/ print = cluster anova
/ save = cluster (ctype)
/ missing = include.
save outfile = 'rdidat.sys'
/ drop = r1 to r77 s.

I am interested in hearing suggestions, comments, criticisms, and so on from researchers attempting to type couples. Please address your correspondence to me at the Center for Communication Research, Vilas Hall 6th Floor, University of Wisconsin, Madison, Wisconsin 53705.

REFERENCES

Adams, B. (1986). *The family.* San Diego: Harcourt, Brace, & Jovanovich.

Allison, P. D., & Liker, J. K. (1982). Analyzing sequential categorical data on dyadic interaction: A comment on Gottman. *Psychological Bulletin, 91,* 393-403.

Altman, I. (1975). *The environment and social behavior.* Monterey, CA: Brooks/Cole.

Altman, I., & Taylor, D. A. (1973). *Social penetration: The development of interpersonal relationships.* New York: Holt, Rinehart & Winston.

Anderson, N. (1968). Likableness ratings of 555 personality trait words. *Journal of Personality and Social Psychology, 9,* 272-279.

Anderson, T. W., & Goodman, L. H. (1957). Statistical inferences about Markov chains. *Annals of Mathematical Statistics, 23,* 89-110.

Argyle, M. (1986). *Happiness in western society.* Lecture given in October 1986, Department of Psychology, University of Wisconsin—Madison.

Argyle, M., & Dean, J. (1965). Eye contact, distance and affiliation. *Sociometry, 28,* 289-304.

Argyle, M., & Ingham, R. (1972). Gaze, mutual gaze and proximity. *Semiotics, 6,* 32-49.

Ashmore, R. D., Del Boca, F. K., & Wohlers, A. J., (1986). Gender stereotypes. In R. D. Ashmore & F. K. Del Boca (Eds.), *The social-psychology of female-male relations* (pp. 69-115). Orlando, FL: Academic Press.

Bach, G., & Wyden, P. (1968). *The intimate enemy.* New York: William Morrow.

Bakeman, R., & Gottman, J. M. (1986). *Observing interaction.* Cambridge, England: Cambridge University Press.

Ball, P., Byrne, J., Giles, H., Berechree, P., Griffiths, J., Macdonald, H., & McKendrick, I. (1982). The retrospective speech halo effect: Some Australian data. *Language and Communication, 2,* 277-284.

Balswick, J., & Peek, C. (1971). The inexpressive male: A tragedy of American society. *Family Coordinator, 20,* 263-268.

Bateson, G. (1938, 1958). *Naven.* Palo Alto, CA: Stanford University Press.

Bateson, G., & Jackson, D. (1968). Some varieties in pathogenic organization. In D. D. Jackson (Ed.), *Communication, family and marriage* (pp. 210-215). Palo Alto, CA: Science & Behavior Press.

Baxter, L. (1985). Accomplishing relationship disengagement. In S. Duck & D. Perlman (Eds.), *Personal relationships* (pp. 243-265). Beverly Hills, CA: Sage.

Bell, R. R. (1979). *Marriage and family interaction* (5th ed.). Homewood, IL: Dorsey.

Bellah, R. N., Madsen, R., Sullivan, W. M., Swidler, A., & Tipton, S. M. (1985). *Habits of the heart: Individualism and commitment in American life*. Berkeley: University of California Press.

Bem, S. (1974). The measurement of psychological androgyny. *Journal of Consulting and Clinical Psychology, 42*, 155-162.

Bem, S. (1984). Androgyny and gender scheme theory: A conceptual and methodological integration. In T. B. Sonderegger (Ed.), *Psychology and gender: Nebraska symposium on motivation* (pp. 179-226). Lincoln: University of Nebraska Press.

Berger, C. (1985). Social power and interpersonal communication. In M. L. Knapp & G. R. Miller (Eds.), *Handbook of interpersonal communication* (pp. 439-500). Beverly Hills, CA: Sage.

Berger, C. R., & Bradac, J. J. (1982). *Language and social knowledge: Uncertainty in interpersonal relations*. London: Edward Arnold.

Berger, P., & Kellner, H. (1975). Marriage and the construction of reality. In D. Brisset & C. Edgeley (Eds.), *Life as theatre: A dramaturgical handbook*. Chicago: Aldine.

Berkowitz, L. (1985). Conversations with Professors Leonard Berkowitz and Harold Kelley: Is there a need for a field of personal relationships? In R. Milardo (Ed.), *Newsletter for the International Society for the Study of Personal Relationships*. Orono: University of Maine.

Bernard, J. (1972). *The future of marriage*. New York: World.

Bernstein, B. (1973). *Class, codes and control*. London: Routledge & Kegan Paul.

Berscheid, E. (1983). Emotion in close relationships. In H. Kelley, E. Berscheid, A. Christensen, J. J. Harvey, T. L. Huston, G. Levinger, E. McClintock, L. A. Peplau, & D. R. Peterson (Eds.), *Close relationships* (pp. 110-168). New York: W. H. Freeman.

Berscheid, E., & Campbell, B. (1981). The changing longevity of heterosexual close relationships: A commentary and forecast. In M. J. Lerner & S. C. Lerner (Eds.), *The justice motives in social behavior* (pp. 205-234). New York: Plenum.

Best, P. (1979). *Relational control in marriage*. Unpublished master's thesis, University of Wisconsin—Milwaukee.

Bienvenu, M. (1970). The measurement of marital communication. *Family Coordinator, 19*, 26-31.

Birchler, G. R., Weiss, R. L., & Vincent, J. P. (1975). Multimethod analysis of social reinforcement exchange between maritally distressed and non-distressed spouse and stranger dyads. *Journal of Personality and Social Psychology, 31*, 349-360.

Bishop, Y. M., Feinberg, S. E., & Hollard, P. W. (1975). *Discrete multivariate analysis*. Cambridge: MIT Press.

Blake, R. R., & Mouten, J. S. (1964). *The managerial grid*. Houston: Gulf.

Blau, P. (1964). *Exchange and power in social life*. New York: John Wiley.

Bochner, A. P. (1983). The functions of human communication in interpersonal bonding. In C. C. Arnold & J. W. Bowers (Eds.), *Handbook of rhetorical and communication theory* (pp. 544-621). Boston: Allyn & Bacon.

Bochner, A. P., & Fitzpatrick, M. A. (1980). Multivariate analysis of variance: Techniques, models and applications in communication research. In P. Monge & J. N. Cappella (Eds.), *Multivariate techniques in communication research* (pp.143-174). New York; Academic Press.

Bochner, A. P., Kaminski, E. P., & Fitzpatrick, M. A. (1977). The conceptual domain of interpersonal communication behavior. *Human Communication Research, 3*, 291-302.

Bolton, C. D. (1961). Mate selection as the development of a relationship. *Marriage and Family Living, 23*, 234-240.

Bott, E. (1971). *Family and social network* (2nd ed.). New York: Free Press.

Bowen, M. (1961). Family psychotherapy. *American Journal of Orthopsychiatry, 31,* 40-60.

Bowers, J. W., Metts, S. M., & Duncanson, W. T. (1985). Emotion and interpersonal communication. In M. L. Knapp & G. R. Miller (Eds.), *Handbook of interpersonal communication* (pp. 500-550). Beverly Hills, CA: Sage.

Bradac, J. (1983). The language of lovers, flovers, and friends: Communicating in social and personal relationships. *Journal of Language and Social Psychology, 2,* 141-162.

Bradbury, T. N., & Fincham, F. D. (in press). Assessment of affect. In K. D. O'Leary (Ed.), *Assessment of marital discord.* Hillsdale: Lawrence Erlbaum.

Brogan, D., & Kutner, N. G. (1976). Measuring sex-role orientation. *Journal of Marriage and the Family, 38,* 31-40.

Broverman, I. K., Vogel, S. R., Broverman, D. M., Clarkson, F. E., & Rosenkrantz, P. S. (1972). Sex role stereotypes. *Journal of Social Issues, 28,* 59-78.

Brown, M. B. (1983). Frequency tables. In W. J. Dixon (Ed.), *BMDP statistical software* (pp. 143-206). Berkeley: Regents of California.

Brown, R. (1986). *Social psychology: The second edition.* New York: Free Press.

Buck, R. (1984). *The communication of emotion.* New York: Guilford.

Buerkel-Rothfus, N. L., & Mayes, S. (1981). Soap opera viewing: The cultivation effect. *Journal of Communication, 31,* 108-115.

Burgess, E. W., & Cottrell, L. S. (1939). *Predicting success or failure in marriage.* New York: Prentice-Hall.

Burgess, E. W., & Locke, H. J. (1948). *The family: From institution to companionship* (1st ed.). New York: American.

Burgoon, J. K., & Hale, J. L. (1984). The fundamental topic of relational communication. *Communication Monographs, 51,* 193-214.

Burgraff, C., & Sillars, A. (1986). *A critical examination of sex differences in marital communication.* Paper presented at the Speech Communication Association, Chicago.

Candland, D. K. (1977). The persistent problems of emotion. In D. K. Candland, J. P. Fell, E. Keen, A. I. Leshner, R. Plutchik, & R. M. Tarpy (Eds.), *Emotion.* Monterey, CA: Brooks/Cole.

Cappella, J. N. (1979). Talk-silence sequences in informal conversations I. *Human Communication Research, 6,* 3-17.

Cappella, J. N., & Greene, J. (1982). A discrepancy-arousal explanation of mutual influence in expressive behavior for adult and infant-adult interaction. *Communication Monographs, 49,* 89-114.

Cappella, J., & Palmer, M. (1987). An approach to the problem of correlated data. Unpublished manuscript, Center for Communication Research, University of Wisconsin.

Cappella, J. N., & Planalp, S. (1981). Talk and silence sequences in informal conversations III: Interspeaker influence. *Human Communication Research, 7,* 117-132.

Carter, H., & Glick, P. C. (1978). *Marriage and divorce: A social and economic study* (2nd ed.). Cambridge: Harvard University Press.

Cattell, R. B. (1958). Extracting the correct number of factors in factor analysis. *Educational and Psychological Measurement, 18,* 791-837.

Christensen, A. (1988). Dysfunctional interaction patterns in couples. In P. Noller & M. A. Fitzpatrick (Eds.), *Perspectives on marital interaction.* Philadelphia: Multilingual Matters.

Christensen, A., & Nies, D. C. (1980). The spouse observation checklist: Empirical analysis and critique. *American Journal of Family Therapy, 8,* 69-79.

Clark, R. A. (1979). The impact of self-interest and desired liking on selection of persuasive strategies. *Communication Monographs, 46,* 257-273.

Cody. M., & McLaughlin, M. (1985). The situation as a construct in interpersonal communication research. In M. L. Knapp & G. R. Miller (Eds.), *Handbook of interpersonal communication* (pp. 263-313). Beverly Hills, CA: Sage.

Cody, M. J., McLaughlin, M. L., & Jordan, W. J. (1980). A multidimensional scaling of three sets of compliance-gaining strategies. *Communication Quarterly, 28,* 34-46.

Cody, M. J., McLaughlin, M. L., & Schneider, M. J. (1981). The impact of intimacy and relational consequences on the selection of interpersonal persuasion tactics: A reanalysis. *Communication Monographs, 29,* 91-106.

Cohen, J. (1960). A coefficient of agreement for nominal scales. *Educational and Psychological Measurement, 20,* 37-46.

Cohen, R., & Christensen, A. (1980). Further examination of demand characteristics in marital interaction. *Journal of Consulting and Clinical Psychology, 48,* 121-123.

Cronbach, L. J. (1955). Processes affecting scores on understanding others and assumed similarity. *Psychological Bulletin, 52,* 117-193.

Cuber, J. F., & Harroff, P. (1965). *The significant Americans: A study of sexual behavior among the affluent.* New York: Appleton-Century-Crofts.

Cummings, E. M., Iannotti, R. J., Zahn-Waxler, C. (1985). Influence of conflict between adults on the emotions and aggression of young children. *Child Development, 21,* 495-507.

Cummings, E. M., Zahn-Waxler, C., & Radke-Yarrow, M. (1981). Young children's responses to expressions of anger and affection by others in the family. *Child Development, 52,* 1274-1282.

Del Boca, F. K., Ashmore, R. D., & McManus, M. A. (1986). Gender-related attitudes. In R. D. Ashmore & F. K. Del Boca (Eds.), *The social psychology of female-male relations* (pp. 121-165). Orlando, FL: Academic Press.

Derlega, V. J., & Grzelak, J. (1979). Appropriateness of self disclosure. In G. J. Chelune (Ed.), *Self disclosure* (pp. 151-176). San Francisco: Jossey-Bass.

Dillard, J., & Fitzpatrick, M. A. (1985). Compliance-gaining in marital interaction. *Personality and Social Psychology Bulletin, 11,* 419-433.

Dindia, K. (1982). Reciprocity of self-disclosure. In M. Burgoon (Ed.), *Communication yearbook 6* (pp. 49-82). Beverly Hills, CA: Sage.

Dindia, K. (1985). A functional approach to self-disclosure. In R. L. Street and J. Cappella (Eds.), *Sequence and pattern in communication behavior* (pp. 121-131). London: Edward Arnold.

Dindia, K. (1986). *A comparison of unidimensional and multidimensional measures of marital quality.* Unpublished manuscript, Department of Communication, University of Wisconsin—Milwaukee.

Doherty, W. J., & Colangelo, N. (1984). The family FIRO model: A modest proposal for organizing family treatment. *Journal of Marital and Family Therapy, 10,* 19-29.

Doherty, W. J., & Rider, R. G. (1979). Locus of control, interpersonal trust, and assertive behavior among newlyweds. *Journal of Personality and Social Psychology, 37,* 2212-2220.

Duby, G. (1983). *The knight, the lady, and the priest: The making of a modern marriage in medieval France.* New York: Pantheon.

Eggeman, K., Moxley, V., & Schumm, W. (1985). Assessing spouses' perceptions of Gottman's temporal form in marital conflict. *Psychological Reports, 57,* 171-181.

Ekman, P. (1980). Asymmetry in facial expression. *Science, 209,* 833-834.

Ellis, D., Fisher, B. A., Drecksel, G., Hoch, D., & Werbel, W. (1976). *Relational interaction coding systems.* Unpublished manuscript, Purdue University, Department of Communication.

Ellis, D., & Hamilton, M. (1986). Syntactic and pragmatic code usage in interpersonal communication. *Communication Monographs, 52,* 264-278.

Elwood, R. W., & Jacobson, N. S. (1982). Spouses' agreement in reporting their behavioral interactions: A clinical replication. *Journal of Consulting and Clinical Psychology, 50,* 783-784.

Ericson, P. M., & Rogers, E. L. (1973). New procedures for analyzing relational communication. *Family Process, 12,* 245-267.

Falbo, T. A. (1977). A multidimensional scaling of power strategies. *Journal of Personality and Social Psychology, 35,* 537-547.

Falbo, T., & Peplau, L. A. (1980). Power strategies in intimate relationships. *Journal of Personality and Social Psychology, 38,* 618-628.

Fine, M. G. (1981). Soap opera conversations: The talk that binds. *Journal of Communication, 31,* 97-107.

Fisher, A., & Beach, W. (1979). Content and relationship dimensions of communication behavior. *Western Journal of Speech Communication, 43,* 201-211.

Fitzpatrick, M. A. (1976). *A typological examination of communication in enduring relationships.* Unpublished Ph.D. dissertation, Temple University.

Fitzpatrick, M. A. (1977). A typological approach to communication in relationships. In B. Rubin (Ed.), *Communication yearbook 1* (pp. 263-275). Rutgers: Transaction.

Fitzpatrick, M. A. (1981). A typological approach to enduring relationships: Children as audience to the parental relationships. *Journal of Comparative Family Studies, 12,* 81-94.

Fitzpatrick, M. A. (1983). Predicting couples' communication from couples' self-reports. In R. N. Bostrom & B. H. Westley (Eds.), *Communication yearbook 7* (pp. 49-82). Beverly Hills, CA: Sage.

Fitzpatrick, M. A. (1984). A typological approach to marital interaction: Recent theory and research. In L. Berkowitz (Ed.), *Advances in experimental social psychology, 18* (pp. 1-47). Orlando, FL: Academic Press.

Fitzpatrick, M. A. (1987a). *The effect of marital schemata on marital communication.* Paper presented at International Communication Association, Montreal, Canada.

Fitzpatrick, M. A. (1987b). Marital interaction. In C. R. Berger & S. Chaffee (Eds.), *Handbook of communication science.* Beverly Hills, CA: Sage.

Fitzpatrick, M. A. (1987c). Power in marital interaction. In P. Noller & M. A. Fitzpatrick (Eds.), *Perspectives on marital interaction.* Philadelphia: Multilingual Matters.

Fitzpatrick, M. A. (1987d). Marriage and verbal intimacy. In V. J. Derlega & J. Berg (Eds.), *Self-disclosure: Theory, research, and therapy* (pp. 133-154). New York: Plenum.

Fitzpatrick, M. A., & Badzinski, D. (1985). All in the family: Communication in kin relationships. In M. L. Knapp & G. R. Miller (Eds.), *Handbook of interpersonal communication* (pp. 687-736). Beverly Hills, CA: Sage.

Fitzpatrick, M. A., Bauman, I., & Lindaas, M. (1987). *A schematic approach to marital interaction.* Paper presented at the International Communication Association, Montreal, Canada.

Fitzpatrick, M. A., & Best, P. (1979). Dyadic adjustment in traditional, independent, and separate relationships: A validation study. *Communication Monographs, 46,* 167-178.

Fitzpatrick, M. A., & Dindia, K. (1986a). Couples and other strangers: Talk-time in spouse-stranger interaction. *Communication Research, 13,* 625-652.

Fitzpatrick, M. A., & Dindia, K. (1986b). *Self-disclosure in spouse versus stranger interaction.* Unpublished manuscript, University of Wisconsin—Madison, Center for Communication Research.

Fitzpatrick, M. A., Fallis, S., & Vance, L. (1982). Multifunctional coding of conflict resolution strategies in marital dyads. *Family Relations, 31,* 611-670.

Fitzpatrick, M. A., & Hein, E. (1986). *First encounters of the close kind.* Unpublished manuscript, University of Wisconsin—Madison, Center for Communication Research.

Fitzpatrick, M. A., & Indvik, J. (1979). *What you see may not be what you have: Communicative accuracy in marital types.* Paper presented at the Speech Communication Association Convention, San Antonio.

Fitzpatrick, M. A., & Indvik, J. (1982). The instrumental and expressive domains of marital communication. *Human Communication Research, 8,* 195-213.

Fitzpatrick, M. A., & Noller, P. (1987). *Marital types and emotional expressivity.* Unpublished manuscript, University of Wisconsin—Madison, Center for Communication Research.

Fitzpatrick, M. A., Vance, L. E., & Witteman, H. (1984). Interpersonal communication in the casual interaction of marital partners. *Journal of Language and Social Psychology, 3,* 81-95.

Fitzpatrick, M. A., & Winke, J. (1979). You always hurt the one you love: Strategies and tactics in interpersonal conflict. *Communication Quarterly, 27,* 3-11.

Folger, J. P., & Poole, M. S. (1984). *Working through conflict.* Glenview IL: Scott Foresman.

Folger, J. P., & Puck, S. (1976). *Coding relational communication: A question approach.* Paper presented at the International Communication Association, Portland, OR.

Folger, J., & Sillars, A. (1980). Relational coding and perceptions of dominance. In B. W. Morse & L. A. Phelps (Eds.), *Interpersonal communication: A relational perspective* (pp. 322-333). Minneapolis: Burgess.

Forgas, J. P. (1981). *Social cognition: Perspectives on everyday understanding.* London: Academic Press.

Frost, J. H., & Wilmot, W. W. (1978). *Interpersonal conflict.* Dubuque, IA: W. C. Brown.

Gergen, K. J., & Jones, E. E. (1963). Mental illness, predictability, and affective consequences for stimulus factors in person perception. *Journal of Abnormal and Social Psychology, 67,* 95-104.

Giddens, A. (1984). *The constitution of society.* Berkeley: University of California Press.

Giles, H., & Fitzpatrick, M. A. (1985). Personal, couple and group identities: Towards a relational context for language attitudes and linguistic forms. In D. Schiffrin (Ed.), *Meaning, form and use in context: Linguistic applications* (pp. 253-277). Washington DC: Georgetown University Press.

Glennon, L. M., & Butsch, R. (1982). The family as portrayed on television 1946-1978. In D. Pearl, L. Bouthilet, & J. Lazar (Eds.), *Television and social behavior: Ten years of scientific progress and implications for the eighties, Vol. 2: Technical Reviews* (pp. 264-271). Rockville, MD: National Institute of Mental Health.

Goodman, L. A., & Kruskal, M. (1965). On the statistical analysis of mobility tables. *American Journal of Sociology, 70,* 564-585.

Goodrich, D. W., Ryder, R. G., & Raush, H. L. (1968). Patterns of newlywed marriage. *Journal of Marriage and the Family, 30,* 383-389.

Gottman, J. M. (1979). *Marital interaction: Experimental investigations.* New York: Academic Press.

Gottman, J. M., & Levenson, R. W. (1988). The social psychophysiology of marriage. In P. Noller & M. A. Fitzpatrick (Eds.), *Perspectives on marital interaction.* Philadelphia: Multilingual Matters.

Gottman, J. M., Markman, H., & Notarius, C. (1977). The topography of marital conflict: A study of verbal and nonverbal behavior. *Journal of Marriage and the Family, 39,* 461-477.

Gottman, J. M., Notarius, C., Markman, H., Bank, S., Yoppi, B., & Rubin, M. E. (1976). Behavior exchange theory and marital decision making. *Journal of Personality and Social Psychology, 34,* 14-23.

Gray-Little, B., & Burks, N. (1983). Power and satisfaction in marriage: A review and critique. *Psychological Bulletin, 93,* 513-538.

Greenberg, B. S. (1982). Television and role socialization. In D. Pearl, L. Bouthilet, & J. Lazar (Eds.), *Television and social behavior: Ten Years of scientific progress and implications for the eighties, Vol. 2: Technical reviews* (pp. 179-190). Rockville, MD: National Institute of Mental Health.

Guetzkow, H. (1950). Unitizing and categorizing problems in coding qualitative data. *Journal of Clinical Psychology, 6,* 47-58.

Gurin, G., Veroff, J., & Feld, S. (1960). *Americans view their mental health.* New York: Basic Books.

Guthrie, D. M., & Noller, P. (1988). Spouse's perceptions of one another in emotional situations. In P. Noller & M. A. Fitzpatrick (Eds.), *Perspectives on marital interaction.* Philadelphia: Multilingual Matters.

Hadley, T., & Jacob, T. (1976). The measurement of family power. *Sociometry, 39,* 384-395.

Hage, J. (1972). *Techniques and problems of theory construction in sociology.* New York: John Wiley.

Hahlweg, K., & Jacobson, N. S. (1984). *Marital interaction: Analysis and modification.* New York: Guilford.

Hahlweg, K., Reisner, L., Kohli, G., Vollmer, M., Schindler, L., & Revenstorf, D. (1984). The development and validity of a new system to analyze interpersonal communication (KPI). In K. Hahlweg & N. S. Jacobson (Eds.), *Marital interaction: Analysis and modification* (pp. 183-197). New York: Guilford.

Haley, J. (1980). *Leaving home: A therapy for disturbed young people.* New York: McGraw.

Hall, E. T. (1966). *The hidden dimension.* Garden City, NY: Doubleday.

Hall, J. A. (1984). *Nonverbal sex differences: Communication accuracy and expressive style.* Baltimore: John Hopkins University Press.

Harper, R. G., Wiens, A. N., & Matarazzo, J. D. (1978). *Nonverbal communication: The state of the art.* New York: John Wiley.

Hart, R. P., & Burks, D. M. (1972). Rhetorical sensitivity and human interaction. *Speech Monographs, 39,* 75-91.

Hart, R. P., Carlson, R. E., & Eadie, W. F. (1980). Attitudes toward communication and the assessment of rhetorical sensitivity. *Communication Monographs, 47,* 1-22.

Hastie, R. (1981). Schematic principles in human memory. In E. T. Higgins, C. P. Herman, & M. P. Zanna (Eds.), *Social cognition: The Ontario symposium, 1* (pp. 155-177). Hillsdale, NJ: Lawrence Erlbaum.

Hawkins, R., & Pingree, S. (1982). Television's influence on social reality. In D. Pearl, L. Bouthilet, & J. Lazar (Eds.), *Television and social behavior: Ten years of scientific progress* (pp. 224-247). Rockville, MD: National Institute of Mental Health.

Haynes, S. N., Chavez, R. E., & Samuel, V. (1984). Assessment of marital communication and distress. *Behavioral Assessment, 6*, 315-321.

Hess, R., & Handel, G. (1959). *Family worlds.* Chicago: University of Chicago Press.

Hicks, M., & Platt, M. (1970). Marital happiness and marital stability: A review of research in the sixties. *Journal of Marriage and the Family, 32*, 553-574.

Higgins, E. T. (1987). Self-discrepancy: A theory relating self and affect. *Psychological Review, 94*, 319-332.

Hill, C. T., & Stull, D. E. (1982). Disclosure reciprocity: Conceptual and methodological issues. *Social Psychology Quarterly, 45*, 238-244.

Hinde, R. A. (1979). *Towards understanding relationships.* New York: Academic Press.

Hunt, M. M. (1962). *Her infinite variety.* New York: Harper & Row.

Hunt, M., & Hunt, B. (1977). *The divorce experience.* New York: McGraw Hill.

Huston, T. L. (1983). Power. In H. H. Kelley, E. Berscheid, A. Christensen, J. H. Harvey, T. L. Huston, G. Levinger, E. E. McClintock, L. A. Peplau, & D. K. Peterson (Eds.), *Close relationships* (pp. 169-219). New York: W. H. Freeman.

Huston, T. L., Surra, C. A., Fitzgerald, N. M., & Cate, R. M. (1981). From courtship to marriage: Mate selection as an interpersonal process. In S. Duck & R. Gilmour (Eds.), *Personal relationships 2: Developing personal relationships* (pp. 53-90). New York: Academic Press.

Indvik, J., & Fitzpatrick, M. A. (1986). Perceptions of inclusion, affiliation, and control in five interpersonal relationships. *Communication Quarterly, 34*, 1-13.

Jacobson, N. S. (1984). A component analysis of behavioral marital therapy: The relative effectiveness of behavior exchange and communication/problem-solving training. *Journal of Consulting and Clinical Psychology, 52*, 295-305.

Jacobson, N. S., Follette, W. L., & McDonald, D. W. (1982). Reactivity to positive and negative behavior in distressed and nondistressed married couples. *Journal of Consulting and Clinical Psychology, 50*, 706-714.

Jacobson, N. S. & Margolin, G. (1979). *Marital therapy: Strategies based on social learning and behavior exchange principles.* New York: Bruner/Mazel.

Jacobson, N. S., & Moore, D. (1981). Spouses as observers of events in their relationship. *Journal of Consulting and Clinical Psychology, 49*, 269-277.

Jaffe, J., & Feldstein, S. (1970). *Rhythms of dialogue.* New York: Academic Press.

Joreskog, K. G. (1969). A general approach to confirmatory maximum likelihood analysis. *Psychometrika, 34*, 183-202.

Jourard, S. (1971). *The transparent self.* New York: Van Nostrand.

Kahn, M. (1970). Nonverbal communication and marital satisfaction. *Family Process, 9*, 449-456.

Kantor, D., & Lehr, W. (1975). *Inside the family.* New York: Harper & Row.

Katriel, T., & Philipsen, G. (1981). "What we need is communication": "Communication" as a cultural category in some American speech. *Communication Monographs, 48*, 301-318.

Kellermann, K. (1984). The negativity effect and its implication for initial interaction. *Communication Monographs, 51*, 37-55.

Kelley, H., Berscheid, E., Christensen, A., Harvey, J. H., Huston, T. L., Levinger, G., McClintock, E., Peplau, L. A., & Peterson, D. R. (1983). *Close relationships.* New York: W. H. Freeman.

Kelly, E. L., & Conley, J. J. (1987). Personality and compatibility: A prospective analysis of marital stability and marital satisfaction. *Journal of Personality and Social Psychology, 52*, 27-40.

Kennedy, J. J. (1983). *Analyzing qualitative data.* New York: Praeger.

Kenny, D., & Judd, C. (1986). Consequences of violating the independence assumption in analysis of variance. *Psychological Bulletin, 99*, 422-431.

Kenny, D. A., & LaVoie, L. (1984). The social relations model. In L. Berkowitz (Ed.), *Advances in experimental social psychology, 18* (pp. 48-101). New York: Academic Press.

Killmann, R. H., & Thomas, K. W. (1977). Developing a forced-choice measure of conflict-building behavior: The "MODE" instrument. *Educational and Psychological Measurement, 37*, 309-325.

Kinder, D. R., Peters, M. D., Abelson, R. P., & Fiske, S. T. (1980). Presidential prototypes. *Political Behavior, 2*, 315-337.

Kipnis, D., Castell, P., Gergen, M., & Mauch, D. (1976). Metamorphic effects of power. *Journal of Applied Psychology, 61*, 127-135.

Knapp, M. L. (1978). *Social intercourse: From greeting to goodbye.* Boston: Allyn & Bacon.

Knoke, D., & Burke, P. J. (1980). *Log-linear models.* Beverly Hills, CA: Sage.

Knudson, R. M., Sommers, A. A., & Golding, S. L. (1980). Interpersonal perception and mode of resolution in marital conflict. *Journal of Personality and Social Psychology, 38*, 751-763.

Kolb, T. M., & Strauss, M. (1974). Marital power and marital happiness in relation to problem-solving ability. *Journal of Marriage and the Family, 36*, 752-766.

Komarovsky, M. (1964). *Blue collar marriage.* New York: Random House.

Kraemer, H.C., & Jacklin, C. N. (1979). Statistical analysis of dyadic social behavior. *Psychological Bulletin, 86, 217-224.*

Kressel, K., & Deutsch, M. (1977). Divorce therapy: An in-depth survey of therapists' views. *Family Process, 16*, 413-433.

Kressel, K., Jaffe, N., Tuckman, B., Watson, C., & Deutsch, M. (1980). A typology of divorcing couples: Implications for mediation and the divorce process. *Family Process, 19*, 101-116.

Kullbeck, S., Kupperman, M., & Ku, H. (1962) Tests for contingency tables and Markov chains. *Technometrics, 4*, 537-608.

Lederer, W. J., & Jackson, D. D. (1968). *The mirages of marriage.* New York: W. W. Norton.

Levenson, R. W., & Gottman, J. M. (1983). Marital interaction: Physiological linkage and affective exchange. *Journal of Personality and Social Psychology, 45*, 587-597.

Levinger, G. (1965). Marital cohesiveness and dissolution: An integrative review. *Journal of Marriage and the Family, 27*, 19-28.

Lewis, R. A., & Spanier, G. (1979). Theorizing about the quality and the stability of marriage. In W. R. Burr, R. Hill, F. I. Nye, & I. L. Reiss (Eds.), *Contemporary theories about the family, Vol. 1* (pp. 268-294). New York: Free Press.

Littlejohn, S. (1983). *Theories of human communication.* Belmont, CA: Wadsworth.

Locke, H. J. (1951). *Predicting adjustment in marriage: A comparison of a divorced and happily married group.* New York: Henry Holt.

Locke, H. J., & Wallace, K. M. (1959). Short marital-adjustment tests: Their reliability and validity. *Marriage and Family Living, 21*, 251-255.

Mahl, G. F. (1956). Disturbances and silences in the patient's speech in psychotherapy. *Journal of Abnormal and Social Psychology, 53*, 1-15.

Mandler, G. (1984). *Mind and body: The psychology of emotion and stress.* New York: W. W. Norton.

Markman, H. J. (1984). The longitudinal study of couples' interactions: Implications for understanding and predicting the development of marital distress. In K. Hahlweg & N. S. Jacobson (Eds.), *Marital interaction: Analysis and modification* (pp. 253-284). New York: Guilford.

Markus, H., & Zajonc, R. B. (1985). The cognitive perspective in social psychology. In G. Lindzey & E. Aronson (Eds.), *The handbook of social psychology* (3rd ed., pp. 137-230). New York: Random House.

Marwell, G., & Schmitt, D. R. (1967). Dimensions of compliance-gaining behaviors: An empirical analysis. *Sociometry, 30,* 350-364.

Mason, K. O., Czajka, J. L., & Arber, S. (1976). Changes in the U.S. women's sex-role attitudes. *American Sociological Review, 41,* 573-596.

McCall, G. J., McCall, M. M., Denzin, N. K., Suttles, G. D., & Kurth, S. B. (1970). *Social relationships.* Chicago: Aldine.

McGoldrick, M. (1982). Normal families: An ethnic perspective. In F. Walsh (Ed.), *Normal family processes* (pp. 399-425). New York: Guilford.

McLeod, J. M., & Chaffee, S. H. (1972). The construction of social reality. In J. T. Tedeschi (Ed.), *The social influence processes* (pp. 50-99). Chicago: Aldine-Atherton.

McLeod, J., Fitzpatrick, M. A., Glynn, C., & Fallis, S. (1982). Television and social behavior: Family influences and consequences for interpersonal behavior. In D. Pearl, L. Bouthilet, & J. Lazar (Eds.), *Television and social behavior* (pp. 272-282). Rockville, MD: National Institute of Mental Health.

Mehrabian, A. (1972). *Nonverbal communication.* Chicago: Aldine-Atherton.

Mendoza, J. L., & Graziano, W. G. (1982). Statistical analysis of dyadic social behavior: A multivariate approach. *Psychological Bulletin, 92,* 532-540.

Millar, F. E., & Rogers, L. E. (1976). A relational approach to interpersonal communication. In G. R. Miller (Ed.), *Explorations in interpersonal communication* (pp. 87-104). Beverly Hills, CA: Sage.

Miller, G. R. (1976). Foreword. In G. R. Miller (Ed.), *Explorations in interpersonal communication* (pp. 9-16). Beverly Hills, CA: Sage.

Miller, G., Boster, F., Roloff, M., & Seibold, D. (1977). Compliance-gaining message strategies: A typology and some findings concerning effects of situational differences. *Communication Monographs, 44,* 37-51.

Miller, G. R., & Steinberg, M. (1975). *Between people: A new analysis of interpersonal communication.* Chicago: Science Research Associates.

Minuchin, S. (1974). *Families and family therapy.* Cambridge, MA: Harvard University Press.

Mishler, E. G., & Waxler, N. E. (1968). *Interaction in families.* New York: John Wiley.

Morley, D. D. (1987). Revised lag sequential analysis. In M. L. McLaughlin (Ed.), *Communication yearbook 10* (pp. 172-182). Newbury Park, CA: Sage.

Morton, T. L. (1978). Intimacy and reciprocity of exchange: A comparison of spouses and strangers. *Journal of Personality and Social Psychology, 36,* 72-81.

Mulac, A., Lundell, T. L., & Bradac, J. (1986). Male-female language differences and attributional consequences in a public speaking situation: Toward an explanation of the gender-linked language effect. *Communication Monographs, 53,* 115-129.

Murray, D. C. (1971). Talk, silence and anxiety. *Psychological Bulletin, 75,* 244-260.

Natale, M. (1975). Convergence of mean vocal intensity in dyadic communication as a function of social desirability. *Journal of Personality and Social Psychology, 32*, 790-804.

Neisser, U. (1967). *Cognitive psychology*. New York: Appleton.

Noller, P. (1980). Misunderstandings in marital communication. *Journal of Personality and Social Psychology, 39*, 1135-1148.

Noller, P. (1984). *Nonverbal communication in marital interaction*. New York: Pergamon.

Noller, P. & Fitzpatrick, M.A. (1988). *Perspectives on marital interaction*. Philadelphia: Multilingual Matters.

Noller, P., & Hiscock, H. (1986). *Fitzpatrick's marital typology: An Australian replication*. Paper presented at the International Conference on Personal Relationships, Herzeya, Israel.

Norton, R. (1983). Measuring marital quality: A critical look at the dependent variable. *Journal of Marriage and the Family, 45*, 141-151.

Nunnally, J. (1967). *Psychometric theory*. New York: McGraw-Hill.

Nye, F. I. (1976). *Role structure and an analysis of the family*. Beverly Hills, CA: Sage.

O'Donnell-Trujillo, N. (1981). Relational communication: A comparison of coding systems. *Communication Monographs, 48*, 91-105.

Olson, D. H. (1977). Insiders' and outsiders' views of relationships: Research strategies. In G. Levinger & H. L. Raush (Eds.), *Close relationships: Perspectives on the meaning of intimacy* (pp. 115-136). Amherst: University of Massachusetts Press.

Olson, D. H. (1981). Family typologies: Bridging family research and family therapy. In E. E. Filsinger & R. A. Lewis (Eds.), *Assessing marriage: New behavioral approaches* (pp. 74-89). Beverly Hills, CA: Sage.

Olson, D. H., & Cromwell, R. E. (1975). Power in families. In R. E. Cromwell & D. H. Olson (Eds.), *Power in families* (pp. 3-14). New York: John Wiley.

Overall, J. E., & Klett, C. J. (1972). *Applied multivariate analysis*. New York: McGraw.

Parsons, T. (1951). *The social system*. New York: Free Press.

Patterson, M. (1983). *Nonverbal behavior: A functional perspective*. New York: Springer-Verlag.

Patterson, M. (1985). The evolution of a functional model of nonverbal exchange. In R. Street & J. N. Cappella (Eds.), *Sequence and pattern in communicative behavior* (pp. 190-205). London: Edward Arnold.

Pearce, W. B., & Sharp, S. M. (1973). Self disclosing communication. *Journal of Communication, 23*, 409-425.

Peplau, L. A. (1983). Roles and gender. In H. Kelley, E. Berscheid, A. Christensen, J. J. Harvey, T. L. Huston, G. Levinger, E. McClintock, L. A. Peplau, & D. R. Peterson (Eds.), *Close relationships* (pp. 220-264). New York: W. H. Freeman.

Phelps, E. (1976). *Programs with and without close male-female relationships*. Unpublished paper, Cultural Indicators Project, University of Pennsylvania.

Planalp, S. (1984). *Relational schemata: An interpretive approach to relationships*. Unpublished doctoral dissertation, University of Wisconsin—Madison.

Pleck, J. H. (1981). *The myth of masculinity*. Cambridge: MIT Press.

Pollard, W. E., & Mitchell, T. R. (1972). Decision theory analysis of social power. *Psychological Bulletin, 78*, 433-446.

Poole, M. S., Folger, J., & Hewes, D. (1983). Coding social interaction. In B. Dervin & M. Voight (Eds.), *Progress in communication science*. New York: Ablex.

Pruitt, D. G., & Rubin, J. Z. (1986). *Social conflict: Escalation, schemes and settlement*. New York: Random House.

Putnam, L., & Wilson, C. E. (1982). Development of a communication in conflict instrument. In M. Burgoon (Ed.), *Communication yearbook 6* (pp. 629-652). Beverly Hills, CA: Sage.

Raush, H. L., Barry, W. A., Hertel, R. K., & Swain, M. A. (1974). *Communication, conflict, and marriage.* San Francisco: Jossey-Bass.

Raush, H. L., Grief, A. C., & Nugent, J. (1979). Communication in couples and families. In W. R. Burr, R. Hill, F. I. Nye, & I. L. Reiss (Eds.), *Contemporary theories about the family* (Vol. 1, pp. 468-492). New York: Free Press.

Reis, H., Senchak, M., & Soloman, B. (1985). Sex differences in interaction meaningfulness. *Journal of Personality and Social Psychology, 48,* 1204-1217.

Reiss, D. (1981). *The family's constructions of reality.* Cambridge, MA: Harvard University Press.

Revenstorf, D. (1984). The role of attribution of marital distress in therapy. In K. Hahlweg & N. S. Jacobson (Eds.), *Marital interaction: Analysis and modification* (pp. 325-335). New York: Guilford.

Roberts, E. J. (1982). Television and sexual learning in childhood. In D. Pearl, L. Bouthilet, & J. Lazar (Eds.), *Television and social behavior* (pp. 209-223). Rockville, MD: National Institute of Mental Health.

Rogers, C. (1961). *On becoming a person.* Boston: Houghton Mifflin.

Rogers, L. E., & Farace, R. V. (1975). Relational communication analysis: New measurement procedures. *Human Communication Research, 1,* 222-239.

Roloff, M. E. (1976). Communication strategies, relationships and relational change. In G. R. Miller (Ed.), *Explorations in interpersonal communication* (pp. 173-195). Beverly Hills, CA: Sage.

Rossi, A. (1985). Gender and parenthood. In A. S. Rossi (Ed.), *Gender and the life course* (pp. 161-192). New York: Aldine.

Rubin, L. (1976). *Worlds of pain: Life in a working class family.* New York: Basic Books.

Rubin, Z., Hill, C. T., Peplau, L. A., & Dunke-Schetter, C. (1980). Self disclosure in dating couples: Sex roles and the ethics of openness. *Journal of Marriage and the Family, 42,* 305-317.

Rummel, R. J. (1970). *Applied factor analysis.* Evanston, IL: Northwestern University Press.

Russell, B. (1938). *Power: A new social analysis.* New York: W. W. Norton.

Sackett, G. (1977). The lag sequential analysis of contingency and cyclicity in behavioral interaction search. In J. Osofsky (Ed.), *Handbook of Infant Development.* New York: John Wiley.

Scanzoni, J., & Fox, G. L. (1980). Sex roles, family and society: The seventies and beyond. *Journal of Marriage and the Family, 42,* 743-756.

Scanzoni, L., & Scanzoni, J. (1976). *Men, women and change.* New York: McGraw Hill.

Scanzoni, J., & Szinovacz, M. (1980). *Family decision-making: A developmental sex role model.* Beverly Hills, CA: Sage.

Schaap, C. (1982). *Communication and adjustment.* Lisse, The Netherlands: Swets & Zeitlinger, B.V.

Schaap, C., Buunke, B., & Kerkstra, A. (1988). Marital conflict resolution. In P. Noller & M. A. Fitzpatrick (Eds.), *Perspectives on marital interaction.* Philadelphia: Multilingual Matters.

Schenck-Hamlin, W. J., Georgacarakos, G. N., & Wiseman, R. L. (1982). A formal account of interpersonal compliance-gaining. *Communication Quarterly, 30,* 173-180.

Scherer, K. (1986). Vocal affect expression: A review and a model for future research. *Psychological Bulletin, 99*(2), 143-165.

Sennett, R. (1978). *The fall of public man.* New York: Basic Books.

Shorter, E. (1975). *The making of the modern family.* New York: Basic Books.

Sillars, A. (1974). Expression and control in human interaction: Perspectives on humanistic psychology. *Western Speech, 38,* 269-277.

Sillars, A. (1986). *Manual for coding interpersonal conflict.* Unpublished manuscript, University of Montana, Department of Interpersonal Communication.

Sillars, A. L., Colletti, S. F., Parry, D., & Rogers, M. A. (1982). Coding verbal conflict tactics: Nonverbal and perceptual correlates of the "Avoidance-Distributive-Integrative" distinction. *Human Communication Research, 9,* 83-95.

Sillars, A., Pike, G. R., Jones, T. S., & Redman, K. (1983). Communication and conflict in marriage: One style is not satisfying to all. In R. Bostrom (Ed.), *Communication yearbook 7* (pp. 414-431). Beverly Hills, CA: Sage.

Sillars, A. L., & Scott, M. D. (1983). Interpersonal perception between intimates: An integrative review. *Human Communication Research, 10,* 153-176.

Sillars, A. L., Weisberg, J., Burgraff, C. S., & Wilson, E. A. (1987). Content themes in marital conversations. *Human Communication Research, 13,* 495-528.

Slater, P. E. (1970). *The pursuit of loneliness.* Boston: Beacon.

Smith, P. M. (1980). Judging masculine and feminine social identities from content-controlled speech. In H. Giles, W. P. Robinson, & P. M. Smith (Eds.), *Language: Social psychological perspectives.* Oxford: Pergamon.

Sneath, P. H., & Sokal, R. R. (1973). *Numerical taxonomy: The principles and practice of numerical classification.* San Francisco: W. H. Freeman.

Snyder, D. K. (1979). Multidimensional assessment of marital satisfaction. *Journal of Marriage and the Family, 41,* 813-823.

Snyder, D. K. (1981). *Manual for the marital satisfaction inventory.* Los Angeles: Western Psychological Services.

Snyder, D. K., & Smith, G. T. (1986). Classification of marital relationships: An empirical approach. *Journal of Marriage and the Family, 48,* 137-146.

Snyder, M. (1981). On the self-perpetuating nature of social stereotypes. In D. L. Hamilton (Ed.), *Cognitive processes in stereotyping and intergroup behavior.* Hillsdale, NJ: Erlbaum.

Spanier, G. B. (1976). Measuring dyadic adjustment: New scales for assessing the quality of marriage and similar dyads. *Journal of Marriage and the Family, 38,* 15-28.

Sprecher, S. (1985). *Emotion in close relationships.* Unpublished Ph.D. dissertation, University of Wisconsin—Madison.

Sprey, J. (1979). Conflict theory and the study of marriage and the family. In W. L. Burr, R. Hill, F. D. Nye, & I. L. Reiss (Eds.), *Contemporary theories about the family* (Vol. 2, pp. 130-159). New York: Free Press.

Stephen, T. (1986). Communication and interdependence in geographically separated relationships. *Human Communication Research, 13,* 191-210.

Stiles, W. B. (1978a). *Manual for the taxonomy of verbal response modes.* Chapel Hill: University of North Carolina, Institute for Research in Social Science.

Stiles, W. B. (1978b). Verbal response modes and dimensions of interpersonal roles. *Journal of Personality and Social Psychology, 36,* 693-703.

Stiles, W. B. (1979). Verbal response modes and psychotherapeutic technique. *Psychiatry, 42,* 49-62.

Stiles, W. B. (1980). Comparison of dimensions derived from the rating versus the coding of dialogue. *Journal of Personality and Social Psychology, 38,* 359-374.

Stiles, W. B., Waszak, C., & Barton, L. (1979). Professional presumptiveness in verbal interactions with college students. *Journal of Educational Social Psychology, 15,* 158-169.

Straus, M. A. (1978). Measuring intrafamily conflict and violence: The Conflict Tactics Scale. *Journal of Marriage and the Family, 40.*

Street, R., & Cappella, J. N. (1985). *Sequence and pattern in communicative behavior.* London: Edward Arnold.

Swafford, M. (1980). Three parametric techniques for contingency table analysis: A nontechnical commentary. *American Sociological Review, 45,* 664-690.

Swenson, C. H., & Gilner, F. (1973). *Manual and test booklet for the Scale of the Feelings and Behaviors of Love.* Unpublished manuscript, Purdue University, Department of Psychology.

Taylor, S. E., & Fiske, S. T. (1978). Salience, attention, and attribution: Top of the head phenomena. In L. Berkowitz (Ed.), *Advances in experimental social psychology* (pp. 249-288). New York: Academic Press.

Terman, L. M. (1938). *Psychological factors in marital happiness.* New York: McGraw-Hill.

Thakerar, J. N., & Giles, H. (1981). They are—so they spoke: Noncontent speech stereotypes. *Language and Communication, 1,* 255-261.

Thakerar, J. N., Giles, H., & Chesire, J. (1982). *Psychological and linguistic parameters of speech accommodation theory.* Cambridge: Cambridge University Press.

Ting-Toomey, S. (1983). An analysis of verbal communication patterns in high and low marital adjustment groups. *Human Communication Research, 9,* 306-319.

Trost, J. E. (1985). Abandon adjustment. *Journal of Marriage and the Family, 47,* 1072-1973.

Tukey, J. (1980). Relationships among multiple dependent variables. In P. Monge & J. N. Cappella (Eds.), *Multivariate techniques in human communication research.* New York: Academic Press.

Turner, R. H. (1970). *Family interaction.* New York: John Wiley.

Vance, L. E. (1981). *Dimensions of autonomy-interdependence reflected in casual marital interactions.* Unpublished master's thesis, University of Wisconsin—Madison.

van Dijk, T. A., & Kintsch, W. (1983). *Strategies of discourse comprehension.* New York: Academic Press.

Vincent, J. P., Friedman, L. C., Nugent, J., & Messerly, T. (1979). Demand characteristics in observations of marital interaction. *Journal of Consulting and Clinical Psychology, 47,* 557-566.

Wackman, D. (1969). *A proposal for a new measure of coorientational accuracy.* Paper presented at the Association for Education in Journalism, Berkeley, CA.

Watzlawick, P., Beavin, J. H., & Jackson, D. D. (1967). *Pragmatics of human communication.* New York: W. W. Norton.

Watzlawick, P., Weakland, J., & Fisch, R. (1974). *Change: Principles of problem formation and problem resolution.* New York: Norton.

Weiss, R. L. (1981). The new kid on the block: Behavioral systems approach. In E. E. Filsinger & R. A. Lewis (Eds.), *Assessing marriage: New behavioral approaches* (pp. 22-37). Beverly Hills, CA: Sage.

Weiss, R. L. (1984). Cognitive and behavioral measures of marital interaction. In K. Hahlweg & N. S. Jacobson (Eds.), *Marital interaction* (pp. 232-252). New York: Guilford.

Weiss, R. L., & Summers, K. J. (1983). Marital interaction coding system-III. In E. E. Filsinger (Ed.), *Marriage and family assessment* (pp. 85-116). Beverly Hills, CA: Sage.

Weiss, R. S. (1975). *Marital separation*. New York: Basic Books.

Werner, C. M., & Haggard, L. B. (1985). Temporal qualities of interpersonal relationships. In M. L. Knapp & G. R. Miller (Eds.), *Handbook of interpersonal communication* (pp. 59-99). Beverly Hills, CA: Sage.

Wheeless, L. R., Barraclough, R., & Stewart, R. (1983). Compliance-gaining and power in persuasion. In R. N. Bostrom & B. H. Westley (Eds.), *Communication yearbook 7* (pp. 105-145). Beverly Hills, CA: Sage.

Willcox, W. F. (1892). *Studies in history, economics and public law*. New York: Columbia University.

Williamson, R. N. (1983). *The theoretical and empirical integration of two approaches to investigating marital interaction*. Unpublished Ph.D. dissertation, University of Wisconsin—Madison.

Williamson, R. N., & Fitzpatrick, M. A. (1985). Two approaches to marital interaction: Relational control patterns in marital types. *Communication Monographs, 52*, 236-252.

Winer, B. J. (1971). *Statistical principles in experimental design*. New York: McGraw-Hill.

Wiseman, R., & Schenck-Hamlin, W. J. (1981). A multidimensional scaling validation of an intuitively derived set of compliance-gaining strategies. *Communication Monographs, 48*, 251-270.

Witteman, H. (1985). *Exploration of Kantor and Lehr's model of family interaction: Conceptual support for the Relational Dimensions Inventory*. Unpublished manuscript, University of Wisconsin—Madison, Center for Communication Research.

Witteman, H., & Fitzpatrick, M. A. (1986). Compliance-gaining in marital interaction: Power bases, power processes, and outcomes. *Communication Monographs, 53*, 130-143.

Witteman, H., & Fitzpatrick, M. A. (1987). A social scientific view of Marriage Encounter. *Journal of Clinical and Social Psychology*.

Wynne, L. C., Ryckoff, M., Day, J., & Hirsch, S. I. (1958). Pseudomutuality in the family relations of schizophrenics. *Psychiatry, 21*, 205-220.

ABOUT THE AUTHOR

Mary Anne Fitzpatrick is Professor of Communication Arts and Director of the Center for Communication Research at the University of Wisconsin—Madison. She is the coeditor, with Patricia Noller, of *Perspectives on Marital Interaction*. She has published more than fifty articles and book chapters on interpersonal communication in the family.

NOTES

NOTES

NOTES

NOTES

NOTES